THE ECONOMY OF COLONIAL AMERICA

"Tolle lege, tolle lege"

Take up & read, take up & read

FROM THE LIBRARY OF

ANNA HAWLEY

THE
ECONOMY
OF
COLONIAL
AMERICA

SECOND EDITION

EDWIN J. PERKINS

COLUMBIA UNIVERSITY PRESS

NEW YORK 1988

Columbia University Press
New York   Guildford, Surrey
Copyright © 1988 Columbia University Press
All rights reserved
Printed in the United States of America

Library of Congress Cataloging-in-Publication Data

Perkins, Edwin J.
The economy of colonial America / Edwin J. Perkins—2nd ed. p.   cm.
Includes bibliographies and index.
ISBN 0-231-06338-5 (alk. paper).   ISBN 0-231-06339-3 (pbk.)
1. United States—Economic conditions—To 1865.   I. Title.
HC104.P47   1988
330.973'02—dc19   87-27980
                                                                           CIP

Book design by Jennifer Dossin

Hardback editions of Columbia University Press books are Smyth-sewn
and printed on permanent and durable acid-free paper

FOR MY FATHER
Paul

CONTENTS

PREFACE

T HIS book is a second, revised edition of a volume published in 1980. Anyone sitting down to read the outpouring of new scholarship on the colonial economy, as I have done over the last year, would be astounded by the range and depth of the literature which has appeared over the last decade. And more studies are in progress and thus destined to enlighten us even further in the very near future. I had anticipated that preparing and drafting a revised edition would be far less time-consuming than the initial project; but I badly misjudged the amount of work involved in bringing myself up-to-date in this burgeoning field. Before the last spelling check was run on the chapter files generated by my personal computer, I had devoted almost as much time to the second edition as to the first.

My initial interest in colonial economic history was stimulated back in 1974 when I was asked to review Joseph Ernst's *Money and Politics in America, 1755–1775*. The excitement of learning about eighteenth-century finance generated further curiosity about the status of scholarly research on other colonial topics. At the same time, I was dissatisfied with the books available to undergraduates on this era for my own economic history course. Since no other historian had yet published a summation and interpretation of recent scholarship in the field, I finally decided to embark on the project myself.

The colonial era is appealing because it represents a study in contrasts. The economy was exceptionally dynamic in terms of population growth and geographical expansion. No major famines, epidemics, or extended wars intervened to reverse, or even slow down appreciably, the tide of vigorous economic expansion. From 1700 to 1774, for example, output expanded twelvefold. At the start of the century, the size of the colonial economy was less than 5 percent of the mother country's; yet on the eve of independence the percentage had risen to nearly one-third, and the colonies were gaining steadily on Great Britain in term of aggregate output.

Despite this broad expansion, however, the fundamental patterns of economic behavior remained fairly constant. In *The Economy of British America, 1606–1789* (1985), John McCusker and Russell Menard observed that there had been "relatively little change in occupational structure or degree of urbanization." They added: "British America was as much (or nearly so) a pre-industrial society in 1775 as it had been in 1650" (p. 70). Workers in the main occupational categories—farmers, planters, artisans, merchants, indentured servants, and slaves—performed similar functions year after year. In comparison with the vast number of institutional innovations in the nineteenth and twentieth centuries, structural change in the colonial economy evolved at a snail's pace. With the exception of the adoption of the pernicious system of black slavery after 1675, few new economic institutions or revolutionary technologies emerged to disrupt the stability of this remarkably affluent commercial/agricultural society. Although fluctuations in the size of harvests and in the level of foreign demand for colonial exports caused fluctuations in the volume of economic output, the patterns of daily activities which developed in the seventeenth century generally prevailed until the 1770s. Living standards rose slowly but steadily at the rate of 4 to 6 percent per decade after 1650.

This book contains a number of noteworthy features. Monetary sums are converted into 1985 dollars so that the figures will be relevant to modern readers. For example, the estimated median income level of £10 for the free white population in the 1770s translates into $900 in 1985 prices (see the appendix for the method of conversion). The focus is primarily rural, reflecting the overwhelmingly agricultural character of the economy. The family farmer thus receives the most extensive coverage in the section on occupational groups. In this context, I have stressed the similarities between the activities of farmers in the northern, middle, and southern colonies rather than their differences. The second edition contains a new chapter on women in the economy; ten years ago little information was available on women, but knowledge has been accumulating rapidly, and my treatment represents, I believe, the first attempt to synthesize the existing literature.

The most influential groups in colonial society were the great planters in the south and wealthy urban merchants in the north. Individual planters and merchants exercised greater political power than economic influence, however. Compared to the twentieth century in which big business, big labor, and big government all wield enormous economic power over the marketplace, the colonial world was governed far more by the free-market forces associated with Adam Smith's classical economic principles. Government expenditures and taxes accounted for a minor percentage of total gross production; labor unions were nonexistent; and, with the exception of some large plantations and iron facilities, business units were universally small. No individual or group of individuals possessed sufficient economic power to influence prices and restrict the supply of goods. In colonial society, impersonal market forces remained predominant.

For the most part, this book describes the economic lifestyles of free white society. The term "colonist" is virtually synonymous with inhabitants of European origin. Thus, statements about very high living standards and the benefits of land ownership pertain only to whites. Occasionally, I have added a qualifying statement at the end of a sentence such as "with the exception of blacks and Native Americans," but it could be validly inserted into thousands of sentences in the text. One chapter does focus, in part, on slaves.

In addition, I often employ a comparative format, with conditions in the thirteen mainland colonies placed in a global framework or contrasted with trends in the modern world. Among the topics are demography, living standards, growth rates, wealth distribution, debtor-creditor conflicts, and the role of merchants and artisans in society. Unless otherwise stated, my vantage point in time is backward from the twentieth century, which is important in understanding why I lean so heavily on terms like "static" and "stable" in describing the economic lifestyles of the colonists. For the modern reader, who is caught up in a era of constant economic change, such a vantage point is, I believe, most effective in communicating how the earlier period differed from our own.

Several scholars went over various chapters and alerted me to additional sources, neglected facts, and questionable analysis. For the first edition, these persons were particularly helpful: Stan En-

german, Alice Hanson Jones, Joseph Ernst, Paul Paskoff, Dennis
Flynn, David Galenson, and Gary Nash. After publication I received
letters from Billy Smith, David Ross, and Harry Fritz, who pointed
out several factual errors in the original text; I hope anyone finding
similar mistakes in this edition (and there are almost certain to be
some) will follow their example and correspond with me about them.
I miscalculated some of Billy Smith's figures by almost one-half in
the original text, and I am glad to have been able to repair the
damage on that score this time around.

Meanwhile, I have accumulated even more debts to another long
list of generous scholars who read and commented on drafts of
chapters, or assisted in other ways, for this second edition: Peter
Bergstrom, Farley Grubb, Julian Gwyn, Ron Michener, Jacob Price,
Oliver Rink, Winifred Rothenberg, Marylynn Salmon, Mary
Schweitzer, Carole Shammas, Timothy Silver, Bruce Smith, Re-
becca Starr, Maris Vinovskis, and Elmus Wicker. Stan Engerman
and Paul Clemens reviewed the entire manuscript. I also appreciate
the confidence expressed by editor Kate Wittenberg at Columbia
University Press, who encouraged me to embark on this second
venture into the realm of the colonial economy. Judy Gladstone was
a great source of stability and friendship during the long months of
research and writing, and I remain thankful for her personal support.

This book represents my best judgment about the most important
features of the colonial economy and their relationship to society in
general and to the movement for independence. Hopefully, it should
remain a good starting point for all readers—undergraduate to accomplished scholar—wanting to learn more about economic activities in the seventeenth and eighteenth centuries. My greatest debt
is to all the economists and historians who have been active in
scholarship over the last quarter-century. To me, their work has
been a source of continuing inspiration, and I trust this new volume
will reveal the extent of their accomplishments to a much broader
audience. While I have tried to include a range of opinions on issues
perennially debated, such as whether the independence movement
had primarily economic origins or what roles various occupational
groups played in the events of the 1760s and 1770s, in the end the
emphasis and interpretation are my own.

THE ECONOMY OF COLONIAL AMERICA

CHAPTER I

POPULATION AND ECONOMIC EXPANSION

T HE colonial economy expanded at a dynamic pace throughout the seventeenth and eighteenth centuries primarily because of the spectacular growth of the free white and black slave populations. During the first century of settlement, the new arrivals were mainly Europeans, either from England or in New York from Holland. White settlers are estimated at 40,000 in 1650; by 1700 the number had grown to 235,000. Natural increase, combined with continued immigration by the English, Scotch, Irish, and Germans, brought the white population up to 1.8 million in 1770. After slavery had taken a firm hold in the southern tobacco colonies in the late seventeenth century, the size of the black population rose from around 13,000 in 1690 up to 465,000 in 1770. From 1660 to 1775 total population grew at an annual rate of increase of slightly over 3 percent, doubling in size every quarter-century. Meanwhile, the native Indian population along the Atlantic coast declined precipitously. Some Indians were killed in hostilities, but most either moved farther inland to avoid the encroachment of Europeans or died after contracting communicable diseases such as measles and smallpox, against which they had developed no natural immunities.

Each geographical region had a very different pattern of population growth. New England received an influx of approximately 20,000 English settlers between 1620 and 1645; thereafter immigration virtually halted, and natural increase was responsible for almost all the region's subsequent expansion. The middle colonies attracted few settlers until late in the seventeenth century, and immigration played an important role in their development well into the eighteenth century. In the Chesapeake tobacco region, immigration from England was the source of all positive growth through the 1670s. The white population was finally able to reproduce itself and expand after 1680, and by the turn of the century, natural increase had become the key factor in white population growth. For the black population, on the other hand, forced immigration continued at a rapid pace from 1680 through the 1740s. With the creation of a more settled slave society by midcentury, natural increase played the more vital role in black demographics. After 1750, however, the impact of immigration—white and black—was diminished, and natural increase was responsible for over 70 percent of the population growth in the thirteen mainland colonies.

In his recent book initiating a series of volumes on the peopling of North America, Bernard Bailyn reminds us that, despite the lessened impact of immigration on a relative scale in the late colonial period, the aggregate number of immigrants in the decade and one-half before independence was nonetheless impressive. Between 1760 and 1775 over 220,000 persons arrived from across the oceans. Among them were 55,000 Irish Protestants, 30,000 Scots, 30,000 English, 12,000 Germans and Swiss, and 84,500 Africans. Indeed, the slave trade still accounted for over 40 percent of black population growth in this period.

On the eve of independence in 1775, the thirteen colonies had a population of approximately 2.6 million, consisting of 2.1 million whites, 540,000 blacks, and 50,000, or fewer, Native Americans. Virginia was the largest colony, with 21 percent of total population, followed by Massachusetts and Pennsylvania with 11 percent each. Philadelphia, with a population of from 30,000 to 35,000 citizens, was on a par with the largest urban areas in England with the exception of populous London. In terms of population, local political institutions, and underlying economic strength, the colonies were by no means dependent on Great Britain for survival or for their prosperity by the mid-eighteenth century, and thereafter they increasingly resented English attempts, both in theory and in practice, to view them as inferior. By 1775, the thirteen colonies already had nearly one-third as many inhabitants as the mother country, and their overall economic output was over 30 percent of Great Britain's.

The implications of American population and economic growth were not lost on Benjamin Franklin, one of the few colonials whose views on scientific matters and political affairs had a genuine following within the European intelligensia. Franklin was an amateur demographer as well, and his commonsense predictions about the future course of the American population and the reasons for its unusual growth have retained their relevancy. In his pamphlet *Observations Concerning the Increase of Mankind*, penned in 1751, Franklin pointed out that at the existing rate of natural increase, augmented by steady immigration, the colonies were doubling in size every twenty years. He added that colonial Englishmen and their slaves were destined to outnumber the inhabitants of the mother country in a few more generations. Therefore, he foresaw pressure building to shift the balance of political and economic power within the British empire across the Atlantic to the colonies.

Franklin cited early marriage and large families as the chief reasons for American growth. The typical number of children in a colonial family he estimated at around 8, compared to only 4 in England and in the rest of Europe. Marriage was more frequent in the colonies too, he argued, because higher wages and the abundance of cheap land made it easier for a man to maintain a wife and raise a family. As indirect evidence of the greater economic opportunities in America, Franklin noted the absence of a permanent class of household servants; in England, persons in service were often forced by circumstance to delay marriage or to remain single.

Despite several instances of overstatement, modern studies of colonial demography have generally verified the soundness of Franklin's judgment. In accord with the experience of most preindustrial societies, and many poor nations today, birthrates in the eighteenth century were very high. Only a small percentage of the population failed to marry. The colonial birthrate was between 40 and 50 per 1,000 inhabitants, with some regions close to the historical biological maximum of 55 per 1,000 for a large population. Birthrates in Europe at the time ranged from 30 to 40 per 1,000. In an early study of a wide sample of New England towns in the period 1720–60, Robert Higgs and Louis Stettler found that the number of children fathered by a married man was about 7 on average, although it sometimes took a second or possibly even a third wife to reach that figure. One wife in six or seven died before the end of her fertile years, with childbirth and its complications the leading cause of death. (Husbands in their twenties and thirties apparently died at almost the same rate from various causes.) The childless marriage was uncommon, and fewer than 15 percent of New England families had less than 3 children.

The age of the partners at marriage was lower in the colonies than in Europe. By the middle of the eighteenth century, women typically married in their early twenties and males in their mid-twenties in most regions, whereas contemporary Europeans often delayed household formation for an extra two or three years. In the southern colonies, native-born women were marrying in their late teens during the last quarter of the seventeenth century and well into the next century. Later, however, as the sex ratio became more balanced, the age of matrimony in the south climbed, and by the last quarter of the colonial era, marriage patterns were not significantly different from those in other regions. Adolescent pregnancies happened, of course, but were relatively rare by modern standards. Although the data are still fragmentary, there is nonetheless some evidence to suggest that the age of puberty for females was as high as 15 or 16 before the mid-nineteenth century, compared to 13 for American girls today. The late onset of fertility may well have accounted for the very low incidence of births to females in their mid-teens.

Just as Franklin had suspected, modern research on colonial demography has revealed a close correlation between early marriage and large families. Colonial households generally contained at least one more child than English households. In premodern Europe, and especially in Ireland, late marriage was the most effective means of limiting population, and even in the present era of sophisticated birth-control technology, the mainland Chinese have relied on delayed marriage as a major tool in slowing population growth.

There is no evidence that colonial couples regularly practiced any method of birth control. In Europe, and especially in France, some historians believe that coitus interruptus was commonly practiced in an effort to restrict pregnancy. Even without contraceptive safeguards, the normal interval between births was at least two years. This spacing was not a result of conscious attempts at family planning, but occurred because colonial babies were invariably breast-fed and most women experience lessened fertility during lactation. Some colonial women did, of course, give birth to 15 or even 20 children; yet these cases were the exception, not the rule. In Hingham, Massachusetts, from 1720 to 1780, Daniel Scott Smith found that women who married before the age of 25 and survived multiple childbirth typically had 3 or 4 children in their twenties and 4 more children after the age of 30. Maris Vinovskis found data suggesting a slight lowering of marital fertility in Massachusetts after 1750, but birthrates remained extraordinarily high compared to Europe because of the early age of marriage.

In research on inheritance, migration, and family formation in Connecticut, John Waters discovered evidence revealing how marriages were consciously shaped by the older generation controlling family wealth. Fathers and grandfathers with property influenced heavily decisions about exactly which of their children would marry, which would remain single and care for aging relatives, and which would migrate to frontier areas. The wealthy tended to marry at younger ages than members of middling families, with poor males the most likely candidates for celibacy. In related work on North Carolina, James Gallman reported that males whose fathers were still alive married at younger ages than the sons of widowers. The death of a father often forced a young man to spend several more years caring for his mother and younger siblings.

While birthrates remained high for the white population, death rates were low in comparison to the experience of most other societies by the eighteenth century. In England death rates were slightly higher than in the northern colonies and about on a par with rates in the Chesapeake in the eighteenth century. In most parts of the world, high mortality rates offset birthrates and held down the growth of population. Whereas up to 40 persons out of 1,000 on the European continent died each year, in the thirteen colonies only 15 to 25 per 1,000 succumbed in the eighteenth century. Death rates fell to low levels in New England within several years after any given area was settled.

In the Chesapeake Bay region, in contrast, the number of deaths was high, and sometimes extremely high, during the first half-century. Russell Menard has calculated that the mortality rate for recent arrivals was 80 percent before 1625, up to 30 percent for the next quarter-century, and finally declined to around 5 percent in the 1660s. As a result of higher death rates, and an unbalanced sex ratio, with many more males than females, families in Virginia and Maryland were initially much smaller than in New England. Men outnumbered women by a ratio of 2.5 to 1 as late as 1700. Many children became orphans in early America and were sent to live with nearby kin, or even placed temporarily in servitude. In some counties in the Chesapeake only one-third of the children who reached the age of 20 could look forward to having both parents still alive. Daniel Blake Smith reported that in some areas along the Atlantic coast, a male reaching the age of 20 could expect to live only into his early forties, whereas members of the same generation in New England lived into their late sixties or early seventies. Darrett and Anita Rutman and Carville Earle have cited some combination of malaria, typhoid fever, and dysentery as primarily responsible for the high death rates in the Chesapeake. After the turn of the eighteenth century, southern death rates generally declined, however, and by the end of the colonial period, they were only slightly higher than those prevailing among their healthier northern neighbors.

The exact reasons for the overall lowering of death rates in the North American environment are still somewhat of a puzzle. Most scholars have cited three factors which, in combination, probably accounted in large part for fewer deaths than in Europe. First, the colonists enjoyed abundant harvests, and the quantity and diversity of foods in their diets made the settlers generally healthier and therefore more capable of warding off potentially deadly diseases. Second, a low population density and a dispersed pattern of rural dwellings discouraged the spread of communicable diseases; incidences of exposure to smallpox, diphtheria, influenza, and other killers were reduced. No catastrophic epidemics were ever endured by the white and black populations on the mainland. Finally, plentiful supplies of wood fuel in most areas meant homes were warmer in winter—certainly warmer than in England, where deforestation was extensive by the eighteenth century. Historians are in general agreement that advances in medical science and treatment were not among the factors contributing to the improved health of the population, however, since colonial doctors were in short supply and their training was often rudimentary. The absence of extensive health services was clearly no handicap given the limited medical knowledge of the era; in Europe, even the best-trained doctors could do little to prevent a high number of deaths from infectious diseases.

Another important category where colonial demography differed from the European experience was a lower infant mortality rate for the white population. The English death rate for children under the age of one was certainly no lower than 20 percent, whereas historians have discovered numerous regions in New England where only 12 to 15 infants out of 100 failed to survive the first year. Again, scholars have attributed the lower infant mortality rate to the good general health of colonial women during pregnancy and throughout the nursing period. Fewer deaths among the young meant that a higher proportion of the population reached reproductive age, and that fact alone helps to explain why the colonies grew so rapidly.

After surviving infancy and adolescence, an individual's life expectancy was unusually long compared to standards in most other parts of the world in the eighteenth century. Indeed, life expectancies for young adults in certain New England towns, quite surprisingly, almost rival the statistics on the current generation of Americans. In many townships, the average age at death for adult males was their early sixties. The data on adult females is conflicting. Some studies suggest a much lower life expectancy, with the explanation that deaths related to childbirth reduced the average age at death to the mid-forties. But Philip Greven in his widely respected study of Andover, Massachusetts, discovered that, over a span of four generations, adult women on average lived into their sixties as well. Moreover, Greven found that despite the assumed greater vulnerability of women during their childbearing years, in actuality more males than females died in their twenties and thirties in the Andover sample.

After 1750, when the sex ratio between men and women was generally equal, the demographic experience of blacks, both slave and free, became more similar to the white majority. Birthrates were likewise near the estimated biological maximum. Death rates for black infants and young children remained 40 percent higher than for whites, however, with over one-half dying before reaching their fifth birthday. According to a study by Richard Steckel, which focused on slave heights, the problem was the extremely poor diet of very young slave children who performed no productive work. In marked contrast, adolescents who had already entered the full-time workforce, usually between the ages of 11 and 14, were fed very nutritious diets, and their growth patterns and mortality rates as adults were similar to the white population. Aided by continued heavy importations of slaves in the eighteenth century, the share of blacks in the overall population rose from 7 percent in 1690 to 21 percent in 1775. Blacks outnumbered whites in South Carolina as early as 1710.

The growth of black population on the mainland stands in sharp contrast to trends in the Caribbean and in the rest of Latin America during the colonial period. In other parts of the western hemisphere where sugar or precious metals were the major products, the black population failed to expand through natural increase, and constant, forced immigration from Africa was required to maintain existing numbers. Birthrates were low and mortality rates were appallingly high—not only for slaves but for whites as well. Although questions remain about all the factors accounting for this demographic pattern, scholars have cited the following as characteristic of Latin American slavery: (1) the sex ratio was unbalanced, with males outnumbering females often by margins of 2 or 3 to 1; (2) the tropical climate played host to more diseases, and crowded conditions on many of the sugar islands provided a less healthful environment; (3) the physical labor associated with sugar cultivation and mining was strenuous and sapped the strength of the average worker after a few years; and (4) the nutritional content of diets in the region was often poor.

By the mid-eighteenth century, conditions in the thirteen mainland colonies were much different. The sex ratio was more evenly balanced, and a close approximation of the extended family model was the basis for social organization in slave quarters on the larger plantations. Allan Kulikoff found that by the 1770s *native-born* black women typically married before the age of 20 and by the age of 45 had produced 7 to 9 children. Most blacks lived on relatively isolated southern farms, and like whites, they had low vulnerability to communicable diseases. Finally, the cultivation of tobacco and most food crops (except rice), while demanding and time-consuming, was not physically debilitating for adults of either sex. Despite persistent myths, there is little evidence that slaveholders took arbitrary or abnormal steps to raise the rate of black fertility. Slaveholders presumably realized that artificial attempts to engage in "slave breeding" were superfluous, since after 1750 the black population was already increasing at a very rapid pace.

Another long-overlooked factor which may have accounted for the sharp difference in fertility rates on the mainland and in the Caribbean was singled out by Stanley Engerman and Herbert Klein. They found that female slaves in the West Indies normally followed the African custom of breast-feeding children for up to two years, whereas slaves on the mainland adopted the European practice of weaning babies within the first year. Since incidences of pregnancy are substantially reduced during the lactation period, this factor alone could account for differences in child spacing. Moreover, some African tribes had strong taboos against renewed sexual intercourse with a woman still breast-feeding her recent child. Engerman and Klein believe these two factors may explain, in part, why fertility rates for slaves were almost two times higher on the mainland than in the West Indies.

Given the size of the continent and the westward march of the frontier after 1776, the physical displacement of the native Indian population during the colonial era was remarkably slight. As late as the 1770s, European settlement was confined largely to a one-hundred-mile band stretching along the Atlantic coast from Massachusetts to Georgia (see the map). Lee Alston and Morton Shapiro calculated that much of the land within the original colonies remained unsettled by the late eighteenth century. The extent of settlement in the three major sections in 1790 was generally as follows: New England—66 percent; middle colonies—20 percent; and southern colonies—25 percent. Farmers tended to cluster within the main river valleys, so that even within the band of European settlement, pockets remained where some Indian tribes continued to live in mostly traditional ways. Probably no more than half a million Native Americans lived within 150 miles of the Atlantic coast when the first European settlements were established, and the majority lived in the southern region. How many Indian tribes in contiguous areas were decimated after contracting communicable diseases such as smallpox and measles is unknown, but most authorities have suggested that this inadvertent form of biological warfare was the most important cause of depopulation after the arrival of Europeans and Africans.

In a study of the ecology of New England, where Native Americans and English settlers coexisted and occasionally interacted during the seventeenth and eighteenth centuries, William Cronon estimated the Indian population of New England in 1600 at between 70,000 and 100,000. A century later, the English and Indian populations in the region were roughly equal, although the former continued to increase while the latter group declined. The economic life of Native Americans was based on some combination of field agriculture, hunting, fishing, and gathering edible plants. Their activities varied according to the seasons, and many tribes in the more southern regions of New England moved the locations of their villages periodically throughout the year. Indian society recognized a given tribe's right to the exclusive use of certain lands lying within broad territorial boundaries, but their concept of property rights did not encompass an individual household's private and permanent ownership of specific fields and forests, with accompanying fences, nor of the livestock raised on those properties.

While the number of Native Americans declined, the black and white populations, on the basis of an unusually high birthrate in combination with an unusually low mortality rate and steady immigration, grew at phenomenal speed, doubling every quarter of a century. The colonial demographic experience is roughly analogous to the situation existing in most underdeveloped countries in the twentieth century. In the poor nations of the world, birthrates of 40 to 50 per 1,000, along with dramatically lowered mortality rates following the introduction of modern medical technology, have produced an explosion in world population. Like the age structure in the less-developed nations today, the colonial population after 1750 was on average quite young, with one-half under 18 years of age.

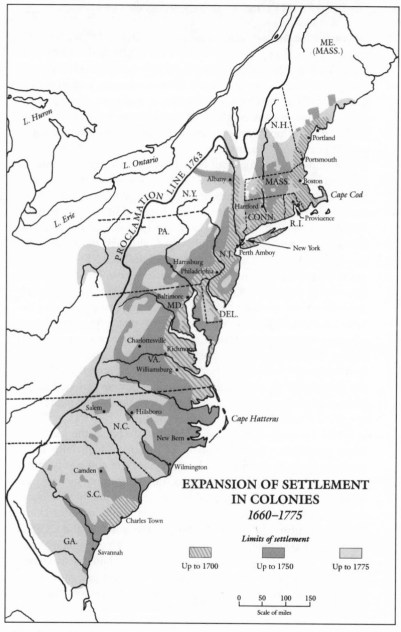

ME.
(MASS.)

L. Huron

L. Ontario

L. Erie

PROCLAMATION LINE 1763

N.Y.

Albany

N.H.

• Portland

• Portsmouth

MASS.

• Boston

Cape Cod

Hartford

CONN.

R.I.

• Providence

PA.

N.J.

Perth Amboy

New York

Harrisburg

Philadelphia •

Baltimore •

MD.

DEL.

Charlottesville •

Richmond •

VA.

Williamsburg •

Salem •

• Hillsboro

Cape Hatteras

N.C.

New Bern •

Camden •

Wilmington

**EXPANSION OF SETTLEMENT
IN COLONIES
*1660–1775***

S.C.

Charles Town

GA.

Savannah

Limits of settlement

| Up to 1700 | Up to 1750 | Up to 1775 |

0   50   100   150

Scale of miles

Redrawn from James A. Henretta, *The Evolution of American Society, 1700–1815* (Lexington, Mass: Heath, 1973), by permission of the publisher.

By comparison, birthrates in the United States have fallen in the 1980s to around the replacement level of 12 per 1,000; at present the median age is around 31, and it is destined to rise higher as the population ages in the decades ahead.

In light of the slow improvements in business technology and agricultural productivity in the seventeenth and eighteenth centuries, it is virtually impossible to overemphasize the importance of population growth in explaining the expansion of the colonial economy. Land and natural resources were abundant and already in place, waiting for development. Labor was the scarce resource in the colonial era, and increases in the size of the labor force led to more extensive settlement and a corresponding expansion in the size and strength of the economy. Population growth was responsible for over 75 percent of the increase in aggregate economic output during the eighteenth century; the contribution from gains in per capita productivity was relatively low even on the basis of the most generous assumptions about its impact.

For every addition to the labor force, gainful employment was normally readily available. By modern standards the range of occupations was narrow, and most young people followed in the footsteps of their parents. Out of every 100 free men who were employed, the vast majority became farmers, while the rest were skilled or semiskilled artisans, day laborers, or seamen; three or four individuals might reach the status of merchant or great planter. In urban areas, the wages earned by skilled workers and laborers were usually higher than the rates paid for comparable work in England, although there is uncertainty among scholars about the magnitude of that margin.

Transatlantic visitors constantly remarked about the few signs of poverty in the colonies. In England, a traveler invariably came across many beggars and paupers on rural roads and in urban streets and alleys. Although scholars such as Gary Nash, Raymond Mohl, Allan Kulikoff, Douglas Jones, and James Henretta have discovered data showing increasing public expenditures for poor relief in Boston, New York, Philadelphia, and several smaller towns, plus an increase in transiency, over the eighteenth century, nonetheless by European standards the colonies contained remarkably few persons who were destitute. Able-bodied workers rarely remained unemployed for long periods of time.

Despite the rapid rise in population, the typical colonial household was able to maintain its already very high material standard of living and even make some improvements. The ability to hold up average living standards in the face of a population boom was a notable achievement. It was a genuine accomplishment that had rarely, if ever, been achieved by any other society before the seventeenth century. During the eighteenth century England was also experiencing per capita income growth, but it achieved steady increases with a rate of population growth only one-sixth that of its mainland colonies.

Before 1600, economic expansion and population growth everywhere in the world had invariably led to a decline in the amount of goods and services available to the average citizen. In Europe, where a large portion of the most fertile land was already under cultivation, increases in population were met by planting new fields that were marginally less productive. As a result, the average yield per acre fell, and the amount of food available for each member of society was less. Eventually, a series of lean crop years produced widespread starvation; or, alternatively, a deadly disease, such as the plague, struck hard at an undernourished population and took away up to one-quarter, or in some cases one-half, of the inhabitants. Paradoxically, those who survived enjoyed improved living standards, since, with population reduced, only the more arable land was regularly cultivated. Soon a new Malthusian cycle of rising population, falling average incomes, and ultimate catastrophe began again.

But in the American colonies that cycle was avoided. As the colonial population rose, settlers were generally able to expand output on new lands that were no less fertile than existing fields. On the frontier, farmers cleared new fields that were more productive than the poorly maintained cropland they had deserted near the coast. Even though population multiplied nearly tenfold in the eighteenth century, food production per capita was clearly sustained. Indeed, food surpluses were so great in the late colonial period that overseas exports of wheat and rice were roughly on a par with the great southern staple—tobacco.

In the more settled areas along the coast, where population pressure caused a decline in the average farm size, most households pursued nonagricultural activities on a part-time basis. Some young men turned to a service or craft occupation permanently. Living standards were maintained, since abundant and relatively inexpensive food could be imported from other locales with steady surpluses. There were no major crop failures in the colonial era—nothing to diminish the optimism of the white settlers about the fundamental stability of their economic world. The colonists anticipated a continuous period of well-being, and the existence of seemingly unlimited new land to the west encouraged them to raise large families, since the opportunities for their heirs did not appear to be restricted by the natural environment.

In comparison with the economies of its more regulated European counterparts, colonial North America was a much closer approximation of the open, free-market society advocated by Adam Smith. In 1776, he published the classic *Wealth of Nations*, which soon became the oracle of capitalism because of its reliance on the unregulated price system to allocate economic resources. Smith argued that, by eliminating artificial monopolies and other forms of governmental interference in the economy (mercantilism), and by generally allowing citizens to pursue independently their own self-interest, a given economy was more likely to approach its maximum potential for the production of goods and services.

Smith cited the colonies in several passages of this treatise as a prime example of the benefits likely to accrue to any society attuned to his basic principles. Two short excerpts illustrate his thoughts: "There are no colonies of which the progress has been more rapid than that of the English in North America"; "Plenty of good land, and liberty to manage their own affairs their own way, seem to be the two great causes of the prosperity of all new colonies." Overall, Smith's general theories about the operations of free markets represent the single best departure point for discussions of the course of colonial development. The recent work of Mary Schweitzer on the Pennsylvania economy, where free-market attitudes and policies held sway over narrower mercantilist thinking, provides a cogent reaffirmation of this viewpoint.

Despite the inconveniences of some British trade and internal regulations, which the colonists often ignored, and which in any event affected no more than 4 to 6 percent of gross colonial output, the thirteen colonies largely fit the Smithian model for economic success. Given the existing technology and the availability of natural resources, this commercial-agricultural society was probably functioning at near optimum efficiency. Indeed, by the mid-eighteenth century, if not earlier, the typical white household in the mainland colonies was almost certainly enjoying the highest standard of living anywhere around the globe.

BIBLIOGRAPHICAL ESSAY

THERE have been no other comprehensive studies of the colonial economy for a student audience similar to this book. Gary Walton and James Shepherd focused primarily on commerce and its contribution to economic expansion in *The Economic Rise of Early America* (Cambridge: Cambridge University Press, 1979). An even earlier analysis of the underlying forces at work in the rise of the overall economy is Stuart Bruchey, *The Roots of American Economic Growth, 1607–1861* (New York: Harper & Row, 1968), although Bruchey's primary emphasis was on the first half of the nineteenth century rather than the colonial period. An excellent interdisciplinary overview of eighteenth-century history with a strong emphasis of economic factors is James Henretta, *The Evolution of American Society, 1700–1815* (Lexington, Mass.: Heath, 1973); an updated, revised, and retitled version is Henretta and Gregory H. Nobles, *Evolution and Revolution: American Society, 1600–1820* (Lexington, Mass.: Heath, 1987). Jacob Price, Richard Sheridan, James Lemon, Richard Dunn, Gary Nash, James Henretta, and T. H. Breen contributed a series of excellent historiographical essays for inclusion in Jack P. Greene and J. R. Pole, eds., *Colonial British America: Essays on the New History of the Early Modern Era* (Baltimore: Johns Hopkins University Press, 1984). The most exhaustive and authoritative source on the colonial economy for graduate students and serious scholars is John McCusker and Russell Menard, *The Economy of*

British America, 1607–1789 (Chapel Hill: University of North Carolina, 1985); see my review of it in *Journal of Economic History* (1986), pp. 279–81, for a more detailed assessment. For additional sources on income growth and economic development, check the references cited in chapter 9 of this book.

A broad introduction to colonial population is found in Gary Nash, *Red, White, and Black: The Peoples of Early America* (Englewood Cliffs, N.J.: Prentice-Hall, 1982). Wilbur Jacobs surveys the debate about the size of the native American population in "The Tip of an Iceberg: Pre-Columbian Indian Demography and Some Implications for Revisionism," *William and Mary Quarterly* (1974), pp. 123–34. A study of the ecology of New England, with substantial data on Indians, is William Cronon, *Changes in the Land: Indians, Colonists, and the Ecology of New England* (New York: Hill and Wang, 1983). The black population of the western hemisphere is covered in Philip Curtin, *The Atlantic Slave Trade: A Census* (Madison: University of Wisconsin Press, 1969). Henry Gemery provides estimates on the number of British citizens traveling to the colonies in "Emigration from the British Isles to the New World, 1630–1700," in Paul Uselding, ed., *Research in Economic History* (1980), 5:179–232, and "European Emigration to North America, 1700 to 1820: Numbers and Quasi-Numbers," *Perspectives in American History* (1984), n.s., 1:283–342. For another ethnic group, see Marianne Wokeck, "The Flow and Composition of German Immigration to Philadelphia, 1722–1775," *Pennsylvania Magazine of History and Biography* (1981), 105:249–78. An earlier article that stimulated much of the recent interest in demography was J. Potter's "The Growth of Population in America, 1700–1860," in D. V. Glass and D.E.C. Eversley, eds., *Population in History: Essays in Historical Demography* (London: Arnold, 1965), pp. 631–88. Bernard Bailyn discusses the last wave of immigration before independence in *The Peopling of British North America: An Introduction* (New York: Knopf, 1986).

Two contemporary discussions of colonial population were Benjamin Franklin's 1751 essay, "Observations Concerning the Increase of Mankind," available in Leonard Labaree, ed., *The Papers of Benjamin Franklin* (New Haven: Yale University Press, 1961), 4:225–34, and Edward Wigglesworth's treatise, *Calculations on*

American Population, with a Table for Estimating the Annual Increase of Inhabitants in the British Colonies (Boston, 1775). Wigglesworth estimated that more Englishmen would reside in the New World than in England by 1825; he was not far off the mark.

Two outstanding books with extensive data on colonial population are Robert V. Wells, *The Population of the British Colonies in America Before 1776: A Survey of Census Data* (Princeton, N.J.: Princeton University Press, 1975); and Alice Hanson Jones, *American Colonial Wealth*, 3 vols. (New York: Arno Press, 1977). The extent of settlement within the colonies is calculated in Lee Alston and Morton Shapiro, "Inheritance Laws Across Colonies: Causes and Consequences," *Journal of Economic History* (1984), 44:277–87.

Much of the scholarly work on colonial demography has focused on New England. The most comprehensive studies of the region are Daniel *Scott* Smith, "The Demographic History of Colonial New England," *Journal of Economic History* (1972), pp. 165–83, and Robert Higgs and Louis Stettler, "Colonial New England Demography: A Sampling Approach," *William and Mary Quarterly* (1970), pp. 282–94. Maris Vinovskis concentrates on a single colony in "Mortality Rates and Trends in Massachusetts Before 1860," *Journal of Economic History* (1972), pp. 184–213; see also his *Fertility in Massachusetts from the Revolution to the Civil War* (New York: Academic Press, 1981). John Waters argues that wealthier individuals married earlier than more common folk in "Family, Inheritance, and Migration in Colonial New England: The Evidence from Guilford, Connecticut," *William and Mary Quarterly* (1982), pp. 64–86. Factors influencing the age of marriage are also discussed in James Gallman, "Determinates of Age at Marriage in Colonial Perquimans County, North Carolina," *William and Mary Quarterly* (1982), pp. 176–91.

Many studies analyze small towns or counties: John Demos, *A Little Commonwealth: Family Life in Plymouth Colony* (New York: Oxford University Press, 1970); Demos, "Families in Colonial Bristol, Rhode Island: An Exercise in Historical Demography," *William and Mary Quarterly* (1968), pp. 40–57; Demos, "Notes on Life in Plymouth Colony," *ibid.* (1965), pp. 264–86; Philip Greven, *Four Generations: Population, Land, and Family in Colonial Andover, Mas-*

sachusetts (Ithaca, N.Y.: Cornell University Press, 1970); Greven, "Family Structure in Seventeenth-Century Andover, Massachusetts," *William and Mary Quarterly* (1966), pp. 234–56; and Kenneth Lockridge, *A New England Town, The First Hundred Years: Dedham, Massachusetts* (New York: Norton, 1970).

Wesley Frank Craven covers one southern colony in *White, Red, and Black: The Seventeenth-Century Virginian* (Charlottesville: University Press of Virginia, 1971). Allan Kulikoff has a wider focus in *Tobacco and Slaves: The Development of Southern Cultures in the Chesapeake, 1680–1800* (Chapel Hill: University of North Carolina Press, 1986); see also his articles, "A 'Prolifick' People: Black Population Growth in the Chesapeake Colonies, 1700–1790," *Southern Studies* (1977), pp. 391–428, and "The Origins of Afro-American Society in Tidewater Maryland and Virginia, 1700 to 1790," *William and Mary Quarterly* (1978), pp. 226–59. Terry Anderson and Robert Paul Thomas discuss mainly white indentured servants in "The Growth of Population and Labor Force in the Seventeenth-Century Chesapeake," *Explorations in Economic History* (1978), pp. 290–312.

Daniel *Blake* Smith discusses death rates in "Mortality and Family in Colonial Chesapeake," *Journal of Interdisciplinary History* (1978), pp. 403–27. Russell Menard adds to our understanding of the lowering of death rates for native-born settlers in "The Growth of Population in the Chesapeake Colonies: A Comment," *Explorations in Economic History* (1981), pp. 399–410. There are valuable essays in Thad Tate and David Ammerman, eds., *The Chesapeake in the Seventeenth Century: Essays on Anglo-American Society* (Chapel Hill: University of North Carolina Press, 1979). A comparative study is Herbert Klein and Stanley Engerman, "Fertility Differentials Between Slaves in the United States and the British West Indies," *William and Mary Quarterly* (1978), pp. 357–74; support for their hypothesis comes from Jerome S. Handler and Robert S. Corruccini, "Weaning Among West Indian Slaves: Historical and Bioanthropological Evidence from Barbados," *William and Mary Quarterly* (1986), pp. 111–17. Another valuable study is Kenneth Kiple, *The Caribbean Slave: A Biological History* (Cambridge: Cambridge University Press, 1984). Richard Steckel explores differences in the mortality rates of black children vs. black adults in "A Peculiar Problem: The Nutrition, Health, and Mortality of American Slaves from Childhood to Maturity," *Journal of Economic History* (1986), pp. 721–41.

For comparative data on Europe, see Carlo Cipolla, *Before the Industrial Revolution: European Society and Economy, 1000–1700* (New York: Norton, 1976); E. A. Wrigley, *Population and History* (New York: McGraw-Hill, 1969); Wrigley, R. S. Schofield, et al., *The Population History of England, 1541–1871* (Cambridge: Harvard University Press, 1982).

For an excellent assessment of the status of research on colonial demography in the late 1970s, plus a comprehensive list of sources, see Daniel *Scott* Smith, "The Estimates of Early American Historical Demographers: Two Steps Forward, One Step Back, What Steps in the Future," *Historical Methods* (1979), pp. 24–38.

For a careful and powerful explanation of how free-market forces operated in one colony, see Mary M. Schweitzer, *Custom and Contract: Household, Government, and the Economy in Colonial Pennsylvania* (New York: Columbia University Press, 1987).

CHAPTER II

FOREIGN TRADE

L IKE other European nations with overseas empires, the British expected their colonies to serve the mother country and to pursue economic activities that on balance contributed to the power of England vis-à-vis its continental rivals. The reigning economic orthodoxy of the day was mercantilism—a rather fluid term (like modern Keynesianism)—which advocated national self-sufficiency and a favorable balance of international trade. With the sales of British goods overseas exceeding the purchases of foreign products, other nations would be forced to settle their deficit accounts through the shipment of specie—gold or silver. According to mercantilist precepts, specie inflows per se strengthened the political and economic power of the recipient and simultaneously weakened those countries losing gold and silver. It is noteworthy that twentieth-century economists generally advocate the maintenance of a favorable trade balance as well, although the goal is no longer to attract gold, since its possession is now considered of little particular value, but rather to boost employment levels and output in the domestic economy.

In the mercantilist world view, colonies were expected to assist the mother country in promoting a favorable balance of trade. The British colonies could help in several ways. First, a colony could contribute directly to Britain's strength by purchasing semifinished and manufactured goods over and above the value of the raw materials and foodstuffs it shipped to the home market, and with the deficit balance paid in specie. Colonies could also contribute by growing products such as tobacco and rice which the mother country could sell in large quantities to the inhabitants of continental powers, thereby draining rivals of their specie holdings. Finally, the colonies could contribute by supplying products within the empire, such as sugar and indigo, which Britain otherwise would have purchased from foreign sources.

To guarantee that trade flows were in harmony with the perceived requirements of their empires, the European colonial powers normally adopted regulations designed to steer commerce into the proper channels. For the first half of the seventeenth century, when the population of Europeans in North America was less than 50,000, Parliament passed a series of Navigation Acts, which established new ground rules for colonial participation in world trade. The major provisions of the acts were as follows: (1) they excluded vessels registered in foreign countries from carrying trade between ports *within* the British empire; (2) they provided that goods manufactured on the European continent could not be imported directly by the colonies but had to pass first through England; (3) they authorized bounties for colonial products especially valued in the home market; and, finally, (4) they specified that certain colonial exports deemed extraordinarily valuable in international trade were "enumerated," which meant that shipment only to Great Britain or other designated ports was permitted. Among the items placed on the list of enumerated goods were furs, ship masts, rice, indigo, and tobacco.

One of the longest-running debates among economic historians revolves around how seriously the various Navigation Acts damaged the colonial economy, and whether resentment over their enforcement was a prime cause of the rift with England in the 1760s and 1770s. The consensus now is that the net burden on the colonies as a whole did not exceed 1 to 2 percent of total income in any given year. The trade regulations actually tended to benefit northern shipping interests, which were protected from competition with French, Spanish, and Dutch vessels. The producers of indigo in the lower south also received bounties for growing plants which yielded dyes valued in the British textile industry.

On the other hand, tobacco growers in Virginia, Maryland, and North Carolina were penalized substantially because they were prevented from selling their output directly to buyers on the continent, where tobacco prices were invariably higher than in England. The extent of the planters' losses was far less than the price differential between Britain and the continent, however, since English and Scottish tobacco merchants provided valuable merchandising services. Indeed, in the years after independence and the ending of trade regulations, most U.S. planters continued to market their tobacco through the British mercantile network voluntarily. The maintenance of old marketing patterns after political separation suggests that the *real* impact of trade regulations on tobacco growers was not extraordinary.

Meanwhile, all regions enjoyed the protection of the British navy on the high seas, and Parliament often reimbursed the colonies for expenses incurred in conducting military operations against various Indian tribes and the French. On the whole, protests about British restrictions on overseas trade played a negligible role in stirring up revolutionary sentiments. The colonists' protests were directed rather at proposals for sharply increased taxes, which were a new feature of Parliament's commercial policies after the conclusion of the French and Indian War in 1763.

The northern colonies lacked the natural resources to yield valuable products unique to the western hemisphere; thus they failed to conform quite as well to the imperial model as did their southern counterparts. Since the northern climate was fairly similar to England, parliamentary leaders attuned to mercantilist thinking viewed these colonies skeptically. They were considered potential competitors of the mother country in overseas commerce as well as possible benefactors. Agriculture in England and the northern colonies was much the same, with basic foodstuffs and livestock predominating.

The basis for direct northern trade with England in the seventeenth century was restricted largely to furs, fish, and ship masts. Furs became an export from New England soon after the Pilgrims landed at Plymouth in 1620. The Pilgrims used their earnings from the fur trade to pay the debts incurred in sailing to the new world and provisioning themselves during the first few years. In the 1630s, the Puritans, who established a much larger settlement in the Boston area, took over the New England fur trade, and they dominated it until beaver were virtually hunted to extinction in southern New England before the end of the seventeenth century. The decimation of the beaver population in the northeast was one obvious manifestation of how the economic activities of Europeans had a strongly negative impact on the natural environment. (Three hundred years

later, here in the late twentieth century, beaver, under the protection
of environmental law, are happily making a comeback in many parts
of New England.)

The most lucrative fur trade during the seventeenth century was
not in English America at all but conducted through Amsterdam
merchants dealing with the Dutch West India Company's colony of
New Netherland. By the 1650s, according to Oliver Rink, local
Dutch merchants were shipping over 45,000 pelts annually out of
the Hudson River valley. Indeed, the lure of profits in the fur trade
and the hope of closing down a smugglers enclave located in New
Amsterdam were the main considerations in the English decision to
pursue a military solution to the half-century-long jurisdictional dispute with the Netherlands in the 1660s. New York remained the
center of the fur trade until the end of the colonial era. The Hudson
River and its numerous tributaries made connections with regions
that were still largely wilderness as late as the 1770s. To prevent
shipments by Dutch descendants to merchants in Holland, Parliament put furs on the enumerated list in 1722. The fur trade represents one field of endeavor where economic cooperation between
the native Indian population and Europeans was sustained over a
long period of time. By the mid-eighteenth century, however, furs
were a relatively insignificant item in the export totals.

When the English arrived in New England, virgin forests covered
up to 90 percent of the land, and some settlers may have envisioned
the development of an extensive timber trade with the mother
country. By the seventeenth century, England had undergone an
extended period of deforestation, and wood, which was the primary
source of construction material for homes, buildings, and ships plus
a major source of energy for household heating and iron manufacturing, was already in short supply. England was heavily dependent
on suppliers in northern Europe and Scandinavia for timber products,
and political leaders considered this reliance a serious handicap for
a strong naval power. But ships were too small and transportation
costs therefore too high to justify the opening of a general transatlantic trade in lumber with the colonies.

Tall, straight white pines, sometimes reaching a height of 120
feet, were prized as ship masts, however. For a large ship, English
shipwrights could use a single American tree to fashion a mast that

was much stronger than masts pieced together from shorter European trees. White pines meeting the proper specifications eventually became enumerated products, and government contracts for supplying the royal navy with ship masts were one of the rewards savored by successful political factions in Massachusetts and New Hampshire. The enforcement of a British rule, which limited the cutting of trees identified by a carved arrow in the bark as solely the property of the crown, proved extremely difficult in the deep forest, and conflicts between imperial officials and colonial poachers, who valued the pines for shingles, clapboard, and barrel staves, persisted into the eighteenth century. For military reasons, therefore, the royal navy valued the northern colonies as a secure source of masts in the event of war on the European continent, but in strictly economic terms, the mast trade with England generated only modest revenues.

By the late colonial period, northern exports to Great Britain and Ireland were still severely limited. The three most important products were whale oil, potash, and flaxseed. The whaling industry expanded swiftly after 1750; twenty years later over 250 vessels set sail each season from New England ports in search of whales. In response to a rise in price of whale oil from £10 ($900) per barrel in the 1720s up to nearly £30 ($2,700) in the 1770s, output climbed to over 11,000 barrels by 1750 and 30,000 barrels in 1775. (For the technique of converting sterling amounts to 1985 dollars, see the appendix.) Before the rise of the petroleum industry in the mid-nineteenth century, whale oil was valued for illumination and lubrication; it was also used to finish leather and to make soap. The head matter of sperm whales also produced fine-quality candles, which were shipped mainly to the West Indies and other coastal ports. Potash, or pearl ash, was another forest product. After burning three to five acres of timber, workers could leach out the ashes with water and extract up to a ton of potash, a chemical used in the manufacture of soap and gunpowder. During the first few years on a farm, when clearing fields was one of the prime activities, potash was often among a household's most valuable products. Flaxseed was grown mainly in the middle colonies and shipped to England, where the seeds were crushed to produce various types of valuable oil.

The northern colonies were much more valuable to England as

an overseas market for home manufactures than as a supplier of raw materials, however. Textiles and metal hardware were the leading British exports to the colonies, both north and south. The importance of the colonies in the export trade of the mother country escalated in the eighteenth century. In 1701 the American colonies (including the West Indies) took only 10 percent of England's domestic exports, but by 1772 the figure had risen to 37 percent. In 1772, for example, Great Britain exported goods valued at £1.7 million ($155 million) to the northern colonies alone; British imports from the same region were only £251,000 ($22.5 million), leaving a favorable trade balance of £1.45 million ($130 million) for the mother country.

The British concern about potential competition from colonial manufacturing was well founded. In certain fields northern business firms were able to produce sufficient supplies not only to meet colonial demand but also to make a dent in the English home market. Thus, Parliament periodically enacted legislation designed to limit the right of the colonists to engage in economic activities that threatened competition with a significant number of English artisans and manufacturers. The aim was to discourage American manufacturing and to preserve colonial markets, especially in finished goods, for British firms; but that goal proved difficult to achieve. Parliament was able to prevent the colonies from exporting manufactured goods back to England and to other foreign ports; however, it generally failed to deter the colonists from producing finished goods for local and regional markets.

The first colonial enterprises seriously affected by export restrictions were hat manufacturers. Concentrated mostly in the Hudson River valley, colonial hatters produced beaver felt hats that, by 1730, had captured a sizable share of the European market. In retaliation, British hatters persuaded Parliament to pass the Hat Act in 1732. It made illegal the export of colonial hats on the grounds that the jobs and profits of English workers took precedence over any benefits accruing to colonial entrepreneurs and European consumers.

The British attitude toward the emerging colonial iron industry was, in contrast, more tolerant. The natural inclination to slow the growth of manufacturing facilities in the colonies was offset by the desire to diminish the mother country's increasing dependence on

Sweden for the iron ingots from which metal products were fabricated. The deforestation of England was an environmental factor which had restrained the production of iron, because wood charcoal was the only energy source technologically perfected for use in refining ore. (Coking coal was not used extensively until late in the eighteenth century.)

The mainland colonies had virtually unlimited timber resources in the vicinity of ore sites, and beginning with the establishment of a furnace at Saugus, Massachusetts, in 1645, colonial iron production had risen to an annual output of 1,500 tons, or around 2 percent of world output, by 1700. Over the next century the center of production shifted southward to Pennsylvania, Maryland, and Virginia. By 1775 the colonies were major producers of iron, with over 80 active furnaces which employed in total up to 8,000 workers. In his comprehensive history of colonial metals, James Mulholland estimated production at 21,000 tons annually. Accounting for 15 percent of world output, the North American colonies ranked third behind Russia and Sweden in the 1770s. They exported to Great Britain pig and bar iron valued at roughly £58,000 ($5.2 million) per year from 1768 to 1772, with about equal amounts shipped from the middle colonies and the upper south.

Because of shortages at home, the British encouraged the establishment of iron furnaces in the colonies, but Parliament still attempted to reserve for English workmen the privilege of fabricating the metal into useful products. A law passed in 1750 eliminated all customs duties on bar and pig iron shipments to England, yet it simultaneously forbade the construction of any new facilities in the colonies for fabricating iron into finished products and stipulated a fine of £200 ($18,000). This ban on the establishment of new fabricating shops was blatantly ignored by the colonists, invariably with the implicit support of royal governors, who normally sought to avoid confrontations with powerful business leaders and who had no effective means of enforcing the prohibition in any event. By the 1770s, Pennsylvania, Maryland, and New Jersey had as many as 175 locations where iron and some steel products were turned out for colonial consumers.

From the perspective of the twentieth century, one of the most serious deficiencies in the mercantilist outlook on economic affairs relates to the issue of the proper role of manufacturing in the colonial empire. The accepted view at the time was that the growth of manufacturing in the colonies represented a threat to business interests in the mother country, and therefore Parliament was obligated to discourage such activities. Among the eighteenth-century students of political economy who suspected that this line of reasoning needed closer scrutiny was, again, Benjamin Franklin. In a pamphlet written in 1760, he argued that the British fear about competition emerging within the empire was largely misplaced.

The bulk of England's trade was actually with her continental rivals, Franklin observed, and these nations had already begun to develop manufacturing sectors. The basis for commerce between prosperous nations with similar economic structures was broader than between nations with wide disparities in environment, incomes, and productive capacities. "A man must know very little of the trade of the world," Franklin wrote, "who does not know, that the greater part of it is carried on between countries whose climate differs very little." Therefore, he concluded, England probably had far more to gain than to lose from any expansion of colonial manufacturing. Once more Franklin's commonsense reasoning has proven compatible with modern theory and practice. Greater opportunities exist today for commerce within the circle of industrialized nations, where incomes are high, than between wealthy nations and underdeveloped and poor countries, where purchasing power is low.

Because of the expansive nature of the colonial economy, aggregate imports from England reached all-time highs in the 1770s. Between 1720 and 1770 per capita imports rose from £0.8 ($72) to £1.2 ($108), an increase of 50 percent. By the latter date, the colonial market accounted for over one-half of all British exports of certain products: wrought copper, wrought iron, beaver hats, cordage, iron nails, linen, wrought silk, printed cottons and linen, and Spanish cloth. As McCusker and Menard have observed, colonial demand grew fast enough to support simultaneously the sales and profits of both British manufacturers and domestic entrepreneurs. The colonists' substitution of domestic goods for imports in some markets failed to diminish overall opportunities for British exporters.

With limited opportunities for exporting directly to England, the northern colonies looked elsewhere for foreign markets. They discovered strong demand for their surpluses in the Caribbean sugar islands, southern Europe, and the Wine Islands. Trade regulations placed few restrictions on the shipment of fish, grain, livestock, lumber, staves, and other basic provisions to ports outside England.

In the 1640s and 1650s, the New England colonies established trading patterns which prevailed throughout the colonial era. The Puritans and their descendants supplied provisions to island societies which concentrated almost exclusively on the cultivation of staples— sugar in the Caribbean and wine grapes in the European outposts off the coast of northwestern Africa. By the eighteenth century, the middle colonies of Pennsylvania, New Jersey, and New York had entered this trade as well, and food shipments were extended to Mediterranean ports, particularly along the southern coast of Spain.

By the 1770s, northern trade routes were firmly established. The middle colonies shipped primarily bread, flour, wheat, and salted beef and pork to southern Europe and the West Indies. The New England colonies sent dried fish to southern Europe, while their exports to the Caribbean included fish, horses, pine boards, cattle, spermaceti candles, and a variety of other products. By the late colonial period, however, New England no longer exported flour and grain; Massachusetts became instead an importer of wheat from other colonies.

From the West Indies, the northern colonies imported mainly rum, molasses, and sugar. In the Caribbean commodity trade, the mainland colonies purchased more than they sold. Most of the rum imported directly or distilled on the mainland was consumed in the colonies, since alcohol consumption per capita was very high. By 1770 about 140 rum distilleries produced about 5 million gallons of rum. W. J. Rorabaugh estimated per capita alcoholic consumption for all persons over the age of 15, including cider, wine, and beer as well as rum, at 5.1 gallons in 1710 and 6.6 gallons in 1770, or 2.3 ounces per day by the later period. (By the 1980s per capita consumption was under one ounce per day.) Most excess colonial production went to Newfoundland, where rum consumption per capita was the highest on the mainland. The rum-for-slaves trade with

Africa, based in Rhode Island, accounted for a very small percentage of mainland rum supplies. The triangular trade among the northern colonies, the West Indies, and England was in truth limited in scope. The vast majority of vessels sailing from colonial ports for the Caribbean returned directly home without ever leaving the western hemisphere.

The northern colonies did generate large surpluses in the commodity trade with southern Europe, however. New England supplied fish, while the middle colonies shipped wheat and flour. The return cargoes of wine and salt were valued at little more than one-sixth of the export figures. The region had on average an annual favorable balance of trade of £198,000 ($17.8 million) from 1768 to 1772. As a result, the northern colonies built up substantial credit balances with mercantile firms in the Mediterranean, and those funds were subsequently transferred to London, where they helped to finance the heavy volume of imports from England. Despite their earnings from the southern European trade, the northern colonies remained in an overall deficit position in their international commodity accounts because of their unfavorable trade balances with the West Indies and, particularly, Great Britain.

The New England and middle colonies paid for these imports primarily with funds earned from providing shipping and financial services in the North Atlantic market. Economists call these earnings "invisible" because they fail to appear in the statistical data routinely compiled on imports and exports. Gary Walton and James Shepherd have shown that these invisible earnings were by no means inconsequential, however. Indeed the northern colonies earned on average more revenues from carrying and insuring cargoes than from sales of any tangible commodity. Colonial ships dominated the West Indian trade, and they played a major role in the commerce with England and southern Europe. In 1772, for example, invisible earnings amounted to about £700,000 ($63 million) for the northern colonies and covered over 50 percent of their deficit in the commodity trade.

The southern colonies fit more readily into the mercantilist mold. They not only provided a growing market for English manufactured goods, but they also produced specialized crops which were heavily in demand in England and on the European continent. The upper south, consisting of Virginia and Maryland, contributed tobacco. This luxury item was actually not consumed heavily by the English in the eighteenth century but was sold instead to French, German, and other European buyers. Thus tobacco became a major factor in Britain's trade balance with its continental rivals. In addition, planters in South Carolina had become large suppliers of two other crops highly valued in Europe—rice and indigo. Like tobacco, rice was extensively reexported to northern Europe, while indigo was prized in the mother country as a dye in the textile industry.

The expansion of the economy in the upper south corresponded with the rising demand for tobacco in Europe. The discovery that Virginia's sandy soils were especially well suited for growing high-quality tobacco transformed the colony. From a struggling settlement on the verge of starvation and abandonment, Virginia became a booming economy in the early 1620s when the price of tobacco temporarily skyrocketed. Although prices declined sharply in the 1630s, profits were substantial enough to attract a continual stream of free immigrants and white indentured servants into the Chesapeake area of Virginia and Maryland.

From 1640 to around the end of the century, tobacco production expanded steadily. Black slaves began to replace white indentured servants in the labor force after the 1680s. Then, in the first quarter of the eighteenth century, production stabilized, and the vigor of the Chesapeake economy was tempered. Jacob Price argues that this period of stagnation was not caused by an inadequate supply of labor, or by soil exhaustion in the older areas, but rather reflected a momentary lull in the growth of foreign demand for tobacco.

After 1725, demand revived, and it grew at a steady pace until the 1770s. Price links the renewed prosperity of the upper-south economy with the spurt in sales generated primarily by the French market. In the late colonial period, the French government, which exercised monopoly rights in purchasing overseas supplies, bought heavily through Scotland's Glasgow tobacco merchants. After 1730, Glasgow merchants diverted much of the tobacco business away from London because their agents in Virginia and Maryland were prepared to offer spot cash at the wharf for a planter's crop, and because they granted liberal credit terms to their colonial customers. Between 1740 and 1770 the population of Virginia rose from 180,000 to 450,000, while tobacco exports jumped from £165,000 to £476,000 ($14.8 to $43.1 million); per capita earnings from tobacco rose by over 15 percent.

The lower south, consisting of the Carolinas and later Georgia, were initially settled after the middle of the seventeenth century by emigrants arriving from Barbados and by families living along Virginia's southeastern frontier. Up to 40,000 Native Americans inhabited the area when the English first arrived, and an active cross-cultural trade in deerskins quickly emerged and persisted for decades. Deerskins were highly valued in England for gloves and leggings because of the softness yet durability of the leather. A second category of products gathered from the pine forests of the lower south were naval stores: mainly turpentine, rosin, tar, and pitch. Converse Clowse and Timothy Silver have described in much detail how these various products were harvested and processed for export. The main applications of these items were as follows: turpentine was burned in lamps; rosin went into candles and soap; tar preserved wood and ropes exposed to air and rain; and pitch coated ship hulls resisted salt water. To encourage production, Parliament authorized the payment of bounties for naval stores in 1704. Although the fees were substantially reduced after 1729, naval stores remained the most valuable export from North Carolina, a colony about which we still know very little, until independence.

In South Carolina, and in the small but growing Georgia settlement, rice and indigo became the two staple crops cultivated widely for the export trade. These were complementary crops because rice grew in swampy lowland areas, while indigo bushes thrived on higher ground. Over the last half-century of the colonial period, the value of these two crops increased rapidly. By the early 1770s exports were £312,000 ($28.1 million) annually for rice and £113,000 ($10.2 million) for indigo. In combination they amounted to over one-half of the value of tobacco shipped from the upper south.

Because the English government appreciated the great value of colonial rice and tobacco in international trade, these two products headed the list of enumerated goods. All tobacco shipments went to Great Britain, where English and Scottish merchants reexported up to 85 percent of the crop to continental buyers in the late colonial period. Similarly, all rice destined for ports in northern Europe also had to pass through Britain; rice bound for southern Europe could proceed directly to its final port of destination after 1731. Roger Ransom has calculated that if the colonists had had the opportunity to send all their crops directly to continental ports, bypassing Britain completely, their sales proceeds from foreign trade would have

TABLE 2.1. Value of Leading Colonial Exports, 1768–1772
(yearly averages in thousands of £)

Food grains		920
Bread & flour	410	
Wheat	115	
Indian corn	83	
Rice	312	
Tobacco		766
Fish		154
Wood products		135
Boards	70	
Staves & headings	65	
Indigo		113
Meat		72
Cured beef & pork	51	
Live cattle	21	
Horses		60
Iron		58
Naval stores		48
Whale oil		46
Flaxseed		42
Potash		35
Rum		22
Total of above		2,471
All other exports		331
Total exports		2,802

SOURCE: Data drawn from Gary M. Walton and James F. Shepherd, *The Economic Rise of Early America* (Cambridge: Cambridge University Press, 1979), table 21, pp. 194–95.

increased substantially. In 1770, for example, he estimated southern revenues might have been as much as £446,000 ($40.4 million) above the £852,000 ($74.2 million) figure actually recorded, or over 50 percent higher. In terms of the overall impact on the colonial economy, the enumeration of southern staples imposed by far the greatest burden. Indeed, the southern colonies assumed roughly 90 percent of the gross burden associated with the Navigation Acts, and regional income may have been penalized by as much as 2.5 percent annually.

Ironically, the financial burden connected with enumeration regulations dwarfed in size the new direct taxes Parliament imposed in the prerevolutionary decade. The English government had proposed to raise no more than £40,000 ($3.6 million) per year from taxes on official stamps, tea, and other colonial imports. Despite the heavy burden on the southern colonies, planters rarely complained about the navigation laws and rarely cited them as a grievance during public debates over the American role in the British empire. Moreover, despite the enumeration handicap, southern planters had higher incomes and held more wealth than northern farmers and many urban merchants. In South Carolina the percentage of slaves in the population was much higher than elsewhere, and the value of exports per white settler was the highest on the mainland by a wide margin. As a result, white South Carolinians enjoyed the highest living standards in the thirteen colonies. Charleston contained the largest collection of wealthy inhabitants, many of them absentee rice and indigo planters who spent up to one-half of the year enjoying life in the port city.

By the 1770s, the sale of food surpluses overseas was the most rapidly expanding export sector for the southern colonies. Because of their heightened interest in enlarging foreign markets for surplus food, the southern colonies had more goals in common with their northern counterparts in the late colonial period than before 1720, when tobacco had been the unchallenged southern export. Rice had become a crop of major importance by midcentury. In response to rising world prices for foodstuffs, wheat and corn production in Virginia and Maryland rose, and sizable amounts became available for sale in overseas markets. In Virginia, grain exports per capita of the free population rose by over 300 percent after 1740, whereas

tobacco exports per capita climbed only 15 percent. David Klingaman has calculated that grain exports jumped from £11,500 ($1
million) in 1740 to £130,000 ($11.7 million) in 1770; by the later
date, the overseas shipments of foodstuffs were valued at one-fourth
of the figure for tobacco.

Much of the grain came from new lands which were better suited
for food crops than for tobacco. In Virginia, settlers opened up the
Shenandoah Valley, just west of the low-lying Blue Ridge Moun-
tains. The valley soils and climate were ideal for wheat, and farmers
had access to distant markets by shipping grain down the Shenandoah River, which flowed north to the Potomac. In Maryland, the
counties contiguous with Pennsylvania were also more adaptable to
grain cultivation, and the high quality of Maryland flour created a
strong demand in the Caribbean sugar islands. The high world prices
for food encouraged many planters in the settled tobacco regions to
shift more land and labor into wheat production for foreign markets.

Since the export of staple crops was so important in the economy
of the southern colonies, historians have too frequently forgotten to
emphasize that the production of foodstuffs for personal consumption was still the chief source of real income for southern as well as
northern farmers. With few exceptions, rural families consumed right
on the farm more of what they produced than the amounts sold on
domestic and foreign markets.

The south was always self-sufficient in food. More acres were
planted in food crops, especially corn, than in tobacco on even the
most specialized Chesapeake plantations. Most families, free and
slave, maintained vegetable gardens and livestock. In this respect,
mainland plantation slavery differed sharply from Caribbean sugar
estates, where little food was grown and provisions were constantly
imported. Klingaman has estimated that the total value of the corn
and wheat grown in Virginia between 1768 and 1772 was £864,000
($78 million) annually compared to tobacco production of only
£493,000 ($44 million). About 90 percent of the corn crop and over
80 percent of the wheat harvest was consumed within the state, with
the remainder exported mainly to the Caribbean. Paul Clemens has
documented how the same forces were at work on Maryland's eastern
shore in this period as well. The increased diversification of agricul-

ture was a key factor in maintaining, and even augmenting, living standards in the upper south during the eighteenth century.

The population of the southern colonies rose from 115,000 in 1700 to over 1 million by the early 1770s, and the region became an increasingly important outlet for English manufacturers. The south alone imported goods valued at £1.6 million ($144 million) from Great Britain in 1772, or 16 percent of the mother country's entire overseas commerce. The southern colonies ran huge trade deficits with England, which coincided nicely with mercantilist policy. However, they generated substantial surpluses in the trade with Scotland to the north, because active Glasgow merchants had captured a large share of the Chesapeake tobacco trade by the early 1770s. As a result the southern commodity trade with Great Britain as a whole was near equilibrium, with the excess funds accumulating in Scotland transferred to London to finance colonial imports of English goods.

Consolidating the trade statistics from all thirteen colonies reveals that they consistently ran deficits in the foreign-trade sector during the eighteenth century. They imported far more goods from overseas sellers than they exported to foreign buyers, and the gap widened in the years just before independence. In the period from 1768 to 1772, the trade deficit averaged £1.05 million ($94.5 million) annually. How did the colonists manage to pay for these excess purchases of foreign goods year after year? In order to assess the status of the thirteen colonies in the international economy, we need to analyze carefully a financial statement listing all the inflows and outflows of monies and monetary claims across their borders from all foreign sources. Economists call such a statement "the balance of payments."

A substantial part of the trade deficit was offset by the invisible earnings generated by colonial ships transporting goods to foreign ports in the North Atlantic. Table 2.2 reveals that invisible earnings alone totaled £820,000 ($73.8 million), accounting for over 75 percent of the trade deficit. Another £140,000 ($12.6 million) inflow was generated by the sales of ships built in colonial shipyards to foreign buyers. When all the transactions associated with the movement of commodities are taken into account, the payments deficit falls to £90,000 ($8.1 million).

Other items also affected the balance of payments. Some of the outflow went to buy labor on either a temporary or a permanent basis. The colonies paid foreigners £80,000 ($7.2 million) for the contracts of indentured servants arriving voluntarily from Europe and another £200,000 ($18 million) to purchase slaves, who came involuntarily, from Africa. According to Julian Gwyn, Parliament authorized the expenditure of approximately £365,000 ($33 million) in the colonies for military defense and for the civil administration

TABLE 2.2. Balance of Payments for the Thirteen Colonies
(yearly average for 1768–1772, in thousands of £)

	Debits	Credits
Commodities		
Export earnings		2,870
Imports	3,920	
Trade deficit	1,050	
Ship sales to foreigners		140
Invisible earnings		
Shipping cargoes		600
Merchant commissions, insurance, etc.		220
Payments for human beings		
Indentured servants	80	
Slaves	200	
British collections and expenditures		
Taxes and duties	40	
Military and civil expenditures		365
Payments deficit financed by specie flows		
and/or increased indebtedness		45

SOURCES: Data compiled from Gary M. Walton and James F. Shepherd, *The Economic Rise of Early America* (Cambridge: Cambridge University Press, 1979), table 9, p. 101; Jacob Price, "New Time Series for Scotland's and Britain's Trade with the Thirteen Colonies and States, 1740–1791," *William and Mary Quarterly* (1975), 32:307–25; Julian Gwyn, "British Government Spending and the North American Colonies, 1740–1775," in Peter Marshall and Glyn Williams, eds., *The Atlantic Empire before the American Revolution* (London: Frank Cass, 1980), pp. 74–84, fn. 7.

of its North American territories. Meanwhile, the British collected about £40,000 ($3.6 million) in taxes and duties in colonial ports, which offset a small portion of those expenses.

After all the debits and credits are listed, the colonies faced a relatively modest annual deficit of approximately £45,000 ($4 million) in their balance of international payments in the period from 1768 to 1772. This amount could be settled either through the shipment of specie or by increasing incrementally aggregate American indebtedness overseas. The data indicate that the colonists selected the latter option and allowed their debts to mount. They did so in large part because, as Jacob Price has shown, of the generous extensions of credit offered by British merchants who were, as a group, anxious to expand their volume of business in the North American market.

Among the most misunderstood and misinterpreted economic developments in the late colonial period relates to the possible role of planter indebtedness to British mercantile firms in fomenting the movement for political independence. Historians have sometimes suggested that resentment over large debts to foreign merchants and the hope of eventually escaping the repayment of outstanding accounts probably had a strong influence on the attitude of planters toward a possible break with the mother country. A close examination of the functioning of the merchandising and financial system for handling southern staples indicates that these alleged motives for separation have been grossly overrated.

The extension of credit to southern planters was a device employed by British merchants, operating in a highly competitive market, to attract business. British merchants earned commissions and profits first on the sale of a planter's produce in the home market and then on the return shipment of finished goods ordered by the planter. Indeed, some scholars believe that the main source of profits for British merchants serving the Chesapeake area came not from tobacco transactions per se but rather from high markups on textiles, hardware, and luxuries sent back to the colonies.

In the last two colonial decades, British merchants offered increasingly liberal credit terms to southern planters, large and small. In Virginia, for example, Emory Evans estimated that outstanding debts in the neighborhood of £2 million ($180 million) were owed by up to 35,000 individuals, with most accounts below £100 ($9,000). Increased debt was not a sign of economic weakness or accelerating dependence, but rather further evidence that planter and merchant alike were confident about the future prosperity of the Chesapeake colonies. Tobacco growers remained in debt year after year voluntarily because they wanted to avail themselves of the benefits accruing from access to relatively easy credit—an attitude little different from millions of modern Americans who stay perpetually in debt to the issuers of thousands of credit cards. An optimist, the tobacco grower used these borrowed funds to maintain consumption, hold up living standards, and occasionally to invest in more land and slaves.

Earlier depictions of desperate planters burdened with uncontrollable debts are overdrawn. The settlement of accounts with British merchants was not difficult if a household had the willpower to break its addiction to living above its means for a year or two. Most of the items ordered from Britain were not necessities but belonged in the luxury, or semiluxury, class—fancy cloth, hand-carved furniture, clocks, jewelry, silverware, and other expensive goods. In certain years, monetary disturbances in Britain caused a brief period of credit stringency and led to strained relations between growers and merchants, but these mild crises failed to disrupt basic trading and financial patterns. Of course, some overly ambitious and imprudent growers overextended themselves in acquiring land and slaves on borrowed money, or simply in high living, and later had to liquidate assets when tobacco prices dropped or crops failed. Commercial agriculture was not a risk-free enterprise—then or now. Even the wealthy were vulnerable.

In a recent book, however, T. H. Breen has attempted to rejuvenate the old argument about a close linkage between rising debt levels and revolutionary behavior, with particular reference to a select group of great planters in Virginia deeply involved in the political affairs of this pivotal colony. These planters continued to market their tobacco through the old consignment system, thus maintaining commercial ties with British mercantile firms thousands of miles across the ocean. He argues that planter attitudes toward their mounting debts underwent a significant shift in the last fifteen years before independence. In correspondence with one another, planters revealed their view of credit extension not as a system based on cold, impartial business calculations but rather as expressions of friendship and personal attachments. They felt that way about loans to each other, and they extended those expectations to British merchants. In addition, the planter mentality became increasingly concerned about the consequences arising from the loss of independence—a loss of autonomy traced back to their continued status as debtors. Debt was a two-way street; it fulfilled immediate desires for consumption and aristocratic lifestyles but it also elicited feelings of dependency and resentment. Thomas Jefferson hated debt with a passion; but naturally he remained indebted.

Breen points to the British credit crisis of 1772, one of the most severe in the eighteenth century, and its repercussions in the Chesapeake. The timing was bad, coming on the heels of the conflicts over the Stamp Act, Townshend duties, and paper money. When merchants cut off credit lines and asked for the settlement of debts, great planters felt insulted and, more important, betrayed by persons previously considered friends. Thereafter, anxieties about mounting debts escalated into near paranoia among prominent Virginia planters who increasingly expressed fears that British merchants planned to entrap them through debt and eventually settle accounts through seizures of properties and estates.

The fear of a British conspiracy was outlandish, of course, but given the course of political events in the past decade, topped off by the crisis of 1772 and calls for the curtailment of debts, Virginians were becoming increasingly suspicious of every aspect of their long-standing relationship with the mother country. While the number of individuals who actually succumbed to such exaggerated rhetoric may have been small, many of them were placed in exceedingly influential positions of political leadership. As a result, tobacco and debt were two economic issues that became "politicized" in the turmoil of Anglo-American relations. Moreover, the impact was certainly felt in concurrent political deliberations, since, as Breen points out, by the early 1770s at least 55 members of the Virginia assembly had debts exceeding £500 ($45,000) to British creditors.

How critical was the foreign-trade sector to the viability of the colonial economy? Some economic historians place great emphasis on the "staples" thesis; among the most prominent proponents are Russell Menard and John McCusker. They believe it remains the most useful analytical tool for explaining the success of the British colonies in the western hemisphere. The staples approach pinpoints European demand for unique and valuable products from distant lands as the original stimulus for the movement of people and capital across the Atlantic Ocean. Historians in this camp extend their analyses by observing that the subsequent growth of various colonial economies coincided with their success in expanding overseas markets for products such as sugar, tobacco, naval stores, lumber, and indigo—plus foodstuffs of all varieties including wheat, flour, rice, Indian corn, preserved meat, and dried fish.

In contrast, other scholars are more attracted by the insights of the "demographic" model which focuses more attention on internal factors—primarily natural population growth and the development of agriculture, local commerce, and crafts. In seeking a practical example to provide support for his general theory about how "population, when unchecked, increases in a geometrical ratio," the economist Thomas Malthus pointed in 1798 to the experience in North America. It was a region where the means of subsistence proved more than ample, and therefore "population has been found to double in twenty-five years."

A modern historian who has mixed Malthusian principles with Frederick Jackson Turner's frontier thesis is Daniel Scott Smith. He noted, for example, that urban areas as a percentage of total population diminished over the course of the eighteenth century, which seems to run counter to arguments about the critical importance of exports and the staples trade during the last three-quarters of the colonial period. Meanwhile, the frontier played a major role in drawing population into the interior. A push-pull mechanism operated: fewer opportunities for employment in the port cities pushed out workers, while expanding opportunities on the agricultural frontier attracted them. This was the underlying force that shaped the extensive growth of the economy in the eighteenth century. North Carolina, with no major port and little involvement in the staples trade, witnessed much faster population growth after 1730, on both an aggregate and a percentage basis, than its neighbor South Carolina, which was heavily committed to rice and indigo. In the middle region, New Jersey grew as rapidly as New York on a percentage basis over the last half-century before independence. Scott discounted the primary role of foreign trade and concluded that "staples were not an engine of economic transformation in the Malthusian era."

At least two broad general statements can be made about the merits of the staples thesis. First, foreign markets clearly made a greater impact on some regions than on others. As a rule, their effect was larger the farther south one traveled. Sugar and tobacco were the driving forces, for example, in the rapid settlement of the West Indies and the Chesapeake Bay regions, respectively. On the other hand, New England had no potential for creating a society based on one or two staples. The middle colonies were aptly named in this instance, for their prosperity was partly a result of external forces and partly a response to internal opportunities. They eventually developed a substantial overseas trade in foodstuffs to the West Indies and to southern Europe, but the existence of those markets was not the rationale for initial settlement in Pennsylvania, New York, and New Jersey.

Second, the timing of the impact of the staples trade varied among regions and local areas. In some locations the greatest impact came long after initial settlement. The effect of the staples trade on Philadelphia, Baltimore, Norfolk, and New York, plus their respective hinterlands, was greatest after 1750 because of sharply increased foreign demand, and thus higher prices, for wheat and flour. Families with easy access to water transportation also responded to new opportunities for the sale of foodstuffs in distant markets. David Klingaman, Paul Clemens, Peter Bergstrom, and others have shown that, by the 1760s, the Chesapeake colonies were steadily shifting more of their land and human resources away from the single-minded pursuit of tobacco as a cash crop and into the cultivation of surplus grains and the production of manufactured goods such as pig iron.

Meanwhile, the coastal trade within the thirteen colonies was growing apace in the eighteenth century. James Shepherd and Samuel Williamson put its magnitude on the eve of independence at £715,000 ($64 million) annually, or about one-fourth of the total value of foreign exports. By the last colonial decade, New England shippers were already heavily engaged in commerce with ports scattered from New York to Charleston and Savannah. Just over half of the vessels departing from Boston harbor were bound for other mainland ports; in nearby Rhode Island the comparable figure was over 60 percent. In Philadelphia and New York, about one-third of the ships owned by local merchants routinely set sail for domestic destinations. Trade, therefore, remained a vital element in the success of the mainland economies, but over the years the location of markets became increasingly internal. Commerce was based upon both regional and international specialization and comparative advantage.

In general, the mainland colonies thrived within the British empire. Most settlers were never too distant from water-transport facilities, whether ocean or rivers, and thus they had ready access to regional and foreign markets. Indeed, the colonists were fortunate to possess two attributes which virtually assured success in an agricultural-commercial society: an endless supply of fertile land given the size of the population and a reasonably efficient distribution system for their surpluses, at home and abroad.

Meanwhile, the colonies were not seriously damaged when Parliament enacted a series of Navigation Acts. From one standpoint, the colonies did suffer losses, since, without any restrictions whatsoever on bilateral trade with other countries, the prices paid for European imports would have been lower, and the prices received for some exports—especially tobacco out of the upper south—would probably have been higher. On the other hand there were substantial benefits associated with participation in the empire. Parliament offered bounties for certain products, such as indigo. The British navy provided protection at sea for all imperial vessels, and at no direct cost to the colonists. By the mid-eighteenth century, incidences of piracy had declined sharply, and the colonists were able to stop relying on armed merchantmen. They constructed new vessels, without heavy guns, that were less expensive and had more cargo space. With risks curtailed, insurance rates declined. The drop in freight rates and other distribution costs increased productivity in shipping and aided the colonial economy.

Colonial shipowners were also permitted to participate fully in the empire's North Atlantic trade. Along with shipowners in the mother country, they enjoyed protection inside the empire from competition with the Dutch, French, Spanish, and other outsiders. The colonists quickly captured a large share of the lucrative North Atlantic trade. The major American ports were busy commercial centers; Boston and Philadelphia, for example, had perhaps 20 to 25 percent of their workers employed in commerce and fishing, with another 5 to 10 percent involved directly in shipbuilding. Ship construction was a flourishing colonial industry, with American shipwrights not only supplying the regional demand for vessels but also selling up to 45 percent, or £140,000 ($12.6 million), of their annual production to overseas buyers in the 1770s.

Yet no analysis of the costs and the benefits of colonial status versus a hypothetical free-trade model can highlight sufficiently the general benefits accruing from a close, often intertwining association with the economy of a mother country which was itself expanding at a respectable pace for an early modern society. Population was rising in England too, and per capita incomes were growing in the eighteenth century, with only the overall rate of growth still in doubt—estimates range from 2 up to 7 percent per decade. By comparison, France and Spain, two other European powers with extensive interests in the hemisphere, were not experiencing similarly steady economic development. Britain and its mainland colonies were expansive societies which stimulated and reinforced one another's progress. On both sides of the Atlantic, merchants and entrepreneurs were permitted greater social status than in most other contemporary societies. The inheritance of English political and economic institutions gave a freer reign to individual initiative and encouraged the colonists to seek property and wealth.

Despite the undeniable importance of foreign trade, we should keep in mind that it represented a minority of colonial gross output. John McCusker and Russell Menard argue that its role in the economy was probably diminishing over the eighteenth century, but that on the eve of independence, foreign and coastal trade still accounted for about 20 percent of economic activity.

Overseas commerce based on the comparative advantages of regional specialization clearly raised income levels, but the real strength of the colonial economy was its prodigious agricultural production for local consumption and urban centers. The value of goods and services for strictly internal consumption outweighed by far the volume of colonial exports. Even without the stimulus of foreign markets, living standards in the eighteenth century would have still ranked among the highest in the world, primarily because of the availability of so much fertile and productive land for the existing population.

Moreover, if foreign markets had stagnated, after perhaps a decade or two of readjustment, the colonies had the wherewithal and institutional flexibility to shift into other economic pursuits aimed at more narrowly serving the domestic market. Unlike the West Indies, for example, the mainland colonies always had the option of devoting even more of their resources to manufacturing and local commerce. They concentrated on staple production because of comparative advantage, but a shift to their *next* best alternatives would not have seriously undermined living standards over the long run. The flexibility of the American economy (then and now) was one of its key strengths over the decades.

At the same time, it would be a mistake to deemphasize too much the role of foreign trade, especially if we take into account its influence on the institutional development of colonial society. Without overseas demand for tobacco, rice, and indigo, it remains questionable whether the institution of slavery would have spread from the Caribbean to the mainland. Slavery was linked to the cultivation of specific crops. Also important was the impact of foreign trade on one very critical part of colonial society—the economic, social, and political elite. The vast majority of individuals in the highest income category, primarily urban merchants and great planters, accumulated wealth as a result of their involvement in foreign commerce.

However marginally foreign commerce affected the lives of the typical farmer, it had a substantial impact on the top 10 percent of wealth-holders. Colonial political leaders were drawn in disproportionate numbers from the elite economic classes. Therefore the vagaries of overseas trade had a much broader influence on the political concerns of the colonial legislatures than was merited strictly on the basis of their effect on the income level of the average citizen. Because these matters affected greatly the status of the economic elite, issues related to foreign commerce played a disproportionate role in the political affairs of the thirteen colonies.

BIBLIOGRAPHICAL ESSAY

JAMES Shepherd and Gary Walton, *Shipping, Maritime Trade, and the Economic Development of Colonial North America* (Cambridge: Cambridge University Press, 1972) is a gold mine of statistical data on foreign trade from 1768 to 1772. Indeed, it remains among the most valuable reference books on the colonial economy, and I relied on it heavily in this chapter. On the explanatory powers of the staples thesis plus a summary of recent scholarship, see John McCusker and Russell Menard, *The Economy of British America, 1607–1789* (Chapel Hill: University of North Carolina Press, 1985); their select bibliography lists the important contributions on colonial commerce, and most other topics, through the mid-1980s. Daniel *Scott* Smith offers a succinct defense of the demographic model in "A Malthusian-Frontier Interpretation of United States Demographic History Before c. 1815," in Woodrow Borah et al., eds., *Urbanization in the Americas: The Background in Comparative Perspective* (Ottawa, Canada: National Museum of Man, 1980), pp. 15–24. Thomas Malthus published in England in 1798 his treatise *An Essay on the Principle of Population, as it affects the Future Improvement of Society* (7th ed., New York: A. M. Kelley, 1971).

The literature on the net effect of the Navigation Acts is extensive. A sample of important contributions includes Oliver Dickerson, *The Navigation Acts and the American Revolution* (Philadelphia: University of Pennsylvania Press, 1951); Lawrence Harper, "The Effects of the Navigation Acts on the Thirteen Colonies," in Richard Morris, ed., *The Era of the American Revolution* (New York: Columbia University Press, 1939), pp. 3–39; Robert Paul Thomas, "British Imperial Policy and the Economic Interpretation of the American Revolution," *Journal of Economic History* (1968), pp. 436–40; and Roger Ransom, "British Policy and Colonial Growth: Some Implications of the Burden from the Navigation Acts," *ibid.*, pp. 427–35. Benjamin Franklin's views on the inappropriateness of limiting colonial manufacturing are found in his essay "The Interest of Great Britain Considered," written in 1760 and published in Benjamin Labaree, ed., *The Papers of Benjamin Franklin* (New Haven: Yale University Press, 1961), 9:47–100; the quoted passage is on p. 77.

For information on New England trade and manufacture, see Bernard Bailyn, *The New England Merchants in the Seventeenth Century* (Cambridge, Mass.: Harvard University Press, 1955); Douglas McManis, *Colonial New England: A Historical Geography* (New York: Oxford University Press, 1975); Thomas Norton, *The Fur Trade in Colonial New York, 1686–1776* (Madison: University of Wisconsin Press, 1974); Oliver Rink, *Holland on the Hudson: An Economic and Social History of Dutch New York* (Ithaca, N.Y.: Cornell University Press, 1986); Charles Carroll, *The Timber Economy of Puritan New England* (Providence, R.I.: Brown University Press, 1973); Richard Kugler, "The Whale Oil Industry, 1750–1775," in Philip Smith, ed., *Seafaring in Colonial Massachusetts* (Charlottesville: University Press of Virginia, 1980); and Daniel Vickers, "The First Whalemen of Nantucket," *William and Mary Quarterly* (1983), pp. 560–83.

Important studies which focus on the Chesapeake region are Russell Menard, "Secular Trends in the Chesapeake Tobacco Industry," in Glenn Porter and William Mulligan, eds., *Economic Change in the Chesapeake Colonies* (Greenville, Del.: Hagley Museum, 1978); Edmund S. Morgan, "The First American Boom: Virginia 1618 to 1630," *William and Mary Quarterly* (1971), pp. 169–98; Jacob Price, "The Rise of Glasgow in the Chesapeake Tobacco Trade, 1707–1775," *ibid.* (1954), pp. 179–99; Price, "New Time Series for Scotland's and Britain's Trade with the Thirteen Colonies and States, 1740–1791," *ibid.* (1975), pp. 307–25; and Price, "The Economic Growth of the Chesapeake and the European Market, 1697–1775," *Journal of Economic History* (1964), pp. 496–511. Other studies include Emory Evans, "Planter Indebtedness and the Coming of the Revolution in Virginia, 1776 to 1796," *William and Mary Quarterly* (1962), pp. 511–33; Evans, "Private Indebtedness and the Revolution in Virginia, 1766 to 1796," *ibid.* (1971), pp. 349–74; T. H. Breen, *Tobacco Culture: The Mentality of the Great Tidewater*

Planters on the Eve of Revolution (Princeton, N.J.: Princeton University Press, 1985); David Klingaman, "The Significance of Grain in the Development of the Tobacco Colonies," *Journal of Economic History* (1969), pp. 268–78; and Peter Bergstrom, *Markets and Merchants: Economic Diversification in Colonial Virginia, 1700–1775* (New York: Garland, 1985). See also Allan Kulikoff, "The Economic Growth of the Eighteenth-Century Chesapeake Colonies," *Journal of Economic History* (1979), pp. 275–88.

Two excellent sources on the lower south are Converse Clowse, *Economic Beginnings of Colonial South Carolina, 1670–1730* (Columbia: University of South Carolina Press, 1971); and Timothy Silver, "A New Face on the Countryside: Indians and Colonists in the Southeastern Forest" (Ph.D. diss., William and Mary, 1985).

Other valuable studies are Jacob Price, "Economic Function and the Growth of American Port Towns in the Eighteenth Century," in Donald Fleming and Bernard Bailyn, eds., *Perspectives in American History* (Cambridge, Mass.: Harvard University Press, 1974), 8:123–88; Richard Sheridan, "The British Credit Crisis of 1772 and the American Colonies," *Journal of Economic History* (1960), pp. 161–86; Geoffrey Gilbert, "The Role of Breadstuffs in American Trade, 1770–1790," *Explorations in Economic History* (1977), pp. 378–87; and James Mulholland, *A History of Metals in Colonial America* (University: University of Alabama Press, 1981).

The data on alcohol consumption are from W. J. Rorabaugh, *The Alcoholic Republic: An American Tradition* (New York: Oxford University Press, 1979). The effects of English settlers on the environment are analyzed in William Cronon, *Changes in the Land: Indians, Colonists, and Ecology of New England* (New York: Hill and Wang, 1983).

OCCUPATIONAL GROUPS

ROM a functional and institutional standpoint, economic life in the thirteen colonies was remarkably stable. During the entire colonial period, occupational roles changed very little, and few new ways of making a living emerged. The vast majority of the male population fit into one of seven work categories: family farmer, southern planter, indentured servant, slave, unskilled laborer, artisan, and merchant. Most women were engaged in activities designed to complement the male head-of-household, whether father or husband. The main duties of women were domestic service, child care, tending livestock, and household production for family consumption or sale in the marketplace. Opportunities for employment differed radically from modern times; no one, for example, was employed in a factory or a bank. From the perspective of the twentieth century, the range of occupations was narrow and rigid; most young people simply followed in the footsteps of their parents in seeking a livelihood. They had limited choices and modest aspirations; for the most part, they expected the future to replicate the past.

Within the last decade scholars have discovered new evidence indicating just how much occupational roles tended to overlap in this preindustrial society. The vast majority of farm families engaged in some type of handicraft production within the household. Women and children were active on a part-time basis at the very least, and adult males usually participated during the off-season. The non-agricultural production of farm families was either consumed within the household or sold in the marketplace for extra income. Few households aimed at total self-sufficiency. Mary Schweitzer found that Pennsylvania households tried to develop skills in two or three areas of economic activity, but few farmers were jacks-of-all-trades.

Paul Clemens and Lucy Simler have identified a group of small tenant farmers in eastern Pennsylvania who alternated their yearly work activities among common wage labor, semiskilled artisanal tasks, and family farming.

Except for the residents of the largest port cities, artisans were, in turn, likely to retain some connection with the land. They frequently owned and cultivated fields on the outskirts of town, and an even higher percentage held livestock, including cows to produce milk and cheese, plus hogs and cattle for meat. Artisans in the highest income groups, such as millers and tanners, invariably had substantial holdings in the countryside. Merchants likewise tended to own land, which was leased to tenants or held in reserve. Fertile land was always a sound investment in settled areas, and it served as a safety net in the event a merchant suffered losses in business ventures and was forced to retreat into agriculture. In the southern colonies, large planters often diversified into several occupational markets; the most common complementary activity was the performance of mercantile services for smaller neighbors.

In the early stages of a colony's settlement, rapid upward mobility was very common. Land was initially easy to acquire, and many families which started with little capital became relatively wealthy after two or three generations. Many indentured servants, who served out terms of 4 to 7 years of quasi-slavery, went on to become tenant farmers, later bought land, and eventually accumulated sizable wealth, sometimes joining the colonial elite.

After the initial fifty years or so of settlement in a colony, however, economic and occupational mobility slowed down. Tenants found it more difficult to escape their dependent status and become independent households. By the last decade of the colonial era, a more ordered, hierarchical society had emerged. Nonetheless, despite the decline in the rate of upward mobility, free whites in the colonies still had many more opportunities for material and social advancement than their counterparts in Europe.

Although occupational roles changed little over the decades, recent research has indicated that slight shifts in employment patterns occurred in some colonies during the eighteenth century. In his detailed study of society and economy in Connecticut, Jackson

Turner Main noted a continuous movement out of farming and into other occupations between 1700 and 1770. The number of farmers declined by approximately one-sixth; meanwhile artisan ranks increased by a similar proportion. The number of men engaged in trade, shopkeepers, and merchants, also climbed—from only 4 to 5 percent of the workforce at the beginning of the century up to 7 percent by the 1770s. On the eve of independence only three-fifths of households could be classified as strictly family farmers in Connecticut. Meanwhile, Allan Kulikoff discovered that, after 1750, planters with large numbers of slaves decided over time to transfer more of those workers—men, women, and youths—into various artisanal activities. The data suggest that the movement of workers out of agriculture and into other occupations (a trend which has continued until the present in American society) had started in most regions long before the impact of advanced industrial technology.

In many recent investigations of colonial society, historians have shifted their attention away from static views of occupational groups and toward the work patterns of individuals over the entire life cycle. At present, we know much more about the course of working lives in New England and the middle colonies than in the south, however, because less work on life cycles has been done in regions where slavery prevailed. In the northern colonies most males were exposed to at least two occupational categories during the course of their working lives. Irrespective of their eventual employment status as adults, youths invariably started as unskilled laborers on neighboring farms or in an artisan's shop. By living at home and contributing to their upkeep, most young people earned enough to save up to one-half of their wages. Their aim was to accumulate a modest sum in anticipation of marriage and starting a household of their own, usually sometime in their mid-twenties.

In certain respects the entry levels of colonial youths into the workforce have clear parallels with employment patterns today. Over the years most young and inexperienced workers have been forced to start employment in jobs requiring low skill levels and little managerial responsibility. Wages in the eighteenth century were lower, of course. Depending on the locale, male youths employed on farms earned from 2 to 3 shillings daily. On the basis of the 12 hour workday common in this earlier era, their wages translate into comparable sums of around 60 cents to $1.00 per hour—a figure one-fifth to one-third of the federal legal minimum wage in 1985. Young women generally earned half that figure, or from 30 to 50 cents per hour.

At the other end of the age spectrum, the retirement patterns of American workers have likewise emerged as a fresh topic for research among economic and social historians in recent decades, but hard data on the colonial era is still scant. Current investigations indicate that able-bodied farmers tended to remain in the workforce longer than members of other occupational groups. Since farming was by far the main colonial occupation, the number of total retirees was probably never very large; yet because so many adults lived into their sixties and seventies, the figure was not negligible. Generally speaking about half of the males 65 to 70, both free and slave, had withdrawn completely from the workforce. In colonial households, the living standards prevailing in retirement, caused by either old-age infirmities or a premature disability, centered on the income potential from accumulated wealth, usually land, and the extent of financial support forthcoming from grown children and other close relatives. A large number of surviving children and a broad network of blood relatives was the colonial substitute for a modern insurance and retirement program.

As they advanced in age, and their responsibilities narrowed to supporting only a spouse, many farmers transferred a large share of their land holdings to their adult children. In return, they received promises, whether informal agreements or written contracts, for a certain level of material support until death. Moving toward the status of semiretirement, many ceased the accumulation of wealth and planted only enough acreage to provide sufficient food for their immediate needs. Estimates of the number of older men completely retired from physical labor are hard to come by, but a figure of around 2 percent of the male workforce seems plausible in the light of current knowledge.

The normal pace of work in most male occupational categories was very slow by modern standards. An informal atmosphere prevailed in the work environment. The majority of workers, whether on farms or in artisan shops, were self-employed. Speed was critical only during the few weeks of the year when crops were harvested. Tenant farmers were not closely supervised. Slaves were perhaps the one exception; however, there was no premium on speed in the tobacco fields since the quality of care for these delicate plants was vastly more important in determining the value of the final crop. In rice-growing areas, work was organized around the task system, which allowed slaves the option of laboring along at a steady pace, and then leaving the fields by midafternoon, or, alternatively, of moving more slowly and stretching the work day out until sunset.

In the artisan shop, work orders came in at irregular intervals. Customers rarely sought immediate service; they were more interested in the quality of the final product. Shops did not maintain uniform working hours; the start and length of the workday varied according to the backlog of jobs and inclination of the owner. Artisans worked haphazardly throughout the day, taking numerous breaks for conversation, a leisurely meal, a rest period, or a drink of cider or rum. Alcohol consumption on the job was routine; if an artisan had a bad hangover from the previous night's bout of drink and merriment, he took the next day off or worked only half-heartedly.

Farm work was likewise irregular in its level of intensity in most regions. Planting and harvesting were periods requiring maximum effort for a few weeks, but months passed when there was little urgency about accomplishing various tasks.

Many weeks were wasted in idle pursuits, either because crops needed little care during the midsummer growing season or because weather conditions in winter made outdoor work impossible or extremely uncomfortable except for brief intervals. Some males took advantage of these predictable interruptions in the farm routine to participate periodically in artisanal or piece-work activity, but few were willing to optimize their labor potential by working steadily every week throughout the year.

In research on Springfield, in western Massachusetts, in the seventeenth century, Stephen Innes outlined the typical workday for one unmarried agricultural laborer, Francis Pepper, who worked in the fields for years under various contractual arrangements. Sometimes he signed on with one employer for three or fours months at a time, but at other times Pepper preferred the flexibility of per diem employment because it permitted him to chose labor tasks and to work periodically for different individuals. A portion of his compensation often came in the form of room and board, which makes the determination of precise wage rates difficult, other than to say that the pay was higher than the actual specie or cash he received. A fairly typical workday for Pepper during the growing season went as follows:

4:30– 5:00 A.M.	rise and tend livestock
5:00– 6:30	field work
6:30– 7:00	breakfast
7:00–11:00	field work
11:00–11:30	cider or rum break
11:30 – 2:00 P.M.	field work
2:00– 3:00	dinner
3:00– 6:00	field work, livestock, tool repair
6:00– 7:00	supper
8:30 P.M.	retire to bed

Unlike most English field laborers, he and other American workers normally did not take a noontime nap.

Beginning in late March, Pepper was involved in preparing the ground with an ox-drawn plow—furrowing and seeding. Usually there was about a two-month lull until harvesting began—first hay, then winter wheat, hay again, spring wheat, barley, oats, peas, and any root crops. After the harvest, Pepper was frequently engaged in slaughtering pigs, carting apples to the cider-mill, threshing and winnowing grain, gathering wood, making shingles, and repairing tools.

An illuminating portrait of the work patterns of one New Hampshire farmer in the third quarter of the eighteenth century is revealed in a recent article by Thomas Thompson. Matthew Patten was a reasonably successful farmer in the vicinity of Bedford (near Manchester), who kept a detailed diary reporting his whereabouts and his daily activities for over three decades, beginning in 1754. He relied on no other source of labor except his wife and children. The most striking fact revealed in the detailed analysis of his lifestyle is that Patten spent only about one-third of his waking hours actually on his farm. He was much involved in hunting, fishing, visiting neighbors, and attending community and church functions such as religious services, weddings, funerals, prayer meetings, and the like. Indeed, during his lifetime, he devoted as much time to local social, political, and religious activities as to farm work.

For about a month every year, Patten was away in Boston or Portsmouth, rides of 25 to 50 miles by horseback, where he bought, sold, and bartered various goods. He traveled to distant locations and stayed away for a week or two at a time, usually in the months of October, November, February, and March. He was always back home for Christmas, of course.

A review of his activities when present on the farm is equally fascinating. Patten spent up to one-fifth of his actual working days on the farm engaged in carpentry. Only a few hours each month went into tending livestock, probably because his wife had assumed the primary responsibility for their feeding and care. During the winter months, when he was not absent on trips to the two port cities, he carted wood for the fireplace much of the time. (On the southeastern frontier of Virginia, Richard Beeman estimated, farmers spent about 40 percent of their working hours from October through March in gathering wood.) In April, Patten was busy preparing his fields and planting seed. But in May and June, he mostly fished with friends who gathered at a favored spot on the local stream, and he went hunting as well. July, August, and September were the three consecutive months he was consistently out in the fields harvesting crops and preparing them for storage.

The hours devoted to farm work varied over his life cycle. Patten allocated more time to economic pursuits just after marriage and while his children were young. As his offspring matured, he gradually lessened the hours spent on the farm and gave more time to recreational, church, and community activities. When all his grown sons were still at home and working the farm, his tasks became largely supervisory, even during the hectic harvest season.

How typical of other New England farmers, or other farmers throughout the colonies, were Patten's work habits? Historians will need more comparative data to make a conclusive judgment, but nothing in his life story appears particularly abnormal or deviant, except perhaps his devotion to various community activities. His income and wealth were neither especially high nor unusually low for the region, which suggests that his experience lies within the range of our expectations. What this review of his lifestyle does tend to support is our broad generalization about the fairly slow and sporadic pace of work in this preindustrial society, which was a function partly of societal attitudes and partly of resource endowments.

One small occupational group does not fit conveniently into the format of the following chapters. In addition to shopkeepers and merchants, another part of the tiny colonial service sector was comprised of professionals and semiprofessionals. The one profession with the greatest social prestige and a reasonably high income, especially in New England, was the ministry. Since many schools and institutions of higher education were established primarily to train ministers—for example, Harvard in 1636 and William and Mary in 1693—this occupational group was also the best educated in the colonies. In fact, the ministry was the only recognized profession to receive what we would consider today genuine professional training.

Connecticut ministers earned annual salaries of at least £100 ($6,750) plus the use of a farm to feed their families. Since there was no moral stigma attached, ministers often purchased a few slaves to grow food crops and to perform household chores. Few ministers ever accumulated huge estates, but most lived comfortable lives. Colonial churchmen enjoyed a higher standard of living compared to the general population than would be true for their counterparts in most American communities today.

Other professional groups had more erratic earning patterns. The incomes of individual doctors and lawyers varied considerably. Some prospered, but others barely eked out a living. The training of doctors was haphazard; most received the benefits of some advanced schooling, and a small minority went to Europe for special training. Lawyers were for the most part self-taught by reading law books and by assisting and observing other lawyers. Except in the large port cities, only a few men were employed full-time in the legal profession. In rural areas the courts were in session only periodically.

Evidence suggests that court calendars were generally quite full, however, for the American population has always been litigious. As is true in the twentieth century, a high percentage of elected political leaders and appointed public officials also practiced law from time to time. Lawyers were on balance, therefore, a relatively prosperous group, but probably only a small percentage of their total wealth actually arose from handling legal cases.

Teachers and tutors, normally males, were at the bottom of the professional classes in terms of earnings potential, which proves, among other things, that certain aspects of American society have changed little over the last 300 years. The educational background of teachers was uneven. The most highly prepared were the very small number imported from England to tutor the children of the very wealthy. Others, however, were barely literate. In New England a teacher hired by a local community to educate its children could expect to earn a yearly salary of about £50 ($4,500). Teaching was typically a part-time position for younger men who hoped to save enough money to escape to some other line of work—or to marry well.

BIBLIOGRAPHICAL ESSAY

THE main sources consulted on occupational patterns were Jackson Turner Main, *Society and Economy in Colonial Connecticut* (Princeton: Princeton University Press, 1985); Mary M. Schweitzer, *Custom and Contract: Household, Government, and the Economy in Colonial Pennsylvania* (New York: Columbia University Press, 1987); Richard Beeman, *The Evolution of the Southern Backcountry: A Case Study of Lunenburg County, Virginia, 1746–1832* (Philadelphia: University of Pennsylvania Press, 1984); Allan Kulikoff, *Tobacco and Slaves: The Development of Southern Cultures in the Chesapeake, 1680–1800* (Chapel Hill: University of North Carolina Press, 1986); Stephen Innes, *Labor in a New Land: Economy and Society in Seventeenth-Century Springfield* (Princeton: Princeton University Press, 1983); and Thomas C. Thompson, "The Life Course and Labor of a Colonial Farmer," *Historical New Hampshire* (1985), pp. 135–55.

For data on wages of laborers and artisans, see Donald Adams, "Prices and Wages in Maryland, 1750–1850," *Journal of Economic History* (1986), pp. 625–45, and Billy G. Smith, "The Material Lives of Laboring Philadelphians, 1750 to 1800," *William and Mary Quarterly* (1981), pp. 163–202.

An unpublished paper which I read just before going to press was "Rural Labor and the Farm Household in Chester County, Pennsylvania, 1750–1820," by Paul Clemens and Lucy Simler, which is scheduled to appear in a forthcoming collection edited by Stephen Innes.

CHAPTER III

FARMERS AND PLANTERS

T H E basic economic unit in colonial America was the farm. Up to 75 percent of the population depended on agriculture for their livelihood. In following this pattern of rural employment, the colonies differed little from contemporary societies around the globe, for productive land was the most valuable economic resource in all preindustrial societies. Yet special circumstances permitted the colonial farmer to achieve an unusually high standard of living. The size of the typical colonial farm was generous, often above 100 acres, and families consistently grew and harvested surpluses. Equally important, farmers had access to adequate transportation and distribution facilities and thus had the opportunity to sell their surpluses in active markets both at home and abroad.

A majority of colonial farmers owned outright the land they tilled. Fertile land was not a scarce resource in North America, and it could be acquired at relatively low prices. Some colonists received title to land free of charge, for example through the headright system which granted 50 acres for every man who arrived in Virginia or through the division of common property in a New England township. On new lands, it normally took hard physical labor and some incidental funds to convert forested areas into arable farms. One man could clear up to 3 acres per month if he left all the tree stumps in the ground.

In the eighteenth century, the value of improved land in some older regions near coastal markets rose substantially. In southeastern Pennsylvania prices tripled between 1730 and 1760, and land prices rose similarly along the southern border of Virginia from the 1740s to the 1770s. On the frontier, new land was always plentiful, however, and despite historical accounts about vast speculative ventures, land prices remained competitively low and well within the means of the average citizen. Historians now are less inclined to believe that, even in New England, population was pressing unduly on the supply of arable land.

Tenancy rates were lower in the mainland colonies than in most other agricultural societies. In England, rural property was concentrated in the hands of the gentry, who lived off the rental income. The freeholder class—namely owner-occupiers with title to 40 acres or more—held only about one-quarter of English farmland. In most regions over 80 percent of all English farm workers were tenants or itinerant laborers. Similarly high tenancy rates were common in most regions of Europe and Asia. As late as the mid-eighteenth century, many English tenants tilled plots in common fields near their villages rather than on farms with permanently fixed boundaries.

The English upper classes relied on this pattern of land tenure to restrict the franchise. Voting rights were extended only to freeholders. In the colonies, however, implementation of the same 40-acre rule did not lead to a similar outcome; instead, it left political power squarely in the hands of the typical white male farmer.

Only in New York were tenancy rates comparable to those in the Old World. The Dutch had created a series of vast estates in the Hudson River valley in the first half of the seventeenth century, and the British continued the estate system after gaining control of the colony in 1664. Despite institutional similarities, the relationship between landlord and tenant differed significantly in New York from European practice. Sung Bok Kim has shown that lease terms were normally quite reasonable, since reliable tenants were in short supply and landlords were interested in promoting settlement on their property. Many tenants were granted leases in perpetuity, with 10 percent of farm output commonly fixed as the annual rental. Even these modest rents were often difficult to collect. Leases were also transferable, and established tenants with improved lands were frequently in a position to sell their rights to new settlers at a solid profit. New York tenant farmers were hardly a downtrodden class; substantial numbers enjoyed a standard of living on a par with freeholders in other colonies.

In a study of Springfield, Massachusetts, from the 1650s to the turn of the century, Stephen Innes found that almost one-third of the town's adult males rented farmland. The vast majority of these renters already owned a farm or shop of their own, however, and only leased to supplement their existing properties. The average leasehold was around 15 acres, which was 20 to 40 percent of the size of the typical farm in that area. Only about 10 percent of the Springfield sample could be classified as genuine tenant farmers, with no outside sources of income.

In her study of the Pennsylvania economy in the eighteenth century, Mary Schweitzer identified a whole series of institutional arrangements between landlords and tenants. Depending upon the terms of a contract, leasehold improvements could be assigned to either landlord or tenant. As in New York, tenants often had the power to demand reimbursement from owners for improvements, and, if it was not forthcoming, to exercise their right to sell their limited interest in the property to third parties. Schweitzer claimed that many families with the financial resources to acquire land on the frontier voluntarily chose tenancy instead, because older farms available for lease in more settled areas had a higher income potential. Artisans were also frequently tenants on small farms by choice, preferring to use their capital for investments in tools, materials, and accounts receivable. In a study of Chester County in southeastern Pennsylvania, Lucy Simler likewise concluded that tenancy "was a rational efficient response to economic conditions" and that both landowners and tenants benefited from the system.

The data on Massachusetts and Pennsylvania elucidate a frequently misunderstood point which bears on the interpretation of colonial tenancy rates. Tenancy was by no means a condition linked solely to poverty; it was, alternatively, a strategy by which enterprising young people and new arrivals with little capital but a strong capacity for work acquired sufficient funds over perhaps a three- or five-year period to purchase a farm of their own. Unlike Europe, where most of the population was locked permanently into tenancy, in the mainland colonies tenant status was often a temporary stepping-stone toward the rank of property holder.

Nonetheless, scattered evidence indicates that the rate of tenancy was probably increasing in many areas during the late colonial period. In studies focusing on the Chesapeake, Gregory Stiverson, Paul Clemens, and Allan Kulikoff concluded that a class of downtrodden tenant farmers, trapped in near-subsistence agriculture, had already emerged. In some Maryland counties which had been settled for several generations, half of the farmers were landless tenants by the 1770s. They cultivated the poorest lands and typically had large households with eight or more members. Movement to the frontier, where land was usually cheap, was a potential escape route, but many tenants were reluctant to migrate because of kinship ties at home and the continuing threat of Indian attacks.

Despite reports of tenancy rates of 30 to 50 percent in selected counties in Maryland, Virginia, and New York, there is no evidence that the incidence of tenancy was approaching this magnitude throughout the colonies. In many areas of the south, tenant farmers made a calculated decision to invest their savings in the acquisition of one or two slaves rather than in land. These farmers had every prospect of eventually rising in the economic order. For every family permanently stuck in tenancy, several others were merely passing through with the genuine prospect of subsequent economic independence.

Since most of the land in colonial North America was owner-occupied, the incidence of at least modest wealth-holding by European standards was surprisingly widespread in all regions, north to south. Peter Lindert and Jeffrey Williamson have shown that the distribution of wealth in agricultural areas changed very little over the eighteenth century. By and large, productivity gains and increases in property values accrued to those families that actually cleared and worked the land, with the exception, of course, of bonded servants and black slaves.

Despite regional variations in soils and climate, farmers everywhere grew sufficient food to feed their immediate families generously and to provide an adequate diet for servants and slaves. In Virginia, Maryland, and North Carolina more acreage by far was planted in corn and other grains than in tobacco. In the south and elsewhere the largest and most valuable portion of a farmer's output was normally consumed right on the farm. Colonial farmers planted a mix of corn, wheat, barley, oats, and rye, plus numerous vegetables in season; they invariably raised livestock as well—cattle and hogs for meat, hides, and dairy products; horses for field work and transportation; and sheep for wool. A few acres of orchard were common. The degree of crop diversification increased in the eighteenth century. As a rule, only a part of a farmer's land holdings was cultivated in a given year. On a typical family farm of 75 to 125 acres, perhaps 15 to 35 acres were actually planted in crops; the remainder was a combination of fallow fields, pasture, and forest.

By European standards, the colonists appeared backward and unsophisticated in the application of farming techniques. Little attention was given to maintaining or increasing the fertility of cultivated land. Fertilizers were applied sparingly, and fields were not plowed or were plowed superficially. Wooden plows were rarely plated with iron or steel coverings. Nonetheless, one agricultural historian, Conway Zirkle, has argued that in many areas deep plowing would have been inappropriate. After centuries of forestation the virgin soil was rich in humus, and extensive plowing would have caused a faster decline in fertility. The heavy concentration of tree roots in recently cleared land also made plowing exceedingly difficult. Since most colonial farms had large stretches of uncultivated land in forest or pasture, owners made a rational economic decision to plant one field for a few seasons and, when its initial fertility began to subside, to move on to another plot.

After a long fallow period, the old fields regained most of their former productivity. Indeed, there was no secular decline in the overall fertility of most colonial farmland. Tobacco fields normally regained over three-quarters of their original fertility. Because of the crop rotation, the overall agricultural output of a typical farm of 75 to 125 acres was not seriously impaired. New England appears to have been the exception, for the soil was poor from the start, and population pressure along the coast reduced the size of the average farm below the acreage required to sustain fertility without systematic care.

An indigenous crop—maize or corn—was a mainstay in the colonial diet. Before the seventeenth century, many Indian tribes near the Atlantic coast had relied heavily on corn for survival. Early European settlers seeking arable land came across some open spaces that Indians had previously cleared for cornfields. The native Americans introduced Europeans to a distinctive method of cultivation.

Young corn plants were "hilled"—that is, soil was hoed up around the base. Indians sometimes practiced multiple cropping, a practice which often served to maintain soil fertility. Bean seeds could be planted in the hills, with the cornstalks performing double duty as bean poles.

Corn was normally one of the first crops planted by new settlers. The technique of hill cultivation was adaptable to fields not fully cleared but containing dying, girdled trees and stumps. Corn was a hardy crop as well, for it was quite resistant to local diseases and insects. Farmers thus counted on it as insurance in the event other grain crops fared poorly. For a small family with limited labor resources, corn was a sensible crop, because, unlike wheat, its harvest season extended over a fairly long time. Corn could be harvested piecemeal in late fall and early winter.

A highly adaptable plant, corn was cultivated extensively from New England to Georgia. One worker was capable of tending 6 to 8 acres and producing 80 to 120 bushels, or enough corn to feed 5 to 7 persons for a year. Corn was consumed directly by humans in southern regions either in cornmeal or off the cob. In the northern colonies and all areas where wheat or rye was grown, much corn was fed to livestock to aid in fattening animals for slaughter. The same procedure of fattening swine and cattle with corn is followed on today's farms.

Wheat was another important crop in the thirteen colonies. Various strains of spring and winter wheat, plus other grains, were of European origin. In the middle colonies and some counties in the upper south, wheat was the main crop; it served not only as the primary source of food on the farm but as the region's principal export as well. Consumers at home and abroad preferred baking with wheat flour over corn or rye flour, and they willingly paid higher prices for its more palatable taste and texture. In Boston the price of wheat was typically 35 to 85 percent above corn in the eighteenth century, according to Karen Friedmann.

In the seventeenth century, spring wheat had been widely and successfully cultivated in New England. The appearance and spread of the wheat blast, now identified as black stemrust, reduced yields sharply, however, and led many farmers to shift to less tasty but hardier rye strains. Rye was nutritionally a good substitute for wheat in the farmer's diet, but unfortunately a poor economic substitute because overseas demand for rye flour was limited.

Although wheat fields became less prevalent in New England, they expanded significantly in the tobacco-growing regions of the south. Chesapeake farmers discovered that winter wheat harmonized well with plantation crops. Carville Earle found that in All Hallow's Parish, Maryland, winter wheat was typically planted in early fall, after the cutting of tobacco and before the gathering of late corn. Wheat required little attention over the winter, and it was harvested in June or July just after tobacco plants had been transplanted from indoor pots out into the open field.

Wheat had a shorter harvest season than corn in all areas; once the grain began to ripen, farmers had to cut it quickly or risk spoilage in the field. Labor resources were thus critical during the harvest season, and wages for temporary workers, usually single males under 25, were high. At this time of the year, wages for unskilled labor could easily double and ranged from 4 to 6 shillings ($13 to $20) per day in most areas. A farmer's wife and older children normally put in a full day's work at harvest. Wheat yielded from 5 to 12 bushels per acre in settled counties up and down the Atlantic coast.

As a rule, families had more land than they could cultivate. Farmers were able to plant and grow more wheat than they could physically harvest. The introduction of the cradle scythe around 1750 boosted production capacity somewhat, but bottlenecks in harvesting technology prevented the emergence of specialized and highly commercial wheat farms. Increased productivity in agriculture came in the nineteenth century after the development of major improvements in harvesting technology, especially the horse-drawn reaper.

In addition to wheat, corn, and rye, a colonial farmer was likely to cultivate a few acres of buckwheat, some barley for brewing beer, and oats and hay for livestock. Diets were supplemented with garden vegetables in season, and farmers maintained small orchards, especially apple trees in cooler climates. Apples were used mainly to produce cider, which became a more common alcoholic drink than beer in the eighteenth century. There were other regional variations, of course; the white potato did better in the colder north, while the more nutritious sweet potato fared better in the south.

The colonial farm normally had varied livestock. The heavy consumption of milk, cheese, and meat was a key sign of the relative affluence of the colonial population. James Lemon has calculated that some farmers in southeastern Pennsylvania could afford the luxury of feeding up to 60 percent of their total grain production to livestock. Robert Mitchell estimated that the bulk of the corn crop in Virginia's Shenandoah Valley ended up as feed for livestock. The typical adult farm resident consumed from 150 to 200 pounds of meat annually, or about one-half a pound per day. Americans at present do not eat significantly more meat than that. Over the years, however, the mix of meats consumed has been greatly altered; modern diets include much more chicken than was true in this earlier era, because of its lower fat content. By comparison, millions of people in the world today rarely consume meat more often than once a week, and as a result, many suffer from serious protein deficiencies.

Cattle and swine were the main sources of meat in colonial diets. These animals were European imports, since Native Americans raised no domesticated animals as a source of meat. Cattle were slaughtered throughout the year, with much of the beef consumed soon after while still reasonably fresh. Hogs tended to be killed in late fall, and their meat eaten during the winter and the next spring, since pork was more safely preserved for human consumption through salting and smoking than beef.

In the south, swine were often allowed to run wild, since they were capable of foraging for natural food in forest areas and protecting themselves from marauding wolves and other predators. In the northern colonies, where winters were harsher, hogs were more likely to be penned up and fed corn and scraps. Hogs are more efficient converters of feed grain into edible meat than cattle; identical amounts of grain produce about 50 percent more pork than beef. Cattle needed good pasturage, and many varieties of superior English grasses and clovers were introduced in the seventeenth century. Every farmer, and most artisans, maintained at least one cow to provide milk, cheese, and butter. Dairy production was low by modern standards, however; a cow that gave over one quart per day was uncommon.

Other livestock on farms were oxen, horses, sheep, and chickens.

Oxen were used exclusively for plowing and pulling heavy carts. Horses were more adaptable, since they could be used for plowing and hauling, plus local and long-distance transportation. Sheep were prized mainly for their wool, and rarely eaten as mutton in the colonies. Wool could be transformed into crude clothing and blankets for home use, or sold in the marketplace. Chickens provided mainly eggs and some meat. Poultry and sheep were both highly vulnerable to natural predators and had to be carefully watched and protected. In a study of the Connecticut economy, Bruce Daniels found that the typical farmer in the 1770s possessed 10 cattle, 16 sheep, 6 pigs, 2 horses, and a team of oxen.

The extent of progress in colonial agriculture over the decades can be judged indirectly by examining changes in the eating habits and diets of Americans. In the seventeenth century, one-pot meals cooked in the fireplace were the rule. Sarah McMahon found that by the mid-eighteenth century, improvements were noticeable; diets were less restrictive and less seasonal. The colonists moved away from meals dominated by bread and salted meats toward more balanced, "deseasonalized" menus. They learned better methods of storing vegetables such as onions, carrots, turnips, and cabbages for winter consumption. The degree of diversity in meals was largely a function of income levels; the upper classes had the widest selection throughout the year, and the poor had the least.

Both McMahon and Carole Shammas concluded that the quality of meals generally improved over the eighteenth century. Cooks became more skillful in preparing various dishes; their concern was no longer with the mere bulk of food on the table but also with its tastefulness. Mealtime was increasingly a form of entertainment and display for relatives and friends. Women sought out tasty recipes in contemporary cookbooks, and they prepared more elaborate and varied menus.

Besides growing sufficient food to provide an ample and nutritious diet for the family unit, most colonial farmers produced for the market. The extent and nature of agricultural surpluses varied according to climate and soils. In the prosperous southeastern counties of Pennsylvania, James Lemon estimated, the typical farmer in the late colonial period had 40 percent of his total output available for sale. In the Shenandoah Valley, Robert Mitchell put the figure at 25 percent during the 1760s. David Klingaman's data suggest that up to 50 percent of the total production of corn, wheat, and tobacco in Virginia was normally sold in overseas markets. Corn and wheat output totaled £864,000 ($78 million) annually in 1768–72, with about 15 percent, or £130,000 ($11.7 million) exported, while tobacco production was £493,000 ($44 million) with virtually the entire crop exported. In other regions where land was less productive, such as in New England or in areas distant from active commercial centers or good transportation, families were closer to subsistence, and the volume of output entering the marketplace was much lower.

In addition to the sale of surplus food crops, farmers often earned supplementary income from a variety of complementary activities. In the middle colonies, farmers produced a substantial amount of flaxseed, while South Carolina planters grew indigo for the English textile industry. The forest was a major source of extra income. In the northern colonies, some farmers turned hardwood ashes into potash, felled tall pines for the mast trade, or sold firewood in nearby towns and villages. Hundreds of miles to the south, farmers in North Carolina relied heavily on the production of naval stores—tar, pitch, rosin, and turpentine—for additional income. Many rural residents were part-time artisans, and they earned supplementary income from a whole host of activities pursued during the winter months and other slow periods on the farm.

In the northern colonies and parts of Virginia and Maryland, farmers marketed surplus wheat, corn, and rye—plus pork and beef. Recent research on local markets by Bettye Hobbs Pruitt indicates that farmers exchanged a fair volume of basic provisions among friends and neighbors. Some provisions were also sold to rural artisans. Surplus foodstuffs went to towns and ports along the coast by wagon and by river transport. Much grain and preserved meat passed directly into the holds of ships and moved to waiting markets overseas. Indeed, Carville Earle, Ronald Hoffman, and Paul Clemens have argued that in many Chesapeake counties after 1750, wheat farmers using wage labor during the harvest season earned greater profits than tobacco growers who relied on slave labor. In southern New England many farmers shifted largely out of grain production and emphasized animal husbandry. In Rhode Island, some land-holders concentrated on raising horses for export to Caribbean sugar plantations.

Generally speaking, the commercial aspects of agriculture were not as evident in the north as in the south, since, by and large, farmers simply raised excess quantities of the same foodstuffs consumed in the household. This factor tends to obscure the market orientation of northern farmers, especially those located in the middle colonies.

Over the last decade academic debate has raged over how best to describe in general terms the nature of this predominantly agricultural society and its prevailing ideology. The course of scholarly debate has been difficult to follow and access, however, because of a lack of agreement among participants about the meaning of certain critical terms such as capitalism, exploitation, exchange relationships, market orientation, and the like.

The depiction of colonial farmers as individuals who typically responded to price signals and opportunities in the marketplace has been questioned by several historians over the last decade. In an article published in 1978, James Henretta argued that communal and family values predominated over individualistic, profit-maximizing impulses in the northern colonies, and as a result, agricultural entrepreneurship was stifled to a significant degree. He cited the absence of crop specialization and the limited impact of foreign markets.

Henretta asserted that the "mentalité" of northern farmers stressed the maintenance of kinship ties between generations; correspondingly, the society placed a much lower priority on individual accumulation beyond the minimal requirements for sustaining future generations. In a subsequent clarification of his views, Henretta reiterated his contention that "the economic behavior of northern farm families was not fundamentally determined by market forces and values," and no significant change occurred until several decades after the close of the colonial era.

Other historians have echoed this theme, but with individual variations. Christopher Clark depicted the rural residents of New England as living in family units which were "not profit-oriented."

Farmers participated in little trading activity requiring cash payment. Their main objective was not strictly the achievement of household self-sufficiency, according to Clark, but a high degree of local independence from the power of outside market forces.

Michael Merrill, Robert Mutch, and Michael Bellesiles have emphasized the prevalence of transactions involving the barter of commodities and the direct exchange of labor among neighbors. Merrill argues that the prevalence of such reciprocal arrangements did not indicate the existence of formal markets. He prefers to call them "exchange relationships," and he differentiates between the goal of property accumulation through slow but steady saving and the narrower aim of short-run profit maximization.

Mutch argues that farm families lived in predominantly "premarket" societies. According to him, households looked inward to meet their immediate needs rather than to outside markets in determining what to produce and how to allocate labor resources; "merchants and farmers lived in separate societies linked only by the impersonal act of exchange." Bellesiles labeled the system of direct reciprocal exchanges on the New England frontier a form of "communal capitalism."

Some scholars have gone a step further and questioned whether the colonial economy could even be described as capitalist in its character and outlook. Rona Weiss maintained that the farmers who owned and worked their own land and the artisans who possessed their own tools were as a class neither workers nor capitalists in a strict sense. Instead they are best viewed, she believes, simply as "petty producers" functioning in what remained fundamentally a feudal world. In a joint publication Michael Bernstein and Sean Wilentz affirmed the correctness of Weiss's attempt to distinguish between rural wages dictated by an impersonal labor market and wages paid alternatively "on the basis of non-capitalist forms of reciprocity and justice."

On another front, Elizabeth Fox-Genovese and Eugene Genovese have extended that general argument to another region by asserting in colorful language that the southern economy based on slave labor never qualified for designation as genuinely capitalist; it was rather "a bastard child of merchant capital and developed as a non-capitalist society." American slaveholders represented a new social class—not feudal, seigniorial, nor capitalist—which was linked to the capitalist world but, according to the Genoveses, was not an integral part of it.

Meanwhile, historians who have interpreted the colonial economy from a free-market and avowedly capitalist viewpoint have countered these claims with arguments and explanations of their own. Among the prominent contributors are James Lemon, Winifred Rothenberg, and Carole Shammas. Lemon concedes that countervailing forces such as the influence of community and church prevented the power of the market from totally dominating colonial society, but "the basic dynamic was toward economic growth, toward success defined by wealth . . . , and toward accumulation as a goal in its own right." Not only the economic leaders, but "all freeholders contributed to the commercialization of land, resources, and society." The basis for economic advancement was the absolute and exclusive right to private property; Lemon has subsequently reiterated his belief that farmers are best viewed as individuals involved in a business enterprise.

Rothenberg defines capitalism as an economic system featuring private ownership, the use of markets to allocate goods and investments, and a legal tradition to enforce contracts. She argues that measured by those criteria, the colonies were clearly capitalist during the eighteenth century. To show the broad influence and integration of the marketplace, Rothenberg reveals how closely the movements of prices for certain basic commodities in rural Massachusetts coincided with price movements in Philadelphia and New York from 1750 to 1775. Coining a phrase of her own to offset Henretta's, she asserts that the mind set prevailing among colonial farmers was a "commercial mentalité."

Shammas challenges old beliefs about the degree of self-sufficiency in colonial households. Acknowledging that the "idea of colonial Americans as commercial primitives . . . has had a long and proud history," she estimates that the typical household spent up to £3.35 ($310) per capita, or one-quarter of personal income, on goods imported across the borders of the colony. The sources of imports were Great Britain, the West Indies, Ireland, continental Europe, and the other mainland colonies. Shammas views colonial farmers, except those on the frontier, as unavoidably involved in a host of market transactions, if for no other reason, because the cost of the equipment required to spin thread, weave cloth, mill grain, and perform all other household tasks was prohibitive. Finally, she notes that farmer's entries in their account books were rarely listed in physical quantities or labor credits but invariably in monetary units, which indicates that the price mechanism and market forces were pervasive in rural areas.

One scholar who has sought to carve out some middle ground in this ongoing debate and to reconcile the controversy has been Bettye Hobbs Pruitt. She has identified contradictory tendencies in northern farm households. Farmers sought independence, true enough, but they also wanted to improve living standards. Therefore, even in instances when farmers had the potential for self-sufficiency, they rarely chose that course because specialization and interdependence at the community level held out the prospect of raising incomes.

Pruitt distinguishes as well between farmers in New England and in the middle colonies. Because of a greater resource endowment, farm households in the middle colonies were simultaneously more self-sufficient and more commercialized than their counterparts in New England—and more prosperous as well. Viewing as futile and illogical all efforts to discuss local exchange and the market mechanism as separate phenomena, Pruitt concludes that "traditionally sharp distinctions between subsistence and commercial agriculture can be set aside as inapplicable to an agrarian economy in which production for home consumption and production for sale or exchange were complementary, not mutually exclusive objectives."

In a recent study of the interaction of culture and commerce in several Massachusetts maritime communities in the first half of the eighteenth century, Christine Heyrman discovered that the area's conversion to a local economy oriented more toward trade than agriculture did not lead, as might have been anticipated, to a breakdown in communal spirit. Tensions developed, but they failed to threaten the stability of the social order. "The profit motive did not dissolve the bonds of communal cohesion." Although wealth inequality increased, the living standard of the typical resident rose in response to new opportunities for investment and employment.

Heyrman added: "Commercial expansion was contained within and molded by an older structure of relationships and beliefs." Her study suggests that the alleged gap between the persistence of communal values and the operation of market forces may not have been so wide.

In this case, as in so many other similar situations, the observer's vantage point can make a critical difference in rendering judgments. Viewed from the twentieth century, northern farmers may appear lethargic and relatively unattuned to market forces in responding to economic opportunities. But in comparison with their predecessors and their contemporaries around the world, it would probably be difficult to identify another group of family farmers who pursued their own self-interest so vigorously. Adam Smith made that same observation in 1776.

Moreover, a heavy emphasis on communal values seems completely inappropriate for the colonial south. Community ties were not as strong in the southern colonies because of a more dispersed pattern of settlement. Plantation owners exhibited obvious entrepreneurial behavior in expanding the size of their bonded workforce to maximize profits. The southern colonies were also actively involved in foreign trade; by the late colonial period a large share of the regional production of four major staples—tobacco, rice, indigo, and wheat—still entered the export market. In varying degrees, most southern farmers were already involved in the commercial aspects of agriculture, while the remainder aspired to acquire the resources, mainly land and bound labor, to expand output and seek outside markets.

The southern colonies also differed from their northern counterparts because three of their main crops—tobacco, rice, and indigo—were unique to the region, and two of them were not foodstuffs. The overall system of production was also quite different. The southern colonies relied extensively, but not exclusively, on bound labor. Starting with white indentured servants in the seventeenth century, the system subsequently shifted to a reliance on black slaves. Actually, only about one-half of southern farmers owned slaves, and most owners held fewer than five persons in bondage. Nonetheless, for the southern economic elite, the slave system was compatible with the creation of large agricultural units with work-forces sometimes numbering in the hundreds.

Tobacco was a plant cultivated in many parts of the world before the seventeenth century, but it grew especially well in Chesapeake soils. The number of European consumers increased steadily after 1620, and they came to prefer Virginia and Maryland leaf because of its texture, taste, and relatively low price. In the upper south, tobacco was the major export throughout the colonial period. (Cotton became an important southern crop only after independence.)

The typical Chesapeake farmer, with only his immediate family as a source of labor, planted about 3 acres in tobacco, along with 10 acres or so in corn and other food crops. Tobacco plants required careful attention during the spring and summer months to obtain a high-quality leaf. The leaves were cut in late summer and hung in the tobacco barn to dry for 3 to 6 weeks. The leaf was then sorted according to grade and packed in hogsheads for transfer, often by rolling them over rough roads, to a certified warehouse on a nearby river. By the eighteenth century, government inspectors were on hand to test the quality of all tobacco scheduled for export, and they did not hesitate to disqualify any hogsheads containing inferior leaf or too much "trash" tobacco. The average farm produced around 2,400 pounds of salable tobacco, and given price levels after 1720, the family received from £10 to £30 ($900 to $2,700) for its efforts, with about £15 ($1,350) the average. Proceeds from tobacco sales typically generated around one-quarter of a family's overall income.

A substantial amount of information about the lives of tobacco farmers in seventeenth Maryland has emerged during the last decade because of the research efforts of numerous historians, among them Paul Clemens, Gloria Main, Russell Menard, Lois Green Carr, and Lorena Walsh. The typical family dwelling of a tobacco farmer in Maryland contained around 350 square feet of living space; it had two rooms, a dirt floor, and a fireplace for cooking and heating. It was constructed of wood shingles (log cabins were rare), and building materials cost not much more than £3 ($270). Furniture was spare; chairs were uncommon, and family members usually sat on beds, chests, stools, and tables. If a family prospered over the course of several generations, it might move up the economic scale to a three-room, brick house with a wood floor, two fireplaces, and up to 800 square feet of living space.

One ambitious Maryland farmer who arrived in the colony in the mid-seventeenth century was Robert Cole. Starting with more capital than the typical immigrant, he brought a wife, four children, and two indentured servants to assist on the farm. His land produced about 5,800 pounds of tobacco annually valued at £25 ($2,250). Historians Menard, Carr, and Walsh estimated that on average 45 percent of the Cole family's income arose from household consumption of food, firewood, and other items produced on the farm; 20 percent of income came from sales to local inhabitants—mainly livestock products such as meat, tallow, hides, butter, and cheese; and 35 percent resulted from tobacco exports.

Like some of his more enterprising counterparts, Cole tended to save a high proportion of the profits from farm operations. His reinvestment of funds in farm improvements and additional bonded labor resulted in steady increases in net worth (assets minus liabilities) from £210 ($19,000) in 1662 to £360 ($32,500) a decade later, a rate of increase of over 5 percent per annum—a figure around double the rate for other Maryland farmers in similar circumstances.

By the third quarter of the seventeenth century, the Cole farm had reached nearly the peak of its economic efficiency. Once a tobacco farmer like Cole was able to produce sufficient grain and vegetables to feed his growing family, to raise numerous livestock, to build a comfortable house with adequate furnishings, and to acquire a varied wardrobe, there were few means available to improve family welfare substantially. The major impact on subsequent generations was the potential for more leisure time, resulting from the continued substitution of bonded workers for family labor and the hiring of white overseers to supervise farm operations. But many reasonably prosperous colonial farmers decided to forego the opportunity for greater leisure, preferring to continue day-to-day managerial control over their properties.

Similar accounts of modest successes in tobacco farming have emerged from Richard Beeman's recent study of Lunenburg County on Virginia's southeastern frontier. Southside Virginia, along the North Carolina border, was settled initially in the 1740s. The key to success there was not land, which was plentiful and inexpensive, but access to labor. Farmers grew mostly food crops for local consumption during the first quarter-century, but they steadily acquired slaves and became increasingly involved in growing tobacco for the export market.

Whereas farmers in the older settled areas of the Chesapeake region were engaging in a more diversified form of agriculture after mid-century, the trend in southside Virginia was just the reverse— toward greater specialization in tobacco. The numbers of families holding slaves rose from just one-fifth in 1750 to over one-half by 1770; by the latter date black slaves had surpassed free whites in the population. Because of the immediacy of its frontier origins and the widespread ownership of property—80 percent of taxpayers in 1770 owned land and had median holdings of over 200 acres— Lunenburg County developed a more egalitarian social and economic order with fewer instances of great wealth or hopeless tenancy, according to Beeman, than prevailed in the older and more established counties in the Chesapeake region.

A greater concentration of even larger wealth was clearly evident in areas long settled near the coast, however. As Allan Kulifoff argues in his recent book on the interrelationships between tobacco and slavery in the Chesapeake, children who inherited both land and slaves were in a favored position, and they generally were able to sustain that advantage for the benefit of future generations. Persons in this group held property ten times more valuable than their nonslaveholding counterparts at every stage in their life cycle. Through inheritance and intermarriage, the leading families consolidated their economic and political power in Chesapeake society. According to Kulikoff, "by the 1750s and 1760s wealthy officeholders and their kindred and friends constituted a distinctive class."

In the seventeenth century, tobacco was marketed almost exclusively under the consignment system. The grower retained ownership and assumed all risks throughout the marketing process, paying transportation and incidental costs until his crop was finally sold in England. The tobacco merchant in Britain negotiated the sale and charged a commission for his services, often 2.5 percent of the gross sales price plus the import duties—in all around 10 percent of the grower's net proceeds. The grower invariably sent along a list of finished goods that the family wanted to purchase for the return trip, and his English consignee had instructions to use the sale proceeds to fill those orders. In supplying these finished goods, the merchant enjoyed either a handsome markup on items sold out of his own inventory or, at least, a second commission for purchasing the requested goods from other suppliers.

In addition, the English merchant frequently offered "advances." He allowed farmers to draw funds prior to the sale of tobacco in Britain, with the understanding that the forthcoming crop would serve as collateral for the loan. When the sale proceeds failed to cover the advance plus the cost of the finished goods requested for return shipment, many tobacco merchants agreed to extend credit to their colonial customers until the next harvest. Convenient credit terms were used to attract more consignments and to hold old accounts, and competitive pressures led tobacco merchants to adopt liberal policies in normal circumstances.

Although the consignment system continued throughout the colonial era, aggressive Scottish merchants invaded the Chesapeake market after 1740 and inaugurated the practice of buying tobacco in the colonies for spot cash or its equivalent. Concentrating mainly on Virginia, the Glasgow merchants opened branch stores along the shores of the major rivers, where they exchanged tobacco for other merchandise. Like their competitors in London, the Scottish firms extended credit to growers in anticipation of the upcoming harvest.

The entrepreneurship of Glasgow tobacco merchants gave growers an alternative marketing channel, and the Scots captured the lion's share of the business by the 1770s, especially within the ranks of the smaller farmers. The offer of spot cash appealed to many growers, because it eliminated the risks and uncertainties associated with future sales by a consignee in a distant overseas market. With slow communications, the news about prevailing prices in London was always weeks out of date, and predictions about future prices in the tobacco market were unreliable. Moreover, the managers of the Scottish stores paid prices for lower and medium grades that were competitive with the net proceeds normally realized from sales in the London market.

Glasgow merchants paid good prices partly because they operated with lower transportation costs. The westbound trip to the colonies from Scotland was often two or three weeks faster than from London because of differences in currents and winds. More important, the turnaround time in Virginia and Maryland was much shorter. Vessels out of London servicing the consignment trade might spend several weeks in Chesapeake waters accumulating a full cargo for the return voyage. But a Scottish ship usually found a full cargo of hogsheads waiting at the wharf of its firm's branch store and ready for immediate loading. With transport costs reduced, the Glasgow tobacco merchants were in a position to offer higher prices to colonial growers. According to Jacob Price, tobacco transactions often resulted in only slight gains for overseas merchants, or even small losses; the great profits in the Chesapeake trade actually arose from the branch stores' sale of English and European goods to growers at substantial markups.

Despite the rise of the Glasgow contingent, some planters still preferred to deal with London commission merchants. Because of market fluctuations, the risk of loss was greater, but so too was the opportunity to realize higher sales revenues and larger profits. Growers who produced premium grades of leaf, for instance in the York River region of Virginia, generally consigned their tobacco to the London market. Many great planters with large shipments and a willingness to accept greater risks also avoided sales to nearby Scottish stores and relied instead on the traditional consignment system. Jacob Price[1] discovered that, by the 1760s, only one-half of the customers of James Buchanan & Co., an important consignment firm, were actually planters; the other half were indigenous Virginia merchants, shopkeepers, lawyers, physicians, and other nonagriculturalists, who had invested in tobacco and shipped their crop overseas for final sale. Nonetheless, consignment sales probably accounted for no more than 20 percent of the total crop on the eve of independence.

The organization of the marketing system for tobacco was one factor accounting for the lack of extensive urbanization in the upper south. Only two Chesapeake cities—Baltimore and Norfolk—had populations over 5,000 as late as 1775, and both were involved heavily in the provisions trade to the West Indies and had few ties with tobacco. One reason for the absence of large commercial centers in the most populous colonial region was the excellent system of natural waterways. The broad rivers of Virginia and the many inlets of the Chesapeake Bay in Maryland were navigable far inland, which permitted large ships to sail upriver to the wharves of individual planters. Meanwhile, larger planters often performed mercantile functions for smaller farmers nearby. Therefore no central collection points for the shipment of hogsheads or the receipt of finished goods were required along the Atlantic coast.

The concentration of merchandising functions in the hands of London and Glasgow tobacco merchants reinforced the decentralized character of the trade in the colonies and rural structure of Chesapeake society. This concentration occurred because tobacco was an enumerated product, and handling it in Britain involved complex procedures. Upon arrival of the cargo, the importer was forced either to pay a heavy duty ranging from 200 to 300 percent ad valorem or to post bond. After carefully examining and grading the tobacco, the merchant was permitted to collect a full drawback of the original import duties on all amounts reexported to the European continent; in some years up to 85 percent was, in fact, reexported. British merchants had access to the financial resources and continental contacts necessary to expedite tobacco transactions. The net result was that indigenous merchants played a minor role in marketing tobacco, and wherever it was the major commercial crop, the growth of urban areas was severely arrested.

Despite the importance of tobacco in the Chesapeake economy, revenues from this staple represented no more than about one-fourth of the median family's annual income. Fluctuations in the market clearly had an impact on a family's welfare, but the level of tobacco prices was not the sole indicator of conditions in the Chesapeake economy. On the downside, a poor harvest of food crops because of bad weather or insects or perhaps the death of livestock from disease could have an equally serious effect on real income. A short harvest could translate into less quantity and variety in diets for every person on a farm, free and slave. Only the great planters who depended on tobacco revenues to support their elevated lifestyle had a huge stake

in the maintenance of high, steady prices in the foreign tobacco
market.

In the lower south, rice and indigo emerged as the main commercial crops. These semitropical plants thrived in the hot and
humid lowlands along the coast of South Carolina and Georgia. The
evidence indicates that greater economies of scale existed in rice
and indigo production than in tobacco, because more of the region's
output can be traced to large plantations with numerous slaves. On
the eve of independence, the value of exports per capita for the
white population from the two southernmost colonies was £9 ($800),
by far the highest total along the coast. As a result, slaveholders in
these two colonies maintained the highest living standards on the
mainland.

Indigo became a major commercial crop after Parliament enacted
a series of laws designed to spur colonial production. Indigo was in
demand because its leaves yielded a brilliant copper or purple dye
highly valued in the English textile industry. Before midcentury,
English clothmakers had purchased indigo mainly from the French
and Spanish islands in the West Indies. Eliza Lucas, who migrated
to South Carolina from Antigua (an island 300 miles east of Puerto
Rico) in 1738 at the age of 16 to assume managerial responsibility
for three of her father's recently inherited plantations, is generally
credited with introducing and sustaining the successful cultivation
of indigo on the mainland.

After Lucas and others had shown that indigo could be grown in
the lower south, Parliament, in sound mercantilist fashion, decided
to take several steps designed to promote its production in British
territory, thereby improving the empire's overall balance of trade.
In 1748 it authorized the payment of a bounty of 6 pence ($2.25)
per pound, later lowered to 4 pence ($1.50). Then in 1764, Parlia-
ment, taking direct aim at French suppliers, imposed a stiff tariff on
foreign imports of indigo into England. With the dual incentive of
a protected market and a generous bounty, colonial planters responded appropriately. Without this program of government subsidies, it remains questionable whether indigo could have been grown
profitably. After the political break with Britain ended the subsidies
in 1776, indigo production declined rapidly and had almost disap-
peared by 1790.

Meanwhile, indigo cultivation expanded rapidly in South Carolina in the third quarter of the century. Like tobacco, it was produced almost exclusively for the export market. The plants grew on high ground unsuitable for rice paddies. Leaves were cut twice in the summer on the mainland, compared to up to four cuttings in the West Indies. Extracting the dye residue from the leaves by boiling in large vats was a complicated chemical process that determined the quality and value of the final product. In addition to raising enough food to feed a family, a skilled slave could care for up to two acres of indigo plants and produce 120 pounds of dye worth £20 to £30 ($1,800 to $2,700) for export in the early 1770s. Few, if any, other crops produced a greater income per acre, or per worker, than indigo during the late colonial period.

In terms of aggregate output, however, rice was the most important crop in the lower south. The land and workers were so productive that large surpluses were available for overseas sale. Like wheat grown in the middle colonies, rice found ready markets in the Caribbean sugar islands and in northern and southern Europe. Rice was grown mainly on plantations located in the swampy lowlands near the Atlantic coast. Following the perfection of the technique of using tidal waters to control grass and weeds in the rice fields, yields improved substantially after midcentury.

Slave labor was used extensively in cultivating this commercial food crop. Two factors appear to have accounted for the slave character of rice agriculture. First, laborers working cooperatively in groups of 5 to 10 and working under the task system were more efficient in growing rice than the individual farmer aided primarily by his immediate family and a few bonded workers. Rice plantations were normally large economic units, and slave populations of 50 to 100 persons were common. The lower south was the only region on the mainland where the black population exceeded the white population. In South Carolina blacks outnumbered whites by a margin of over 50 percent.

Second, the coastal lowlands had a reputation as an unhealthful region teeming with a host of mysterious fevers. Fearful whites often spent part of the year in Charleston, hoping to escape the diseases associated with the swampy rice fields. For reasons inexplicable at the time, black workers seemed on the whole more immune to disease on rice plantations, and thus planters viewed blacks as better suited than white workers to this form of agriculture.

Only in modern times have medical researchers discovered a probable biological explanation for this previously perplexing difference in the health pattern of the races. Although the chemical mechanism is still not fully understood, it has been fairly well established that individuals whose blood molecules reveal the so-called sickle cell trait exhibit an unusually high degree of immunity to malaria. If husband and wife are both carriers of this blood trait, some of their children may inherit the serious genetic disease called sickle cell anemia (about one in 400 black Americans have the disease at present). While members of other races in rare cases also possess this blood characteristic (the author is one), the incidence of sickled cells is concentrated in the descendants of black Africans.

One hypothesis holds that through a process of Darwinian natural selection over thousands of years, persons with the sickle cell mutation fared better in the malaria-infested regions of West Africa, and they gradually became a significant part of the general population. At present, up to 10 percent of the Afro-American population are carriers of the sickle cell trait, and assuming a similar proportion of colonial slaves were carriers too, it follows that some blacks were less susceptible to chronic malaria than others, and were in fact healthier and more productive workers in the rice fields.

The strain of white rice widely grown in the lower south was not a native plant. Historians are unsure, however, whether Europeans or Africans were most responsible for developing the technology of rice agriculture in South Carolina in the late seventeenth century. The white settlers who came to the mainland from the Caribbean sugar islands knew little about rice growing, but many West Africans were already familiar with the techniques of dike building, flooding, weeding, and harvesting. Thus some blacks may have taught their white masters much about the cultivation of this crop. Peter Wood and James Clifton have emphasized the probable contributions of slaves to rice culture, but Philip Morgan disputes the extent of their knowledge, since only about 15 percent of the blacks brought to South Carolina were from rice-growing areas in Africa.

Rice was a very profitable crop in the late colonial period. Prices rose steadily over the decades, climbing by over 50 percent between 1730 and 1775; output jumped from an annual average of 62,000 barrels in the 1740s to 125,000 barrels in the early 1770s. Philip Morgan estimates that the rate of profit on a 200 acre rice plantation with 40 slaves was 25 percent in the 1770s. Yields were from 2 to 4 barrels per acre, and most plantations had 3 acres under cultivation for each field hand. Based on an average price of £2.3 ($207) per barrel from 1768 to 1772, revenues generated annually by the typical slave ranged from £9.2 to £27.6 ($830–$2,485), with around £15 ($1,350) probably the average figure, according to my analysis of trade data in the study by James Shepherd and Gary Walton.

In addition to an environment uniquely suited to growing certain semitropical crops, the southern colonies provided the setting for a distinct economic and political elite—the planter class. The planter elite played a major role in the tobacco regions of the upper south, and it dominated the rice and indigo agriculture of South Carolina and Georgia. In North Carolina, wealthy planters were less numerous, yet they were still the most influential political force within the colony.

To rise in the social and economic order, a settler had to accumulate both land and slaves. Although no agreement exists among historians about the requirements for full-fledged planter status, by the time a man had acquired 500 acres and 20 slaves, he had clearly become an important member of local society. Below the elite on the economic and social ladder were many aspiring settlers who owned a few slaves and who still worked in the fields themselves performing the same tasks as their bonded workers. The great planters, who did no physical labor but supervised the work of overseers, were the model for other ambitious whites to imitate. T. H. Breen estimates that 3 to 10 percent of households in Virginia qualified for great planter status after 1750.

Great planters held enormous political power in the southern colonies. They spent much of their free time in leisure, educational pursuits, and participation in public life; Thomas Jefferson and George Washington functioned within this elite circle. By the mid-eighteenth century, southern legislatures were largely composed of wealthy planters, who also filled most of the important judicial and administrative offices. Because of planter dominance, the south mirrored more closely than the north the structure of society in the mother country. In England, the landed gentry remained the most potent force in government affairs.

Yet substantial differences existed between the English gentry and the colonial planter—in the sources of political power and, more important to this study, the performance of economic functions. The colonial elite exercised governmental control with the active support of the general population. Unlike England, where the franchise was narrowly restricted, most farmers in the colonies were eligible to vote, and, in a very deferential manner, they normally elected wealthy neighbors who were well qualified to protect local interests. In the south, the great planters became the representatives of small farmers in public affairs.

In the scope of his economic activities, the colonial planter was likewise quite different from the English gentry. In the mother country, the gentry were primarily landlords who rented small farms to a large number of tenant families. Because peers viewed non-agricultural work as socially degrading, English landlords refused to become extensively involved in mercantile activities. The great planters in the mainland colonies were, in contrast, deeply involved not only in the management of their estates but simultaneously in a wide range of complementary enterprises. Few southerners achieved great wealth through agriculture alone; great planters were simultaneously land developers, moneylenders, lawyers, and part-time merchants.

The planter class in the southern colonies was never isolated from the mundane world of business. Most planters were active entrepreneurs who were inclined to engage in any form of economic activity that promised to pay an adequate return on the time and money invested. Most owners handled the business affairs and record keeping for their own estates. In the absence of active commercial centers, southern planters typically performed a number of ancillary mercantile functions. Many planters became middlemen between neighboring farmers and established merchants in overseas ports. They bought small lots of tobacco from lesser neighbors and sold to them, in turn, finished goods imported from Britain. Occasionally, a planter loaned surplus funds to nearby friends or extended credit to small farmers.

One of the most prominent Virginia planters during the first half of the eighteenth century was William Byrd II, whose Westover plantation home above the James River remains one of that state's major architectural showcases. Our knowledge of Byrd's lifestyle is unusually complete because he was a prolific writer and because his personal diary written in a secret code was deciphered and published in the twentieth century.

Byrd was full of paradoxes. In his Virginia habitat, he was an enormously wealthy man with thousands of acres of land and hundreds of slaves. He was a member of the upper chamber in the legislature and a powerful man in the political affairs of the colony. He accumulated a substantial library, hired European tutors to educate his children in intellectual and cultural matters, and kept up as best he could on current events at home, in England, and on the continent. Every morning he spent time reading the Bible, passages in Greek and Hebrew, plus some poetry. In his own territory, he appeared at first glance to be almost the mirror image of a respectable English gentleman.

But when he went back to visit friends and relatives in the mother country, he was—like virtually every other colonial—not taken very seriously. In English society, "colonials," whether from North America, India, or any other location, were invariably viewed as pretentious upstarts. On a comparative basis, Byrd's wealth was barely middling; his political influence where it really counted—in England—was negligible; and his social position was inferior. Cultural refinement was virtually impossible from the British perspective, for Byrd lived literally thousands of miles from London and sophisticated society. Moreover, to accumulate and perpetuate his wealth, he relied on an unsavory slave system, and probably even more damning, he was actively involved, along with hired white overseers, in the management of his own fields and his black labor force. (British investors in sugar plantations in the Caribbean, which relied even more heavily on slavery, normally remained absentee owners and were thus less tarnished by their association with slave labor.) At home in Virginia, he was a representative of the economic,

political, and social elite, but in Britain, Byrd—and his fellow planters—had to struggle for even a semblance of recognition.

In an article discussing the role of market forces in the lives of
William Byrd II and other great planters, Michael Greenberg described the southern elite as a mix of aristocratic aspiration and
bourgeois reality. Byrd aimed at economic success through competition in the marketplace while he attempted to create an aristocratic
lifestyle. In his relationship with his black slave force, he was motivated both by paternalism (visiting the sick every day) and by
unrestrained profit-seeking—two strategies which were by no means
incompatible, as historians ranging from Robert Fogel and Stanley
Engerman to Eugene Genovese have shown. Despite the concern
with the health of field hands, Byrd also could display cruelty in
relations with slaves; according to his own accounts, the serving girl
Jenny was repeatedly beaten with tongs, strapped, and on one
occasion branded with a hot iron, for various minor offenses such as
acting unmannerly, dropping water on the sofa, and other small
complaints. The great southern planters combined traits of refined
gentry and calculating merchant. The precursor to modern large-
scale agriculture—with its emphasis on commercial specialization,
distant markets, and heavy capital investments in men or machinery—is found in the behavior of the great planters of the colonial
era.

A brief glance at the correspondence of William Fitzhugh, a
Virginia tobacco grower and part-time lawyer who managed the
family estate in the late seventeenth century, provides further insight
into the economic status and lifestyle of the great planters. In a letter
written in April 1686, Fitzhugh described in great detail the extent
of his holdings along the Potomac River in northern Virginia:

> The Plantation where I now live contains a thousand Acres, at least
> 700 Acres of it being rich thicket, the remainder good hearty
> plantable land, . . . together with a choice crew of Negroes, . . .
> twenty-nine in all, with Stocks of cattle and hogs at each Quarter;
> upon the same land is my own Dwelling house, furnished with all
> accommodations for a comfortable and gentile living, . . . with 13
> Rooms in it, . . . nine of them plentifully furnished with all things

necessary and convenient, and all houses for use well furnished with brick Chimneys, four good Cellars, a Dairy, Dovecoat, Stable, Bar, Henhouse, Kitchen and all other conveniences, . . . a large Orchard of about 2500 apple trees most grafted, . . . a Garden a hundred foot square, . . . together with a good Stock of Cattle, hogs, horses, Mares, sheep and etc.

As Fitzhugh's description of his estate indicates, the economic position of the planter class was manifest primarily in the grandeur of the family residence, the elegance of its furnishings, and the capital invested in a whole series of productive assets on the estate. A luxurious standard of living in this era was reflected in the finery of dress, the spaciousness of the home, the stylishness of the furniture, the craftsmanship revealed in the silverware, and the convenience of having servants perform all the routine household tasks.

This account of Fitzhugh's status points up as well the extent to which the great strength of the colonial economy rested on its formidable agricultural base. The elegant lifestyles of the great planters derived from the production of a few staple crops in heavy demand overseas. But other members of this agricultural society likewise benefited from the large output generated by land resources. The unusually high living standard enjoyed by the typical family farmer was linked to the copious output of more mundane crops such as corn, wheat, and rye. Steady grain surpluses supported a large population of livestock and gave the colonists a generally protein-rich diet. In our modern economy, only a small percentage of total grain output is consumed directly by the human population; today field crops serve mainly as raw material for the production of meat and dairy foods. While the same statement could not as yet be made about our colonial ancestors, they were already moving in that direction.

With around three-fourths of the population engaged primarily in agriculture, the production of farms and plantations overshadowed by a wide margin the contributions of all other economic sectors to the enhancement of colonial living standards.

BIBLIOGRAPHICAL ESSAY

AMONG the best sources on colonial farming are the innovative studies of historical geographers. James Lemon, *The Best Poor Man's Country: A Geographical Study of Early Southeastern Pennsylvania* (Baltimore: Johns Hopkins University Press, 1972) is one outstanding book. Other valuable volumes in the same genre are Douglas McManis, *Colonial New England: A Historical Geography* (New York: Oxford University Press, 1975); Carville Earle, *The Evolution of a Tidewater Settlement System: All Hallow's Parish, 1650–1783*, Dept. of Geography Research Paper no. 170 (Chicago: University of Chicago, 1975); Robert D. Mitchell, *Commercialism and Frontier: Perspectives on the Early Shenandoah Valley* (Charlottesville: University Press of Virginia, 1977); and Roy Merrens, *Colonial North Carolina in the Eighteenth Century: A Study in Historical Geography* (Chapel Hill: University of North Carolina Press, 1964).

For overviews of farming over longer periods, see two classics and two newer studies: Lewis Gray, *History of Agriculture in the Southern United States to 1860*, 2 vols. (Washington, D.C.: Carnegie Institute, 1933); Percy Bidwell and John Falconer, *History of Agriculture in the Northern United States, 1620–1860* (New York: Smith, 1941); John Schlebecker, *Whereby We Thrive: A History of American Farming, 1607–1972* (Ames: Iowa State University Press, 1975); and John Shover, *First Majority—Last Minority: The Transformation of Rural Life in America* (Dekalb: Northern Illinois University Press, 1976). Articles which touch on environmental issues are E. L. Jones, "Creative Disruptions in American Agriculture, 1620–1820," *Agricultural History* (1974), pp. 510–28, and Conway Zirkle, "To Plow or Not to Plow: Comment on the Planter's Problems," *ibid.* (1969), pp. 87–89. The relative prices of various grains in one urban market are listed in Karen Friedmann, "Victualling Colonial Boston," *ibid.* (1973), pp. 189–205.

On the issue of tenancy, these sources were valuable: Sung Bok Kim, *Landlord and Tenant in Colonial New York: Manorial Society, 1664–1775* (Chapel Hill: University of North Carolina Press, 1978); Gregory Stiverson, *Poverty in a Land of Plenty: Tenancy in Eighteenth-Century Maryland* (Baltimore: Johns Hopkins University Press,

1977); Stephen Innes, "Land Tenancy and Social Order in Spring-field, Massachusetts, 1652 to 1702," *William and Mary Quarterly* (1978), pp. 33–56; Innes, *Labor in a New Land: Economy and Society in Seventeenth-Century Springfield* (Princeton: Princeton University Press, 1983); Lucy Simler, "Tenancy in Colonial Pennsylvania: The Case of Chester County," *William and Mary Quarterly* (1986), pp. 542–69; and Mary Schweitzer, *Custom and Contract: Household, Government, and the Economy in Colonial Pennsylvania* (New York: Columbia University Press, 1987). An analysis of the distribution of wealth is Jeffrey Williamson and Peter Lindert, *American Inequality: A Macroeconomic History* (New York: Academic Press, 1980).

On northern farming, I found especially useful Carl Bridenbaugh, *Fat Mutton and Liberty of Conscience in Rhode Island, 1636–1690* (Providence, R.I.: Brown University Press, 1974); Howard Russell, *A Long Deep Furrow: Three Centuries of Farming in New England* (Hanover: University Press of New England, 1976); and Jackson Turner Main, *Society and Economy in Colonial Connecticut* (Princeton: Princeton University Press, 1985). Sarah F. McMahon has provided data on meals and diets in "Provisions Laid-Up for the Family: Towards a History of Diet in New England, 1650–1850," *Historical Methods* (1981), pp. 4–21, and "A Comfortable Subsistence: The Changing Composition of Diet in Rural New England," *William and Mary Quarterly* (1985), pp. 26–65. See also Carole Shammas, "The Domestic Environment in Early Modern England and America," *Journal of Social History* (1980), pp. 3–24.

The research on Chesapeake farmers and planters is fairly extensive. Thomas J. Wertenbaker, *The Planters of Colonial Virginia* (Princeton: Princeton University Press, 1922) is an older book that remains useful. Among the most valuable recent studies are Gloria Main, *Tobacco Colony: Life in Early Maryland* (Princeton: Princeton University Press, 1982); Paul Clemens, *The Atlantic Economy and Colonial Maryland's Eastern Shore: From Tobacco to Grain* (Ithaca: Cornell University Press, 1980); Richard Beeman, *The Evolution of the Southern Backcountry: A Case Study of Lunenburg County, Virginia, 1746–1832* (Philadelphia: University of Pennsylvania Press, 1984); T. H. Breen, *Tobacco Culture: The Mentality of the Great Tidewater Planters on the Eve of Revolution* (Princeton: Princeton University

Press, 1985); and Allan Kulikoff, *Tobacco and Slaves: The Develop-ment of the Southern Cultures in the Chesapeake, 1680–1800* (Chapel Hill: University of North Carolina Press, 1986). Two studies that focus on individual planters are Pierre Marambaud, *William Byrd of Westover, 1674–1744* (Charlottesville: University Press of Virginia, 1971) and Richard B. Davis, ed., *William Fitzhugh and His Chesa-peake World, 1676–1701* (Chapel Hill: University of North Carolina Press, 1963). The conflict between aristocratic ambitions and com-mercial success is examined in Michael Greenberg, "William Byrd II and the World of the Market," *Southern Studies* (1977), pp. 429–56. Good data on smaller farmers come from Edward Papenfuse, Jr., "Planter Behavior and Economic Opportunity in a Staple Econ-omy," *Agricultural History* (1972), pp. 297–311; Stiverson, "Early American Farming: A Comment," *ibid.* (1976), pp. 37–44; D. Alan Williams, "The Small Farmer in Eighteenth-Century Virginia Pol-itics," *ibid.* (1969), pp. 91–102; and Russell Menard, Lois Green Carr, and Lorena S. Walsh, "A Small Planter's Profits: The Cole Estate and the Growth of the Early Chesapeake Economy," *William and Mary Quarterly* (1983), pp. 171–96.

Menard has also produced some solid figures on tobacco prices; see his "Farm Prices of Maryland Tobacco, 1659–1710," *Maryland Historical Magazine* (1973), pp. 80–85, and "A Note on Chesapeake Tobacco Prices, 1618–1660," *Virginia Magazine of History and Bi-ography* (1976), pp. 401–10.

For research on southern wheat production, see David Klingaman, "The Significance of Grain in the Development of the Tobacco Colonies," *Journal of Economic History* (1969), pp. 268–78, and Carville Earle and Ronald Hoffman, "Staple Crops and Urban De-velopment in the Eighteenth-Century South," *Perspectives in Amer-ican History* (1976), 10:7–77.

For information on the marketing and financing of the tobacco crop, see Stuart Bruchey, *The Colonial Merchant: Sources and Read-ings* (New York: Harcourt, Brace, & World, 1966); Warren Billings, ed., *The Old Dominion in the Seventeenth Century: A Documentary History of Virginia, 1606–1689* (Chapel Hill: University of North Carolina Press, 1975); and T. M. Devine, *The Tobacco Lords: A Study of the Tobacco Merchants of Glasgow and Their Trading Activities, c 1740–1790* (Edinburgh: John Donald, 1975). Over the years, numerous articles have appeared in the *William and Mary Quarterly:* Jacob Price, "The Rise of Glasgow in the Chesapeake Tobacco Trade, 1707–1775" (1954), pp. 179–99; Price, "Buchanan & Simson, 1759–1763: A Different Kind of Glasgow Merchant Trading to the Chesapeake" (1983), pp. 3–41; Price, "The Last Phase of the Virginia-London Consignment Trade: James Buchanan & Co., 1758–1768" (1986), pp. 66–98; and Samuel Rosenblatt, "The Significance of Credit in the Tobacco Consignment Trade: A Study of John Norton & Sons, 1768–1775" (1962), pp. 383–99.

For coverage of the rice and indigo economies, see Lelia Sellers, *Charleston Business on the Eve of the American Revolution* (Chapel Hill: University of North Carolina Press, 1934); Peter Wood, *Black Majority: Negroes in Colonial South Carolina from 1670 through the Stono Rebellion* (New York: Knopf, 1974); Daniel Littlefield, *Rice and Slaves: Ethnicity and the Slave Trade in Colonial South Carolina* (Baton Rouge: Louisiana State University Press, 1981); and Julia Floyd Smith, *Slavery and Rice Culture in Low Country, Georgia, 1750–1860* (Knoxville: University of Tennessee Press, 1985). Important articles are James Clifton, "The Rice Industry in Colonial America," *Agricultural History* (1981), pp. 266–83; Henry Dethloff, "The Colonial Rice Trade," *ibid.* (1982), pp. 231–43; David Coon, "Eliza Lucas Pinckney and the Reintroduction of Indigo Culture in South Carolina," *Journal of Southern History* (1976), pp. 61–76; and Peter Coclanis, "Rice Prices in the 1720s and the Evolution of the South Carolina Economy," *ibid.* (1982), pp. 531–44. For information on the importance of sickle cell trait, see Kenneth Kiple, *The Caribbean Slave: A Biological History* (Cambridge: Cambridge University Press, 1984).

For discussions of the mentalité of northern farmers, start with James Henretta, "Families and Farms: Mentalité in Pre-Industrial America," *William and Mary Quarterly* (1978), pp. 3–32; Christopher Clark, "Household Economy, Market Exchange, and the Rise of Capitalism in the Connecticut Valley, 1800–1860," *Journal of Social History* (1979), pp. 169–89; Michael Merrill, "Cash is Good to Eat: Self-Sufficiency and Exchange in the Rural Economy of the United States," *Radical History Review* (1977), pp. 42–71; Robert Mutch,

"Yeoman and Merchant in Pre-Industrial America: Eighteenth-Century Massachusetts as a Case Study," *Societas* (1977), pp. 279–302; and Michael Bellesiles, "Community Strategies for Dealing with Poverty: The New England Frontier, 1760–1820," unpublished 39-page paper distributed at the University of California's economic history conference, Laguna Beach, May 1986.

Other publications with a more explicit Marxist tone include Elizabeth Fox-Genovese and Eugene Genovese, *Fruits of Merchant Capital: Slavery and Bourgeois Property in the Rise and Expansion of Capitalism* (New York: Oxford University Press, 1983); Rona Weiss, "Primitive Accumulation in the United States: The Interaction Between Capitalist and Noncapitalist Class Relations in Seventeenth-Century Massachusetts," *Journal of Economic History* (1982), pp. 77–82, and "The Market and Massachusetts Farmers, 1750–1850: A Comment," *ibid.* (1983), pp. 475–78; Michael Bernstein and Sean Wilentz, "Marketing, Commerce, and Capitalism in Rural Massachusetts," *ibid.* (1984), pp. 171–72.

The contrary argument is found in James T. Lemon, "Comment on James A. Henretta's Families and Farms: Mentalité in Pre-Industrial America'," with reply by Henretta, *William and Mary Quarterly* (1980), pp. 688–700, and "Letter to Editor," *ibid.* (1985), pp. 555–59; Winifred Rothenberg, "The Market and Massachusetts Farmers, 1750–1855," *Journal of Economic History* (1981), pp. 283–314, and "Markets, Values, and Capitalism: A Discourse on Method," *ibid.* (1984), pp. 174–78; Carole Shammas, "How Self-Sufficient Was Early America?" *Journal of Interdisciplinary History* (1982), pp. 247–72, and "Consumer Behavior in Colonial America," *Social Science History* (1982), pp. 67–86. Other pertinent publications include Bettye Hobbs Pruitt, "Self-Sufficiency and the Agricultural Economy of Eighteenth-Century Massachusetts," *William and Mary Quarterly* (1984), pp. 333–64, and "Letter to Editor," *ibid.* (1985), pp. 559–62; Christine L. Heyrman, *Commerce and Culture: The Maritime Communities of Colonial Massachusetts, 1690–1750* (New York: Norton, 1984).

CHAPTER IV

INDENTURED SERVANTS
AND SLAVES

S OME Americans were able to increase their income and wealth by acquiring legal claims on the labor services of other human beings, both black and white. The two systems of bonded labor—indentured servitude and slavery—had many characteristics in common in terms of day-to-day appearances, but striking differences in the expectations of participants and in the final resolution of their lives. Because of a lack of knowledge about the functioning of markets for indentured servants, previous historians have generally erred in stressing the similarities rather than the extreme differences between the two labor systems, particularly in regard to the issue of exploitation.

Indentured servants served masters for a period of 4 to 7 years, whereas slaves were bound not only for their own lifetimes but in perpetuity—since their children, grandchildren, and all future generations were likewise doomed to enslavement. The indenture system was, for up to 90 percent of its participants, a market-driven, unexploitative arrangement that financed the movement of thousands of willing migrants to the colonies; all parties involved in a indenture contract received the benefits bargained for in advance—or the terms customarily granted in the colony of disembarkation. The slave system, on the other hand, exploited the labor of its victims and transferred financial benefits to owners. Succinctly stated, indentured servitude was a path of upward social and economic mobility for most participants, while slavery, in the North American context, was an absolutely hopeless dead end in terms of any potential for steady advancement.

The opportunities for greater profits from rapidly increasing the size of the tobacco crop for overseas export was the catalyst for the expanded use of bonded labor in Virginia after 1630. Labor was the scarcest economic resource in colonial America, and the opportu-

nity to enlarge the supply of workers through the acquisition of indentured servants and slaves proved irresistible. Vast acreage was of
only modest value without complementary laborers to clear the
fields, plant the seeds, nurture their growth, and harvest the crops.

Before 1680, when Virginia and Maryland were undergoing the
early waves of settlement, the most common form of bound labor
was the white indentured servant. Indeed, up to two-thirds of the
English migrants who came to Virginia between 1630 and 1680 arrived in servile status. In return for the cost of a complete outfit of
clothes, a steady diet, and transportation across the Atlantic, the
servant signed a legal contract, or indenture, which permitted the
sale of his or her labor to the highest bidder in the colonies for a period usually running from 4 to 7 years. Estimates of outfitting and
transportation costs vary from £6 to £10 ($540–$900), or about 75 to
130 percent of median incomes in the Chesapeake in the seventeenth century. The labor contracts of servants sold at varying
prices depending on the age, sex, length of contract, skills of the
servant, and on the local demand for bound labor. The contract
normally specified the conditions of work and stipulated that the
servant was entitled to fair treatment, including an adequate diet,
sufficiently warm clothing, decent lodging, and, for males, a generous supply of alcohol.

Most contracts called for the payment of a sizable bonus, either
in land or in money, upon the successful completion of the labor
term. This feature provided an incentive for servants to remain
faithful workers throughout the indenture. In the seventeenth century, these freedom dues gave thousands of indentured servants
the means to become eventually independent farmers and property
holders. Gloria Main estimates the typical payment at £3.5 ($315)
in the early eighteenth century in Maryland.

The institution of indentured servitude, a temporary status
somewhere between slavery and freedom, was perfectly acceptable
in colonial society. The system was unique to the English colonies,
with characteristics in common with the apprenticeship tradition in
Europe, whereby adolescents bound themselves to an employer in
return for an opportunity to learn the skills of a given trade, and
with the English system of life-cycle servitude in husbandry as out-

lined in recent work by Ann Kussmaul. In the colonies, servant contracts were normally acquired by farmers who sought males to provide extra labor in the field and females to assist in caring for children and routine household chores.

In the Chesapeake region, servants made a good return cargo for vessels engaged in the tobacco trade. Most were young, the majority males, between the ages of 15 and 25. Although a few isolated cases involved kidnapings, the vast majority entered into contracts voluntarily. Scholars are still debating the social origins of indentured servants; the most recent evidence indicates that they were drawn from a wide spectrum of British society and in fairly equal numbers from the ranks of farmers and artisans, unskilled laborers, and domestic servants. The one clear exception to the generalization about the voluntary character of indenture relates to the roughly 30,000 criminals languishing in English jails who were transported to the colonies for sale between 1718 and 1775. This criminal element represented about 10 percent of the total transatlantic trade in servants.

For most indentures who came to North America voluntarily, the lure was the potential benefits of a new life in an atmosphere where labor was in heavy demand and where the opportunity to reside on land owned by the household unit, after a few years of servitude, was genuine. At home in Europe, the likelihood of eventually rising to the status of landowner was almost nil. Moreover, servants were actually selling only a claim on their surplus production, for in this era of relatively low per capita output, most of the fruits of their labor were normally returned in the form of food, clothing, shelter, health care, and freedom dues. By the late eighteenth century, around three-quarters of their output went toward routine maintenance. Despite their servile status, the living standards of colonial indentures were probably not much, if at all, below the conditions they had experienced back home. From an economic standpoint, their short-run sacrifices were minimal and their long-run opportunities for advancement much enhanced.

The competitive features of the indenture market have been outlined in recent work by David Galenson, Robert Heavner, and Farley Grubb. In general, they have argued that variations in indenture contracts were based on rational economic considerations. In analyzing a sample of nearly 3,000 extant contracts housed in London, Galenson found that the terms of a given contract were the result of negotiation between the potential immigrant and a host of merchant contractors. Workers who were likely to be the most productive—on the basis of such factors as knowledge of a valuable trade or more advanced age (above 25)—were in the best position to bargain for shorter contracts and higher freedom dues. Galenson listed literacy as a positive factor in the servant's bargaining position. But Heavner's research on the Philadelphia market in the 1770s suggested that literacy had little effect on the value of labor contracts. In Galenson's sample the literacy rate for men was almost 70 percent, a rate considerably higher than for the English population as a whole. Just over one-half of the servants in his sample listed trades, with the percentage rising with the age of individuals.

Other factors affecting the length of the indenture were the immigrants' selected destination and their sex. Youths under the age of twenty who chose the West Indies sugar islands, where the opportunities to acquire land were diminishing and the climate was less healthful, bargained for shorter contracts than youths headed for the mainland. In the seventeenth century females received terms about one and a half years shorter than males. Buyers valued them more highly at the time because of the great imbalance of the sexes in the Chesapeake. By the eighteenth century, however, the sex ratio was moving into equilibrium, and females served only a few months less than males. By the 1770s, in fact, Grubb found that Irish women normally served slightly longer terms than their male counterparts.

In the tobacco colonies, planters constantly complained about the poor quality of their servant labor. Masters invariably described their white indentures as lazy, ignorant, and alcoholic idlers, who were universally ungrateful, unruly, and irresponsible. In the eighteenth century, planters depicted black slaves in virtually identical words, which suggests that the status of subservience alone could explain the persistence of contemptuous white attitudes toward black slaves in eighteenth-century America, and for years thereafter.

Masters could use corporal punishment and could go to court to enforce the terms of a labor contract. If a servant failed to perform assigned duties clearly within the scope of the indenture agreement, or attempted to flee, or when a female servant became pregnant by someone other than her employer, the master could ask a judge to impose penalties. Whippings could be ordered for members of both sexes. The most serious penalty was an extension of a servant's contract for additional years; merely the threat of extension was usually sufficient to keep most servants in line.

At the same time, the indentured servant, unlike slaves, had the option of taking a cruel and overbearing master to court for breach of contract. Servants typically asked judges to instruct masters to abide by the terms of the indenture or, if serious injury had already occurred, to reduce the length of service. Pregnant servants raped by their owners could sue for child support. Suits for the nonpayment of freedom dues were fairly common.

After 1680 black slaves steadily replaced indentured servants as the primary source of bound labor in the southern colonies. Although the number of English departing for the mainland colonies declined sharply from 1690 to 1760, Scotch-Irish and German migration rose substantially, especially into Pennsylvania. Many new arrivals were actually redemptioners, persons who brought their own clothing and supplies but had insufficient funds to pay the full price of a transatlantic passage. In these cases, the term of their labor contract was adjusted to correspond with the amount still due for transportation to the colonies. A fair number of German redemptioners came in family units and went into service that way.

Much research on redemptioner immigration to Pennsylvania in the eighteenth century has been conducted by Farley Grubb. Because redemptioners had at least limited financial resources before embarking for the colonies, they were usually able to exert greater control over the transfer process. Passengers were not auctioned off immediately upon arrival at the dock, but given several weeks to come up with funds to satisfy the unpaid balances due the transatlantic shipper. Money was raised either from relatives already in the area or arose as a result of negotiations with a number of potential masters. "The redemptioner method was a loan transaction secured by human capital collateral," according to Grubb, and it facilitated "a more efficient match between servants and masters" than had prevailed in the indenture system operating in the Chesapeake region in the prior century.

Given a few weeks' leeway, redemptioners had the chance to seek out potential owners pursuing diverse occupations, living in different sections of the province, and possessing compatible ethnic and religious backgrounds—an critical factor for many of the 80,000 Germans, mainly Protestants, who came to Pennsylvania between 1725 and 1775. Before midcentury most redemptioners were European farmers who migrated as families. They sought out masters in frontier areas where opportunities to acquire land of their own at reasonable prices within a matter of months or years was most favorable. Both Grubb and Marianne Wokeck found that after 1750, however, persons who braved the Atlantic were more often single, and fewer than a third had farming backgrounds. Unmarried males tended to link up with artisans in small towns and in Philadelphia, while young women went into domestic service in these same urban areas. (For additional information on the lives of female servants, see chapter 6.)

In research on immigration patterns in the last decade and one-half before independence, Bernard Bailyn observed that about 125,000 persons arrived from Great Britain, and one-half were servants or redemptioners. Persons from London and other urban areas in southern England usually headed for Pennsylvania, Maryland, and Virginia, whereas residents of northern England and Scotland, who traveled more often in family groups, chose more often New York and North Carolina. Maryland was the most popular destination for indentured servants and the final destination of two-fifths of the English in the 1760s and 1770s.

The trade in convicts began in 1718. Surviving records list the names of 17,740 men and women transported from jails in and around London alone, and the total size of the convict trade from Britain as a whole has been estimated to be on the order of 30,000 persons. Felons convicted of minor crimes served 7-year indentures, while those guilty of major crimes were indentured for 14 years. In work on the convict trade in Maryland, the final point of sale for over 9,000 contracts form 1746 to 1772, Kenneth Morgan found that, among males, the average price for a criminal was about one-third of the price for a slave of comparable age. Most colonial buyers purchased the contract of only one convict out of any given cargo. But one local entrepreneur, John Tayloe II, the owner of a large estate and over 300 black slaves, financed the importation of two shiploads of London convicts in 1773–74. He kept a few servants for his own use and sold the remainder to other Maryland planters.

One of the most fascinating aspects of recent research on the system of bonded labor has been the discovery that not only immigrants but numerous native-born American youths were also involved in indenture contracts. In Pennsylvania, Mary Schweitzer has asserted that various types of labor contracts, covering anywhere from six months to several years, were nearly as common to the life experiences of colonial youths as formal schooling has become for modern generations. Moreover, the work days and living conditions of native-born servants were not significantly different from the lives of their free peers. Servants simply became additions to the employing household, eating the same meals as other family members and sharing the same housing and bedding. The indenture contract was akin to the legally enforceable and fairly prevalent apprentice contract, under which an artisan agreed to teach a youth a specific craft in the return for labor services and the payment of a fee by the youth's parents or relatives.

Orphaned minors and the children of indigent parents with poor prospects were prime candidates for court-approved indentured status, with the length of the contract often running until the age of 21. Contracts were fully reassignable to third parties, and Schweitzer detected a substantial amount of trading among families as labor requirements changed with the passage of time. Judges permitted native males to work off accumulated debts under indenture contracts at rates of up to £7 ($630) per year—versus only £4 ($360) for recent immigrants. Persons seeking capital to buy land or tools at some specific date in the future occasionally agreed to indenture contracts stipulating the payment of substantial freedom dues. Since there were no legal barriers to such arrangements and very little, if any, social stigma associated with temporary servile status after the contract expired, the labor arrangements available to colonial youths were in many ways more varied and flexible than those prevailing in our present economy.

There are no good modern parallels to the colonial practice of placing children and youths in the homes of unrelated persons under indenture contracts, although the system of assigning minors to foster homes during periods of prolonged family crisis probably comes the closest. In the modern instance, however, the compensation for housing a youth comes from the payment of government maintenance fees rather than from the labor services supplied by the new member of the household.

Despite the continued functioning of the indentured and redemptioner systems until the 1770s, the impact of later arrivals from Europe on the colonial labor market, even in Pennsylvania, was never as great in the eighteenth century as it had been in the early settlement of Virginia and Maryland. By 1774, only 2 percent of the colonial population were indentured servants. The opportunities for upward mobility were also lessened for indentured servants, although not necessarily for redemptioners, in the late colonial era.

This institution of voluntary temporary servitude, with transactions between most participants normally occurring in a free-market environment, was primarily a feature of the British colonial system in the western hemisphere. In total about 350,000 white servants arrived in North America over the course of the entire colonial period. In the seventeenth century most immigrants were English, but in the next century the main points of departure were Ireland, Scotland, and Germany. The French employed the indenture system on a limited scale, and the Spanish not at all. Meanwhile, the mere existence of a recognized class of Europeans living in a state of "quasi-slavery" clearly made it much easier for the white majority to accept with so few reservations the permanent enslavement of another race with an entirely different culture.

Black slaves were the second-largest group of workers in colonial America, after yeomen farmers. They functioned mainly as field hands, house servants, and occasionally artisans. By 1770, blacks composed over 20 percent of the colonial workforce; in Virginia, Maryland, and North Carolina they numbered 320,000 and constituted 38 percent of the population, while in South Carolina, where settlement began in the late seventeenth century, they outnumbered whites by roughly 50 percent. In the north only New York City plus Newport and Providence, Rhode Island, had slave populations of over 10 percent; the vast majority of northern blacks were involved in domestic service. Most of the very wealthy merchants in the north owned slaves; indeed slaveholding was a common characteristic of the elite classes in north and south.

Prior to 1675 only a handful of Africans were imported into the Chesapeake colonies, and their status was initially determined by legal customs similar to those applied to English indentured servants. After a normal term of service, these early arrivals were either released from their obligations by grateful masters or were given an opportunity to purchase their freedom. These ex-servants formed the core of a very small class of free blacks which survived in the midst of a society subsequently committed to racial slavery and white supremacy.

In research on the lives of black yeoman farmers on Virginia's eastern shore in the mid-seventeenth century, Timothy Breen and Stephen Innes found that several black families enjoyed a substantial degree of economic success for one or two generations. A few black farmers "owned sizable tracts of land, competed with their white neighbors in the marketplace, built up large herds of livestock, and, if resources allowed, purchased their own dependent laborers." Andrew Johnson, who arrived in Virginia in 1621, was among the most prosperous black farmers. By the 1650s the Johnson family owned 900 acres of land and claimed ownership of at least one other black man, John Casor, as a slave for life.

The beginning of the shift from a dependency on indentured servants to a reliance on slaves in the tobacco colonies occurred in Virginia in the last quarter of the seventeenth century and followed from a combination of economic, political, and social factors. Tensions between large property holders, who were tied closely to the established government, and a group of lesser rivals on the frontier, who gained the active support of a sizable number of discontents from the lower classes, including numerous servants and ex-servants, led to Bacon's Rebellion in 1676. Once the king's representatives had reestablished control over government, the colonial leadership realized the probable benefits of shifting away from a reliance on potentially rebellious servants and moving toward a permanent labor force of enslaved Africans, who had been deprived of all political and civil rights by 1660. Free blacks such as the Johnson family on the eastern shore faced an increasing number of racial barriers, in law and custom, which prevented their full participation in Chesapeake society. By the turn of the century, the free black population had left the area or fallen into poverty. In 1699 the Virginia assembly gave every newly freed slave only six months to leave the colony. The slave codes of 1705 recognized blacks as legally inferior human beings, preventing thereby any outside chance that Virginia would evolve into a society with equal economic and political opportunities for members of both races.

Edmund Morgan has suggested that the creation of a large class of permanent slaves, easily distinguished by skin color, was one factor accounting for the surprisingly high degree of solidarity among all sectors of the southern white community after 1680. Indeed, the emergence of a cohesive free society based on the subjugation of black slaves may explain, Morgan hypothesized, why many wealthy planters were so readily attracted to radical concepts such as republicanism and white male political equality in the eighteenth century.

Meanwhile, improving economic conditions in the mother country after 1675 reduced the number of English willing to sign indenture contracts in order to reach the colonies. With the decline of the indenture market, the continued expansion of tobacco fields required the substitution of a new labor supply. Black slavery was one alternative since it was already a well established institution in the Caribbean and other colonized areas of the western hemisphere. Thus imitation, not innovation, guided the course of Chesapeake labor policy.

Finally, Russell Menard found that the price of permanent slaves, with lower yearly upkeep, was only 2 to 3 times higher than the cost of gaining the more temporary services of indentures in the 1690s. The profit motive therefore clearly favored the substitution of black labor for white. In contrast to the declining supply of servants, the number of Africans available for purchase rose steadily. Yet, the thirteen colonies were only a small fraction of the overall hemispheric slave market, since no more than 6 percent of the Africans forcibly transported across the Atlantic came to the English mainland. The number of slaves imported to North America was about 250,000, with over half arriving after 1740.

The constant infusion of fresh supplies of Africans held down market prices of slaves and made them competitive with servant contracts. Robert Paul Thomas and Richard Bean demonstrated that every aspect of the slave trade—from procurement, to transport, to distribution—was characterized by highly competitive markets, with a large number of active participants. Given an open-market structure, average prices for slaves exceeded only modestly the average costs of delivery to the western hemisphere. A normal profit rate of 8 to 12 percent was probably the rule. Reports of phenomenally high profits in the slave trade, at one time a major theme in historical accounts of this era, are now largely discounted.

One topic which has recently drawn the attention of economic historians has been the incidence of slave mortality on transatlantic voyages. In the seventeenth century, up to one-quarter of all slaves boarded in Africa died enroute. By the eighteenth century, mortality rates had fallen to about 10 percent. Despite this improvement, the figures were still much higher than prevailed, for example, in the indentured servant trade with Europe, where Grubb found death rates as low as 4 percent in the eighteenth century. The overcrowding of slaves, a policy allegedly motivated by reckless greed, was originally assumed to be the reason for such high death rates. In recent years, however, researchers have discovered no correlation between the degree of crowding and mortality rates. Raymond Cohn and Richard Jensen have suggested that mortality rates were related rather to several variables: the port of departure in Africa, the date of sailing, the length of the voyage, which varied with wind and weather, and, most crucial of all, the amount of provisions loaded onboard—a decision made by shipping entrepreneurs. Joseph Miller disputes this hypothesis about the importance of supplies; nonetheless, he agrees that slavers attempted to operate rationally in this realm of uncertain and risky business ventures.

The final irony remains that the major beneficiaries of this barbaric system of forced African labor were the consumers of sugar and tobacco. These products had been luxuries in Europe before colonization, but they fell sharply in price over the decades and had become habitual necessities for the middle and even lower classes in many parts of western Europe by the eighteenth century. As a result of the slave trade, Thomas and Bean sarcastically observed, European consumers found "dental decay and lung cancer" available at bargain prices.

In a subsequent research project, Thomas and Bean offered an explanation for the timing of the shift from servants to slaves in the Chesapeake region. Plantations in the Caribbean area began the shift in the 1640s, but on the mainland the transition did not come until almost half a century later. First, they found no evidence that black slaves were inherently more productive in raising any specific crop, such as sugar or tobacco, or in working on large economic units. For them, the key to understanding lay in the relative prices of slaves and servants in the two markets.

The West Indies shifted to slavery in the 1640s because the price of Africans fell sharply while the contractual terms necessary to attract English servants became more costly. By the 1640s, most of the arable land on the British Caribbean islands was already occupied, and these locations offered diminishing opportunities for white immigrants. Meanwhile, economic conditions in England had improved by the 1660s, and it became more difficult to recruit indentured servants on favorable terms.

The Chesapeake region did not shift to slavery at this point, however, because labor prices in that market continued to favor servants. The net cost of transporting slaves (operating expenses plus mortality rates) to the mainland colonies remained £3 to £4 ($270–$360) higher than to the Caribbean. In addition, the contractual terms necessary to attract servants to the Chesapeake, which had a reputation for a more healthful climate and plentiful opportunities to acquire land, were still attractive to planters.

In the 1680s and 1690s, wages in England rose again, and even greater inducements were necessary to lure indentured servants. Meanwhile, the opening up of North Carolina and Pennsylvania to settlement raised the costs of enforcing indenture contracts, because the lure of inexpensive land and the improved chances of evading capture, in combination, encouraged servants in the Chesapeake colonies to attempt escape. Slave prices held steady, and the costs of preventing successful escapes of blacks remained low. Daniel Littlefield reports that in South Carolina only 2 or 3 per 1,000 slaves were listed as runaways in a given year. By the 1690s, the relative cost of slaves was lower than for white servants on the mainland. As a result, slavery expanded.

According to Galenson, the shift came in two stages. First, planters substituted slaves for servants in the tobacco fields; but they continued to purchase the contracts of English servants possessing artisan skills well into the next century. With the emergence of a stable, native-born slave society in the eighteenth century, slaveholders decided to remove an increasing number of slaves from the fields and to train them in crafts such as carpentry and metal fabrication. Allan Kulikoff's research on slave lives confirms the existence of this trend. After midcentury planters no longer wanted to buy the contracts of numerous English artisans; their plantations were in the process of becoming completely self-contained and self-sustaining economic units.

By the eighteenth century, planters found investments in slave labor much more profitable than investments in servants. Ralph Gray and Betty Wood examined in detail the transition to slavery in Georgia in the 1740s and discovered substantial differences in yearly expenses. The Georgia trustees estimated the annual cost of upkeep for a male servant at £9 ($810) compared to only £3.46 ($310) for a slave (table 4.1).

A close analysis of the data reveals, however, that three items— meat, cheese, and beer—accounted for almost all the disparity in maintenance costs between servants and slaves. The allotments of the most basic foodstuffs and clothing were virtually identical. An English servant expected a liberal 200 pound allowance of beef and pork, or seven times the allotment for blacks. But remarkably, alcohol consumption accounted for 60 percent of the estimated differential; indeed beer rations alone were 37 percent of the estimated expenses for maintaining an indentured servant. The cost of supplying servants with alcohol was just a shade below the minimum requirements of slaves. Despite the much smaller sums expended on slaves, it is questionable whether the overall combination of food and clothing left slaves with living standards in Georgia that much inferior to white servants. To the extent that the absence of gallons of beer from the yearly allotment protected a laborer from the potentially debilitating effects of alcoholism, which was a genuine threat throughout colonial America, a slave was in some cases physically healthier than an indentured servant.

Because the economy was overwhelmingly agricultural, slaves performed most of the same labor tasks as white farmers. The skill level of white and black farm workers was essentially the same. Slaves cleared land, prepared the soil for planting, tended the fields, and harvested the crops. On large Chesapeake plantations, slaves labored throughout the day in work gangs. Not only men but black women were regular field hands; indeed the high participation rate

TABLE 4.1. Yearly Maintenance Costs for Servants and Slaves—
Georgia in the 1740s

Item	SERVANTS		SLAVES	
	Amount	Cost	Amount	Cost
Rice	114 lbs.	£0.26	114 lbs.	£0.26
Peas	114 lbs.	0.17	114 lbs.	0.17
Flour	114 lbs.	0.50	114 lbs.	0.50
Basic Foodstuffs		£0.93		£0.93
Meat	200 lbs.	£1.67	30 lbs.	£0.25
Corn	–	–	13 bu.	0.98
Beer		3.39	–	–
Cheese	18 lbs.	0.60	–	–
Butter	9 lbs.	0.36	–	–
Sugar		0.23	–	–
Soap		0.40	–	–
Clothing		1.42		1.30
Total		£9.00		£3.46

SOURCE: Ralph Gray and Betty Wood, "The Transition from Indentured to Involuntary Servitude in Colonial Georgia," *Explorations in Economic History* (October 1976), 13:353–70.

of slaves of both sexes in the labor force accounts in large part for the economic viability of the slave system. Youths went to work in the fields as part-time helpers sometime after the age of 7 and became full-time workers between 11 and 14. Older slaves worked as long as they were physically able, although at least half were retired from any strenuous work after the age of 65. Owners tried to keep workers active on a year-round basis. Slaveholders had a fixed investment in a human machine, and in an effort to minimize down-time, they planned work schedules so that during the winter months blacks were kept busy mending fences, removing tree stumps, and performing other productive tasks.

The skill level of blacks and whites differed more in the rice-growing areas of the lower south because slaves performed most of the field work. In this region slaves normally labored under a work regimen called the task system. In research on the work and culture of lowcountry blacks, Philip Morgan came across testimony from a writer styled "Scouts Americanus" who published, in Scotland in 1773, an account of his observations:

> Their work is performed by a daily task, allotted by their master or overseer, which they have generally done by one or two o'clock in the afternoon, and have the rest of the day for themselves, which they spend in working on their own private fields, consisting of 5 or 6 acres of ground . . . , they have also the liberty to raise hogs and poultry. . . . They do not plant . . . for subsistence, but for amusement, pleasure, and profit.

The task system was so ingrained in work patterns in the coastal areas of the lower south, according to Morgan, that it was universally applied to other crops as well, including corn.

In legislation designed to restrict the private market activities of rural slaves, South Carolina enacted a law in 1751 which forbade slaves to sell surplus output to anyone other than their masters. Despite restrictions, some owners permitted slaves to acquire a fair amount of personal property. Morgan cited one unusual case involving a slave named Sampson who saved enough money to buy a substitute—another slave named Tom—resulting in Sampson's manumission.

In a subsequent study of Charleston, Morgan has brought the differing lifestyles of the colony's urban slaves into much sharper focus. By the 1770s a majority of the city's population was slave— 6,000 residents on a permanent basis and perhaps 1,500 transients. In the dead of summer, when many whites left to seek relief from the heat and humidity, there were weeks when blacks constituted up to 80 percent of the local population. Many, if not most, of these slaves exercised a fair degree of independence in their work lives because they were encouraged to "hire out" their labor to third parties. Under the self-hire system, the wages slaves collected from outside employers were divided with their owners according to some prearranged formula. These urban blacks lived in what Morgan calls a "twilight zone" between freedom and slavery.

Charleston's slaves frequently earned wages from their involvement in skilled crafts. One sample of 372 male slaves spanning the period from 1730 to 1799 revealed representatives in over 50 occupational categories. The number of participants in the ten largest occupations were the following: 73 carpenters, 64 boatmen, 33 coopers, 24 shoemakers, 22 bricklayers, 22 household butlers, 12 tailors, 11 laborers, 9 barbers, and 8 painters. The most common occupations of female slaves were domestic service, seamstress, cook, washerwoman, and market vendor. In addition to greater choices in the selection of employers, Charleston's slaves also retained enough spending money to purchase at least a limited volume of personal goods and services. Numerous inns and alehouses catered to black customers; allowing easy access to alcohol translated into a loosening of control over slaves, which whites did not tolerate in other southern environments. Incidents of illicit interracial sex were also more frequent in this urban society, leading to the birth of many mulattos. Some mulattos eventually gained their freedom and became slaveholders themselves. Morgan concluded that slaves in Charleston were generally "confident and secure" in comparison with their counterparts in the Caribbean region. The lax system of urban slavery in this southern port was strongly entrenched by the late colonial era and revealed no signs of unusual stress or threatened disintegration.

According to Allan Kulikoff's study of the evolution of slave society in the Chesapeake region, the productivity of slave labor rose over the course of the eighteenth century because of the decreasing percentage of untrained, unacclimated, and less easily disciplined Africans in the black population. By 1740, only 17 percent of adult blacks in Virginia had arrived in the colony within the last decade. Whereas early in the century males outnumbered females by 50 percent, by the 1770s the sex ratio had finally come into near balance.

The rising number of native-born slaves and the more balanced sex ratio were two factors leading to the emergence of an identifiable Afro-American culture in the Chesapeake. Early in the eighteenth century, most slaves had lived on small plantations and were isolated from contact with other blacks. Over the century the size of many plantations increased, however, and these larger units provided the environment for the development of a settled community and a unique black culture. Unlike the majority of whites, who lived isolated from each other in separate family units on separate farms, the slaves on these plantations increasingly lived in the more communal atmosphere of slave quarters. By the 1770s over half of the slaves in the southern colonies lived on plantations with ten or more bonded workers. Cabins in the slave quarters usually contained about 300 square feet with a dirt floor; they were furnished with straw bedding, barrels for seating, a few pots and pans for cooking, and a grindstone or millstone for converting corn to meal. Kulikoff argues that after midcentury, the more concentrated pattern of black settlement, in comparison with the dispersed nature of the white population, resulted in the more advanced development of kinship ties among blacks.

One question which has perennially emerged in discussions of colonial agriculture is why slave labor was confined almost exclusively to the production of southern crops, such as tobacco, rice, and indigo. No laws or customs discouraged the purchase and use of slaves in the northern colonies. Except for a very small number of Quakers in the middle colonies, few whites recognized slavery as a serious moral issue. For example, Puritan ministers in New England frequently owned one or two house slaves. Instead the adoption of a labor system was strictly a matter of economics: where slavery proved profitable, whites adopted it; and where it proved too costly, they relied instead on free labor. Slavery was not used extensively in northern agriculture because it was less profitable in regions relying exclusively on the production of wheat and other grain crops.

The northern Chesapeake, where wheat and tobacco were both grown, reveals sharp differences in labor requirements. Carville Earle and Ronald Hoffman found that although the two crops demanded about the same amount of aggregate labor to produce comparable output, the timing varied significantly. Tobacco required constant attention during the growing season, but often the time consumed was only a few hours per day. Free white laborers customarily expected wages for an entire day, not a fraction thereof. Consequently, the hiring of free labor to tend tobacco fields was prohibitively expensive. In a separate article, Earle estimated the cost of hiring free labor to bring in a tobacco crop at £11 ($1,000) per year versus only £5 ($450) for slave labor, based on £2 ($180) of depreciation and £3 ($270) for maintenance.

Wheat, in contrast, was labor intensive only during the planting and harvest seasons and needed little care during the interim. Workers hired at the beginning and end of the grain cycle were fully utilized from sunup to sundown. Earle and Hoffman noted that even wheat farmers who already owned slaves still found it profitable to hire supplementary labor during the harvest season. Thus, wheat farmers beyond the tobacco-growing regions of Virginia and Maryland generally found slave ownership less profitable than the reliance upon wage labor, which was provided in large part by local youths and single adult men. This factor explains why slavery, with the exception of house servants and dairy workers in some parts of Rhode Island, failed to expand to the northern colonies.

Leaving aside the morality of the slave system, from a strictly economic standpoint mainland blacks had an enviable standard of living compared to most agricultural workers in other parts of the world, including Africa and South America. Moreover, neither lengthy investigation nor complex quantification are necessary to support this sweeping generalization; the evidence is implicit in the demographic data. The rate of natural increase for the black population was high by any standard.

Slaves on the mainland rarely feared economic deprivation. Like their masters, they had access to sizable plots of productive land for the cultivation of food crops. Meat and fish, while not plentiful, were a regular feature of slave diets on at least a weekly basis—which could not be said of most of the planet's inhabitants at the time. Richard Steckel has conducted research on slave diets and reached some surprising and paradoxical conclusions. On the basis of infant mortality rates, he concluded that slave children consumed generally inadequate diets, but later, as they entered the workforce, their nutritional status underwent a dramatic and positive transformation. Teenage slaves normally experienced a rapid growth spurt in height. Upon reaching 20, they had usually recovered from previous deficiencies and were generally healthy as adults.

In a review of shipping manifests, Steckel found that adult slaves born in the new United States in the late eighteenth century were about two inches taller than slaves imported from Africa; Afro-Americans were also slightly taller than contemporary Europeans. The data indicate that as teenagers and adults, slaves consumed diets with relatively high amounts of protein, minerals, and vitamins. As a result, the overall health of adult blacks acclimated to North America was relatively good, and about the same as whites. True, slaves missed out on most of the luxuries available to other members of this relatively affluent preindustrial society, such as a varied wardrobe, improved housing and furnishings, a large quota of meat, and gallons of beer, cider, and rum; but the basic necessities of life in terms of diet, clothing, and shelter were not lacking and indeed were quite liberal by contemporary world standards.

Unlike whites, however, slaves had no opportunity to reap additional benefits from their own productivity. After 1670 they had no hope whatsoever of acquiring land and improving their economic or social status, irrespective of individual effort. Nonetheless, the greatest tragedy of slavery was not the everyday treatment of its immediate victims; rather it was the reality that all future generations could look forward to nothing other than dependency, humiliation, and subjugation. In sum, the second largest group of workers in North America contributed greatly to the exceptional prosperity of the colonies, yet they had permanent and perpetual limitations placed upon their participation in its material rewards.

BIBLIOGRAPHICAL ESSAY

AN excellent survey of the historical literature on bonded labor published through the early 1980s is Richard Dunn, "Servants and Slaves: The Recruitment and Employment of Labor," in Jack P. Greene and J. R. Pole, eds., *Colonial British America: Essays in the New History of the Early Modern Era* (Baltimore: Johns Hopkins University Press, 1984), pp. 157–94.

For information on indentured servants, the starting point is now the work of David Galenson and Farley Grubb. Galenson's contributions include *White Servitude in Colonial America: An Economic Analysis* (Cambridge: Cambridge University Press, 1981); "British Servants and the Colonial Indenture System in the Eighteenth Century," *Journal of Southern History* (1978), pp. 41–66; "Immigration and the Colonial Labor System: An Analysis of the Length of Indenture," *Explorations in Economic History* (1977), pp. 360–77; "White Servitude and the Growth of Black Slavery in Colonial America," *Journal of Economic History* (1981), pp. 39–47; and "The Rise and Fall of Indentured Servitude in the Americas: An Economic Analysis," *ibid.* (1984), pp. 1–26.

Grubb's contributions are "Immigration and Servitude in the Colony and Commonwealth of Pennsylvania: A Quantitative and Economic Analysis" (Ph.D. dissertation, University of Chicago, 1984); "Immigrant Servant Labor: Their Occupational and Geographic Distribution in the Late Eighteenth-Century Mid-Atlantic Economy," *Social Science History* (1985), pp. 249–75; "The Incidence of Servitude in Trans-Atlantic Migration, 1771–1804," *Explorations in Economic History* (1985), pp. 316–39; "Colonial Immigrant Literacy: An Economic Analysis of Pennsylvania-German Evidence, 1727–1775," *ibid.* (1987), pp. 63–76; "Colonial Labor Markets and the Length of Indenture: Further Evidence," *ibid.*, pp. 101–6; "The Market for Indentured Immigrants: Evidence on the Efficiency of Forward-Labor Contracting in Philadelphia, 1745–1773," *Journal of Economic History* (1985), pp. 855–68; "Redemptioner Immigration to Pennsylvania: Evidence on Contract Choice and Profitability in the Late Eighteenth Century," *ibid.* (1986), pp. 407–18; and "Morbidity and Mortality on the North Atlantic Passage: Evidence from

Eighteenth-Century Immigration to Pennsylvania," *Journal of Interdisciplinary History* (1987), pp. 565–86.

An older work, which was the standard for several decades, is Abbot E. Smith, *Colonists in Bondage: White Servitude and Convict Labor in America, 1607–1776* (Chapel Hill: University of North Carolina Press, 1947). More recent work on the tobacco region includes Russell Menard, "Immigration to the Chesapeake Colonies in the Seventeenth Century: A Review Essay," *Maryland Historical Magazine* (1973), pp. 323–29, and "From Servant to Freeholder: Status Mobility and Property Accumulation in Seventeenth-Century Maryland," *William and Mary Quarterly* (1973), pp. 37–64. For information on a significant aspect of the servant trade in the Chesapeake in the eighteenth century, see Kenneth Morgan, "The Organization of the Convict Trade to Maryland, 1718–1776," *ibid.* (forthcoming).

Robert Heavner covers one of the middle colonies in *Economic Aspects of Indentured Servitude in Colonial Pennsylvania, 1771–1773* (New York: Arno Press, 1977) and "Indentured Servitude: The Philadelphia Market, 1771–1773," *Journal of Economic History* (1978), pp. 701–13. Additional information on this market is found in Marianne Wokeck, "The Flow and Composition of German Immigration to Philadelphia, 1727–1775," *Pennsylvania Magazine of History and Biography* (1981), pp. 249–78. For data on the migration of servants in the late colonial period, see Bernard Bailyn, *The Peopling of British North America: An Introduction* (New York: Knopf, 1986).

On the social origins of indentures, see Mildred Campbell, "Social Origins of Some Early Americans," in James M. Smith, ed., *Seventeenth Century America: Essays in Colonial History* (Chapel Hill: University of North Carolina Press, 1959), pp. 63–89; James Horn, "Servant Emigration to the Chesapeake in the Seventeenth Century," in Thad Tate and David Ammerman, eds., *The Chesapeake in the Seventeenth Century: Essays on Anglo-American Society* (Chapel Hill: University of North Carolina Press, 1979), pp. 51–95; Galenson, "Middling People or 'Common Sort'?: The Social Origins of Some Early Americans Reexamined," with a rebuttal by Campbell, *William and Mary Quarterly* (1978), pp. 499–540; and Galenson,

"The Social Origins of Some Early Americans: Rejoinder," with a reply by Campbell, *ibid.* (1979), pp. 264–86. For information on migrants from the continent, see Grubb, "The Social Origins of Eighteenth-Century German Immigrants," unpublished paper delivered at annual meeting of Historians of Early Republic, Washington, D.C., 1985. For a review of the treatment and status of servants in England, see Ann Kussmaul, *Servants in Husbandry in Early Modern Europe* (Cambridge: Cambridge University Press, 1981).

Two books that discuss the transition from servants to slaves in the upper south are Edmund S. Morgan, *American Slavery—American Freedom: The Ordeal of Colonial Virginia* (New York: Norton, 1975), and John Rainbolt, *From Prescription to Persuasion: Manipulation of Seventeenth-Century Virginia* (Port Washington, N.Y.: Kennikat Press, 1974); see also Timothy Breen, "A Changing Labor Force and Race Relations in Virginia, 1660–1710," *Journal of Social History* (1973), pp. 3–25, and Russell Menard, "From Servants to Slaves: The Transformation of the Chesapeake Labor System," *Southern Studies* (1977), pp. 355–90.

Other important contributions on servants and slaves in the upper south are Allan Kulikoff, *Tobacco and Slaves: The Development of Southern Cultures in the Chesapeake, 1680–1800* (Chapel Hill: University of North Carolina Press, 1986); Gloria Main, *Tobacco Colony: Life in Early Maryland* (Princeton: Princeton University Press, 1982); Paul Clemens, *The Atlantic Economy and Colonial Maryland's Eastern Shore: From Tobacco to Grain* (Ithaca: Cornell University Press, 1980); and Timothy H. Breen and Stephen Innes, *Myne Owne Ground: Race and Freedom on Virginia's Eastern Shore, 1640–1678* (New York: Oxford University Press, 1980). Two articles surveying the Chesapeake region are Menard, "Maryland Slave Population 1658 to 1730: A Demographic Profile of Blacks in Four Counties," *William and Mary Quarterly* (1975), pp. 29–54, and Kulikoff, "The Origins of Afro-American Society in Tidewater Maryland and Virginia, 1700 to 1790," *ibid.* (1978), pp. 226–59.

For information on the lower south, the sources are Daniel Littlefield, *Rice and Slaves: Ethnicity and the Slave Trade in Colonial South Carolina* (Baton Rouge: Louisiana State University Press, 1981); John D. Duncan, "Servitude and Slavery in Colonial South Carolina,

1670–1770" (Ph.D. dissertation, Emory University, 1971); Philip D. Morgan, "Work and Culture: The Task System and the World of Lowcountry Blacks, 1700–1880," *William and Mary Quarterly* (1982), pp. 563–99; Morgan, "Black Life in Eighteenth-Century Charleston," *Perspectives in American History*, n.s. (1984), 1:187– 232; Peter Wood, *Black Majority: Negroes in Colonial South Carolina from 1670 through the Stono Rebellion* (New York: Knopf, 1974); and Julia Floyd Smith, *Slavery and Rice in Low Country Georgia, 1750– 1860* (Knoxville: University of Tennessee Press, 1985). For an account of the shift from servants to slaves in the lower south, see Ralph Gray and Betty Wood, "The Transition from Indentured to Involuntary Servitude in Colonial Georgia," *Explorations in Economic History* (1976), pp. 353–70.

Much of our knowledge of slave conditions still comes from studies focusing mainly on the first half of the nineteenth century: U. B. Phillips, *American Negro Slavery* (New York: Appleton, 1918); Kenneth Stampp, *The Peculiar Institution* (New York: Vintage, 1956); and Robert Fogel and Stanley Engerman, *Time on the Cross* (Boston: Little, Brown, 1974). Strong rebuttals to certain aspects of the last book are found in the Paul David et al., eds., *Reckoning with Slavery* (New York: Oxford University Press, 1976).

On the debate about mortality rates on slave ships, see Raymond Cohn and Richard Jensen, "The Determinants of Slave Mortality Rates on the Middle Passage," *Explorations in Economic History* (1982), pp. 269–82; Joseph Miller, "Mortality in the Atlantic Slave Trade: Statistical Evidence on Causality," *Journal of Interdisciplinary History* (1982), pp. 331–36; Charles Garland and Herbert Klein, "The Allotment of Space for Slaves Aboard Eighteenth-Century Ships," *William and Mary Quarterly* (1985), pp. 238–48; and Klein, *The Middle Passage: Comparative Studies in the Atlantic Slave Trade* (Princeton: Princeton University Press, 1978). On the health and diets of slaves, see Richard Steckel, "Slave Height Profiles from Coastwise Manifests," *Explorations in Economic History* (1979), pp. 363–80, and "A Peculiar Population: The Nutrition, Health, and Mortality of American Slaves from Childhood to Maturity," *Journal of Economic History* (1986), pp. 721–41. Two important studies by Robert Paul Thomas and Richard Bean are "The Fishers of Men:

The Profits of the Slave Trade," *Journal of Economic History* (1974), pp. 885–914, and "The Adoption of Slave Labor in British America," in Henry Gemery and Jan Hogendorn, eds., *The Uncommon Market: Essays in the Economic History of the Atlantic Slave Trade* (New York: Academic Press, 1978), pp. 377–98. Another important contribution is David Galenson, *Traders, Planters, and Slaves: Market Behavior in Early English America* (Cambridge: Cambridge University Press, 1986).

For a survey of scholarship on colonial slavery through the 1970s, see Peter Wood, " 'I Did the Best I Could for My Day': The Study of Early Black History During the Second Reconstruction, 1960 to 1976," *William and Mary Quarterly* (1979), pp. 185–226. Other valuable articles pertinent to this chapter are Ira Berlin, "Time, Space, and the Evolution of Afro-American Society on British Mainland North America," *American Historical Review* (1980), pp. 44–78; and Carville Earle, "A Staple Interpretation of Slavery and Free Labor," *Geographical Review* (1978), pp. 51–65.

CHAPTER V

ARTISANS AND MERCHANTS

ARTISANS and merchants constituted from 15 to 20 percent of the white occupational group. Although widely distributed throughout the economy, they tended to congregate in villages, towns, and port cities. Given the absence of factory work in the colonial era, urban areas were commercial and handicraft centers, populated by merchants, artisans, mariners, and common laborers. The term "merchant" was loosely applied to persons ranging from poor storekeepers on the frontier to wealthy shipowners in the major ports. Artisan was likewise a category that cut a broad swath. It encompassed low-paying trades requiring minimal skills and little capital investment such as tailors, cordwainers (shoemakers), and weavers; in the middle income ranks were carpenters and metal workers. An elite group of artisans with higher incomes included millers (grain and wood), tanners, silversmiths, and clockmakers.

Artisans comprised a crucial segment of the labor force in the colonies. Working largely with wood, leather, and metal materials, these skilled and semiskilled workers provided specialized services for the local community and sometimes engaged in small-scale production for regional markets. With the exception of hats and later shoes, few items were produced for the export market.

Estimating the number of persons performing artisan work is difficult, however, because many farmers and members of their families participated in this labor market on a part-time or seasonal basis. Women, for example, were frequently involved in textile production in the home. A few slaves on large plantations acquired artisan skills. Conversely, most artisans in villages and towns cultivated a few acres of farmland near their home or workplace and held livestock. In towns and cities, artisans often doubled as shopkeepers. In this book, artisans are defined as skilled workers, invariably males, who earned over 50 percent of their income from nonfarm pursuits.

They headed from 10 to 15 percent of colonial households, and their percentage of the workforce rose slightly over the course of the eighteenth century as the pace of economic activity quickened. In New York port, one-third of all taxpayers were artisans.

The wages of artisans in the colonies were generally quite good. The demand for skilled labor grew steadily and held up wage rates. In England and continental Europe, workers had banded together into associations called guilds that, by restricting entry into a craft and through various licensing agreements, acted to limit artificially the supply of skilled labor. (The American Medical Association has employed similar techniques successfully in the twentieth century.) In the colonies, no artificial market restraints were required to maintain wages, and the guild system was never permanently established. How much colonial artisan wages exceeded rates paid in England remains in doubt. Contemporaries cited figures 30 to 50 percent higher in the colonies. But Stephen Innes in his study of seventeenth-century Springfield, Massachusetts, found that artisans earned from 3 to 4.5 shillings ($13–$20) per day according to skill levels, or about the same as comparable workers in England. Colonial annual earnings were greater, nonetheless, because Springfield artisans worked more days and longer hours. In research on Philadelphia artisans in the 1770s, Billy Smith uncovered similar income levels—about £45 ($4,000) annually for a master shoemaker and £60 ($5,400) for a master tailor. In Maryland, Donald Adams found that unskilled field workers normally earned from 2 to 2.5 shillings ($9–$11) per day throughout the colonial era, which suggests that the premium for skilled work over unskilled labor was on the order of 20 to 100 percent depending on the requirements of a given trade.

The successful colonial artisan was an independent, self-employed worker who owned his own tools and furnished his own materials. Work was performed in the home or on the job. On occasion two craftsmen joined together to create a small shop. The artisan was also a small business entrepreneur, for he usually had a sizable investment in equipment and tools, managed his own work schedule, and kept his own account book. Most artisans owned sufficient property to qualify as voters in local and provincial elections.

Artisans often took on apprentices as helpers and trainees. In the European tradition, the apprentice's parents normally paid the artisan a fee for agreeing to assume responsibility for teaching their son a marketable skill. A contract, similar to an indenture, was negotiated between the parties; it required the artisan to feed and house the youth and to teach him a useful trade in return for labor services. Contracts often terminated when the apprentice reached the age of twenty-one. Benjamin Franklin was one famous colonist who began his career as an apprentice in a print shop.

The range of nonfarm occupations for men in the colonies was wide and varied. The largest number of skilled and semiskilled workers were found in the towns and cities, where in response to larger markets, the greatest degree of specialization also existed. In a study of Germantown, Pennsylvania, which lay five miles northwest of Philadelphia, Stephanie Wolf used tax records to compile a list of occupational categories in 1773, when the town's population was approximately 2,200. While not inclusive, the Germantown data provide a fairly representative sample of colonial craft and service occupations (table 5.1).

Some urban areas attracted a concentration of specialized workers. In Pennsylvania, the town of Lancaster attracted large numbers of weavers in the woolen and linen trades plus gunsmiths. Lynn, Massachusetts, became a center for shoe production, generally a cooperative family activity. Under the domestic or putting-out system, merchant-entrepreneurs organized production, financed the inventory of materials, and provided outside markets. The shoemaker and his family periodically received payment for finished shoes on a piecework basis. Blanche Hazard credited Lynn with the production of approximately 80,000 pairs of shoes for domestic and foreign markets in 1768.

Skilled workers who fabricated metal products earned among the highest wages. According to James Mulholland, the staple of blacksmiths was domestic hardware, including door hinges, latches, and kitchen utensils. They also produced horseshoes and small farm implements. Coppersmiths concentrated on tea kettles, warming pans, and equipment used in preparing alcoholic beverages and other liquids. Specialized metal workers produced locks and cutlery.

Silversmiths melted coins to create jewelry, luxury tableware, and other expensive items.

In port towns the shipping trade attracted a host of skilled workmen and mariners. In Philadelphia, where occupational data from the tax rolls of 1774 has survived, mariners constituted 9 percent of identifiable workmen; among them were 83 ship captains, 22 pilots, and 199 general seamen. Members of the shipbuilding and fitting-out crafts made up another 5 percent of the city's labor force. These artisans were ship carpenters, ropemakers, sailmakers, caulkers, joiners, and the like.

TABLE 5.1. Artisan Occupations Listed
by Germantown, Pennsylvania, Taxpayers in 1773

	NO. WORKERS		NO. WORKERS
Fabric crafts		*General crafts*	
Stocking weaver	20	*and industries*	
Weaver	11	Clockmaker	5
Tailor	12	Bookbinder	3
Hatter	6	Painter	3
Dyer	4	Printer	2
Leather crafts		*Woodworking*	
Cordwainer	17	*and building crafts*	
Tanner	10	Cooper	26
Saddlemaker	8	Mason	10
Skinner	7	Carpenter	9
Food production		Joiner	8
Butcher	10		
Miller	6	*Transportation*	
Baker	4	*and services*	
		Coachmaker	8
Metals crafts		Carter	8
Blacksmith	11	Wheelwright	6

SOURCE: Stephanie Grauman Wolfe, *Urban Village: Population, Community, and Family Structure in Germantown, Pennsylvania, 1693–1800* (Princeton, N.J.: Princeton University Press, 1976), pp. 106–7, table 10.

Shipbuilding in colonial America was in the hands of individual shipwrights, who operated small yards with few, if any, permanent employees. Working largely under contracts from merchants at home and abroad, a builder rarely produced more than two ships a year, although the pace of work in the colonies was considered faster than in England. Work was seasonal, with little activity during the winter months.

Because of labor efficiencies and lower material costs, especially timber, colonial ships were built at prices £2 to £4 ($180—$360) less per ton than in England. By the late colonial era, slightly over one-half of all ship sales were to buyers in Britain and other parts of the empire. By that date, perhaps one-third of all British-owned ships had been built in colonial shipyards.

In addition to drawing up the building plans, the shipwright organized and coordinated the work of other artisans. At different stages of construction, he hired skilled workers to perform specific tasks. No more than 10 to 15 workers were normally in the shipyard at any given time. The daily wages of these laborers were generally high, but irregular employment patterns and the seasonal nature of ship construction prevented them from earning yearly incomes much above those of other skilled artisans.

Although the largest concentrations of artisans lived in urban areas, others were scattered throughout the countryside. Millers who ground grain into flour were virtually everywhere, and they were normally prosperous citizens who also owned farmland in the area. Operators of sawmills were common as well. In both instances proprietors had an investment in dams, canals, waterwheels, and related equipment.

In districts remote from trading centers, a versatile artisan with skills in several crafts could earn a modest living. Some were itinerant workers. In Granville County, North Carolina, located 150 miles inland from the Atlantic coast, Carl Bridenbaugh counted at least 41 artisans between 1749 and 1776, including numerous carpenters, joiners, blacksmiths, wheelwrights, coopers, a haberdasher, a weaver, a tailor, a bricklayer, and a silversmith. Similarly, James Lemon found that about 20 percent of taxpayers in rural Lancaster County, Pennsylvania, listed artisan occupations in 1759. Yet, except for millers, artisans usually held a rank in society below independent farmers, primarily because most owned little land.

In a careful study of household labor patterns in Chester County in southeastern Pennsylvania, Paul Clemens and Lucy Simler identified one group of rural artisans who lived as tenants on small farms, units generally ranging in size from 2 to 20 acres. Landlords normally charged modest rents because the contractual arrangement required these artisan tenants to make themselves available as hired field workers to the owner during the critical planting and harvesting seasons. In one instance, a weaver was granted access to a garden plot, the fruit of six apple trees, and enough pasturage to keep one cow and one pig plus free firewood—and all for the yearly fee of only £4.75 ($425). As part of the rental agreement, the weaver was required to help the landlord with the hay and wheat harvest at a wage of 3 shillings ($13.50) per day, a rate which included meals but not liquor. These settled rural artisan households thus had three sources of steady income: the sums earned from practicing their regular craft; the monies earned from seasonal labor in the landlord's fields; and finally any income, whether received in kind or cash, generated from cultivating their own fields, maintaining a few livestock, or picking fruit.

One group of artisans did not conform to the picture we have painted thus far of the independent worker. Especially during the last quarter century of the colonial era, slaves on the larger plantations were increasingly trained to perform skilled work. Although they lacked independence, these black workers possessed artisan skills. Initially, they received training as carpenters and coopers, but later their expertise was extended to a full range of skills useful in plantation agriculture. On some units in the Chesapeake, up to one-third of the slave population was engaged primarily in artisan activities. In one exceptional case, Allan Kulikoff described how up to 75 slave artisans regularly worked at an ironworks in Snowden, Maryland, in the 1760s and 1770s. Women were likewise transferred out of the fields and into the full-time production of thread and cloth. As in free society, slave parents tended to select their own children as trainees and thus to transmit acquired skills into the next generation. In some urban areas, especially Charleston, the practice of permitting slave artisans to hire themselves out to third parties for wages shared with their masters was already common.

Paralleling the experience of other occupational groups in colonial North America, the artisan's lifestyle altered little over the decades. Technological change was slight. The pace of work was slow by modern standards. The products of farm and forest were fashioned by hand, using simple tools and traditional processes. Skilled workers were associated with every stage of creating a finished product from the simplest procedures to the application of more advanced techniques. Artisans, whether free or slave, enjoyed the pride of craftsmanship so lacking in modern factories dominated by machinery.

In the major port cities, white artisans held a middle rank in the community between the dominant merchant class and the "lower orders," composed of propertyless day laborers and seamen. Although merchants retained most of the important public offices, most free artisans qualified as voters and some were active in local political affairs. Few were seated, however, in the provincial legislatures. In the last two decades before the break with Britain, artisans increasingly participated in the independence movement. They served often on the extralegal citizens committees formed to implement and enforce the various nonimportation agreements aimed at British goods after 1765.

Artisans and merchants frequently split into opposing camps over the continuance of the trade boycotts periodically implemented to pressure Parliament to rescind legislation calling for increases in imperial taxes. After the first few months of the boycott, the merchants who had relied upon sales of British imports faced difficult times, since they were unable to replenish inventories. As time passed, these merchants normally pressed for modifications in the nonimportation agreements or their outright abandonment. Merchants who were associated primarily with the West Indies trade rather than with British imports were not greatly affected by boycotts, however, and they tended to maintain their support for nonimportation.

Meanwhile, American artisans prospered from the boycott of British finished goods. In the absence of foreign competition, they generally expanded the volume and range of their business activities and reaped the benefits of higher prices for their output. Given these circumstances, it is easy to understand why the artisan class participated so willingly and so enthusiastically in the various efforts to punish the British through the tactic of the trade boycott.

During the last quarter-century, scholarly research has focused much more extensively on the economic, political, and social role of artisans and common laborers in colonial urban society. Indeed, a number of historians have been actively examining the hypothesis that social and economic tensions within the major port cities contributed significantly to the revolutionary spirit and the independence movement. The list of scholars includes Gary B. Nash, Billy Smith, Charles Olton, Eric Foner, and Dirk Hoerder. Their focus is primarily on the allegedly mounting dissatisfaction of the middle and lower classes with the distribution of wealth and property, which was skewed heavily in favor of the merchant class, and such issues as the rising cost of living, increased incidences of poverty and unemployment, higher domestic taxes, and imprisonment for debts.

Hermann Wellenreuther has challenged this radical framework for interpreting the politics of independence. He argues that explanations based on domestic economic rivalries are unconvincing. Wellenreuther discounts historical interpretations focused on the alleged emergence of class consciousness within urban society. Convinced that artisans' protests were based on a broader perspective, he maintains that the most crucial factor was a "heightened awareness among individual crafts of their particular position within imperial as well as the colonial markets."

Although it remains difficult to assess the impact of this line of inquiry on historical interpretations of political events in the 1760s and 1770s, one fact remains indisputable: artisans played a much larger role in the public affairs of the thirteen colonies than their counterparts in any other society around the globe. From a comparative perspective, their economic, social, and political status was unrivaled anywhere. The same claim can be made—and even more emphatically—for the colonial merchant class.

The mercantile community was geographically dispersed throughout the thirteen colonies. The thousands of small firms involved in the commercial sector coordinated the flow of trade inside the domestic economy and with numerous overseas markets. The mercantile network reached from the major port cities through the towns and villages and out to the frontier. What linked together these disparate businesses was the extension of credit—money to finance inventories at the wholesale level and sales to consumers at the retail level. Credit was the glue that held together the mercantile community and prompted its participants to espouse similar views on the enforcement of contracts and the repayment of debts.

The various firms involved in the distribution of goods can be divided into two groups: traders and merchants. Traders sold strictly to final consumers, whereas merchants were simultaneously wholesalers and retailers. The frontier and other remote areas were the domain of traders. Country storekeepers were the main retail outlets. Typically, they transacted business with neighboring farmers within a radius of 10 or 20 miles, frequently extending credit in the process. Storekeepers maintained only a small inventory of goods, which fit into a corner of their crude dwellings. To feed their families and guarantee survival, they also cultivated a few acres of reliable food crops, such as corn or rye, and kept livestock. Despite their place on the lower rung of the mercantile ladder, country storekeepers provided critical services for the local economy. They were often the only convenient source of goods from the outside world, whether 50 or 3,000 miles away, and they provided a limited market for the farm surpluses of their neighbors. Another category of traders were roving peddlers, who wandered throughout the rural areas and sometimes ventured into the towns and cities.

In small towns, the volume of business was sufficient to attract genuine merchants. They were intermediaries in the mercantile chain. Small-town merchants bought in larger lots from their counterparts in more populous towns and cities and then sold on a wholesale basis to country storekeepers and on retail terms to residents in their own locality. Because of the seasonal pattern of harvests in this predominantly agricultural economy, small-town merchants usually needed to offer credit terms of three to nine months to buyers in order to sustain business throughout the year.

These merchants, in turn, required similarly liberal financing from distant suppliers in the port cities. Long chains of credit, which were offered to induce sales, were thus standard practice in the entire mercantile system, and the original source of much financing could be traced back through the commercial network to English merchants and manufacturers. In London and other English trade centers, the capital required to finance trade was more readily available, a condition reflected in the colonial marketplace through low interest rates and lenient repayment terms.

The distribution of goods and services was uniformly a small-scale and highly personal form of economic activity. Mercantile firms were organized as proprietorships or as partnerships, often with close relatives. Owners invariably managed the daily operations of their business enterprises; hired managers were rare, except in instances when a woman had inherited ownership of an ongoing firm. All business was conducted at one location, and the volume of transactions was low by modern standards, sometimes only two or three sales per day. The number of full-time employees in even the largest mercantile firms were few—besides the partners, perhaps one or two men acted as clerks and bookkeepers.

With the exception of some firms in the largest port cities, successful colonial merchants rarely specialized in any single line of goods. They handled instead a wide range of merchandise originating in diverse markets. These all-purpose merchants were routinely involved in a host of commercial activities, including occasionally the production of certain goods for distant markets. Since they often accepted payment in kind when customers were short of coin or currency, merchants frequently bartered items already in stock for new additions to existing inventories. Most items fell within the classifications of food, spices, alcohol, textiles, hardware, farm tools, and general household goods. In the major ports, the leading merchants were engaged extensively in foreign commerce, and most mercantile fortunes arose from profits earned in overseas ventures.

In a recent study of the merchant community in Philadelphia in the late colonial period, Thomas Doerflinger discovered that, whereas the wealthiest firms conformed to the all-purpose model, a substantial number of small to intermediate merchants did, in fact, specialize in certain geographical markets and specific types of goods. Much of Philadelphia's trade was divided into two distinct spheres:

one group of merchants concentrated on the importation of dry goods from England and a different group specialized on the export of provisions to the West Indies and southern Europe.

The degree of geographical specialization was pronounced, and Doerflinger attributed its persistence largely to financial constraints. Young merchants at the beginning of their careers had access to limited amounts of capital and credit and thus were forced to restrict the scope of operations. Other merchants forced to specialize in certain markets and lines of goods included older firms battered over the years by the vicissitudes of war, depression, or bad luck at sea. In addition, Doerflinger noted that specialization had emerged in one clearly identifiable trade sector where the volume of commerce was already extremely large and growing rapidly. The export of flour from Philadelphia rose to such proportions after 1750 that its sheer magnitude encouraged the emergence of a few highly specialized flour wholesalers who served as intermediaries between inland collection points and the city's exporters.

Determining the precise extent of mercantile specialization in other colonial port cities must await further study. In their study of merchant activity in Charleston, South Carolina, in the mid-eighteenth century, Stuart Stumpf and Jennings Marshall discovered a fair degree of concentration in the port's slave trade; eight firms handled 50 percent of the business, with two alone accounting for over 20 percent of all slave imports. Three other firms devoted their energies largely to the export of deerskins, a leather treasured for its softness and durability. Although the data remain incomplete, Bruce Wilkenfeld and Philip White, in separate research projects, have suggested that a greater degree of specialization was also present in the New York commerical community before independence than was previously supposed. Wilkenfield found that smaller firms were more likely to trade in furs, rum, and wine rather than dry goods and general mechandise.

Irrespective of the degree of diversity or specialization, the wealthiest merchants in the major port cities were extensively involved in shipments to distant ports, either overseas or along the Atlantic coastline. Merchants who regularly exported to the West Indies, southern Europe, and other mainland colonies usually owned a few ships outright, and they also took fractional interests—ranging from perhaps one-eighth to one-third—in other vessels and their cargoes. Often the value of an outbound cargo exceeded the construction cost of the ship. Spreading risks through the device of arranging fractional interests was an age-old procedure used around the globe to compensate for the absence of financial service firms offering marine insurance. With fractional shares held by several investors, if one ship and its cargo was lost at sea, the entire loss would not fall on the shoulders of a single merchant and threaten that firm with bankruptcy. In contrast, merchants involved heavily in the importation of dry goods from England normally had a much smaller investment in ships and cargoes. In separate studies of the ownership patterns of vessels serving the ports of Philadelphia and Charleston, Doerflinger and Jacob Price discovered that direct shipments between the colonies and the mother country tended to cross the Atlantic in transport facilities owned more often by British shippers than by colonial merchants.

Established merchants rarely traveled overseas with their cargo. Sometimes they made prior arrangements with other independent merchants in distant ports to act as agents on a commission basis. Under these arrangements, goods were consigned to foreign merchants who handled all transactions for a negotiated percentage of the sales price, somewhere from 3 to 10 percent. It was often difficult, however, to establish business contacts with foreign merchants who were reliable and trustworthy, which explains why much overseas commerce was conducted among relatives by blood or marriage. On other occasions, merchants designated the ship captain as the person to handle business affairs in the foreign port. If the captain was a poor businessman, merchants might send out an additional passenger called a supercargo, who was authorized to assume responsibility for all business matters.

Commerce across long distances was an inherently risky proposition. Because communications were slow, information about conditions in overseas markets was invariably weeks or months out of date. Meanwhile, interruptions in the regular flow of trade caused the prices of commodities to fluctuate sharply. Merchants sending out goods to a foreign market on the basis of a rumored shortage often learned later that others, either by luck or greater enterprise, had already satisfied the local demand. As a precautionary measure, merchants sometimes instructed ship captains and supercargoes to sail for other nearby ports, especially in the Caribbean, if prevailing prices for the outbound cargo were depressed in the first designated market. The most successful merchants gave their overseas representatives instructions that contained a reasonable degree of flexibility about prices and routes.

A fine example of the wide-ranging activities of one group of all-purpose merchants is provided by the Brown family of Providence, Rhode Island. James Hedges has written extensively about this prominent New England family, which later donated funds for the establishment of the venerable Brown University. Although the family had settled in Rhode Island in the 1640s, its fortunes improved dramatically in the 1720s after James Brown married the daughter of one of Providence's leading shipowners. James was appointed captain of one of his father-in-law's vessels, and he gained business experience on trips to the Caribbean where provisions such as grain, meat, live horses, dairy products, and lumber were exchanged for molasses and rum.

In 1728, James Brown settled down to become a resident merchant in his own right. The trade with the sugar islands continued, and his brother Obadiah, after serving as supercargo on several voyages, joined the firm. In later decades, the family partnership began the direct importation of hardware, textiles, and other finished goods from England. Much of this merchandise was resold to inland storekeepers at markups of 60 to 75 percent with 4 months credit at 6 percent interest.

For a short time, the Browns were involved in the slave trade. The partners financed three voyages to Africa in the 1760s—one ship was lost at sea, a second lost money after suffering many deaths in passage, and a third trip returned a small profit. After this third voyage, the family ceased its participation in the slave trade until one last voyage was undertaken late in the century. The absence of profits was one factor in their decision, but moral considerations may have played a role as well, for Moses Brown eventually became a leading abolitionist and a sponsor of legislation curbing the slave trade in Rhode Island.

Beyond their regular mercantile activities, the Browns also became investors in a series of manufacturing enterprises. These ancillary ventures were closely connected with their merchandising business. The main motive for building a small slaughterhouse was to provide a steady source of salted pork and beef for the outbound voyage to the sugar islands. Similarly, the family opened a rum distillery to process molasses and sugar imported from the Caribbean.

In the 1750s, the family built a small factory to produce high-quality candles from the head matter of sperm whales. The Browns' own vessels supplied some of the head matter for the spermaceti candles, but most of the pure white oil came from other whalers. The partners' candles quickly established a solid reputation in the New York and Philadelphia markets. To promote consumer identification with their product and increase sales, the Browns adopted the strategy of affixing the family's label to every box of candles shipped to out-of-town agents. This practice of putting a brand label on an item produced in bulk was uncommon, since most goods were sold strictly on the basis of their generic names.

The Browns extended their investments into iron production in the 1760s. In this venture, the family initially took a half-interest in a new partnership with four other Rhode Island businessmen. Three of them withdrew after two years, and the family assumed complete control. The Browns were optimistic about the profit potential in iron. Demand was strong both in England and at home. In the domestic market, they had already developed ties with commission merchants in New York and other cities who were eager to handle their output.

The furnace constructed near the village of Hope on the Pawtuxet River shared many characteristics with iron plantations in other colonies. The site was rural, since the ore, adequate supplies of wood for conversion into charcoal, limestone, and water power were all required at a common location. It was impractical to move either the ore or wood fuel any more than a few miles, because before the building of canals and railroads in the nineteenth century, overland transportation costs were prohibitive. Iron plantations in eastern Pennsylvania—the center of the colonial industry—were usually situated in remote, heavily wooded locations. The Hope site was, however, near Providence in an area long settled and partially cleared. Therefore, the partners negotiated contracts with local farmers to gain access to timber stands in the surrounding area.

In comparison with other colonial enterprises, iron production was a large-scale operation. The funds needed to develop a site were substantial, for capital went into acquiring mineral and timber rights, into the construction of a furnace and supplementary machinery, and often into housing for the workforce. The residents on these iron plantations were usually expected to grow at least a portion of the food required to sustain them throughout the year. The Hope furnace employed up to 75 men, with one-half of the workers normally engaged in gathering wood from nearby timber lands. Cordwood was converted into charcoal before entering the furnace in an extremely delicate and critical process. To serve as choppers, ore diggers, carters of wood and ore, molders, and firemen, the Browns had to recruit laborers with varying skills and to entice them with relatively high wages. Finding men who were competent and sober was invariably a difficult task.

In addition to a sizable workforce, the investors had to seek out capable supervisors to oversee day-to-day operations. The Hope partners hired one man, Rufus Hopkins, to serve in the capacity of general manager; his primary responsibilities were procuring timber, digging out ore, and handling the bookkeeping. The Browns discovered it was more difficult to locate an accomplished founder who could oversee the technical aspects of the refining process. Because of limited knowledge about metallurgy, iron refining was as much art as science in the colonial era. A successful founder was usually an experienced worker who had learned, largely through trial and error, how to combine charcoal and ore to produce iron with the anticipated characteristics. According to Paul Paskoff, the conversion of cordwood into charcoal was one of the most critical stages in the overall process because of the constant danger of fire and because bad charcoal produced poor-quality iron.

The Hope partners hired one founder who was unable to produce high-quality iron on a consistent basis, and he was replaced in 1768 by James Studefont, who had previously been employed at an iron plantation near Salisbury, Connecticut. From that date until independence, the Hope furnace was a steady producer of pig iron. One experiment to cast high-quality pots and kettles at the Hope site was judged a failure. On another occasion, the partners considered a plan to operate a forge to complement the iron furnace. Some colonial forges merely removed the impurities from pig iron and refined the metal into what was commonly called bar iron, while others went one step further and actually fabricated bar iron into finished goods. In the end, however, the Browns decided to restrict their operations largely to the production of basic pig iron.

The Browns marketed their iron through three distribution channels. Most pig iron was sent out on consignment to other mercantile firms in New York and England. A portion went to local merchants in Rhode Island, who were seeking a variety of salable commodities to include in cargoes destined for London and other foreign ports. Finally, the partners sold iron directly to the owners of independent forges in the New England area. In one complex business arrangement, the Browns sent pig iron to a forge in Massachusetts, received back refined bar iron in payment, and then hired several experienced workers to transform the bar iron into finished nails.

Since it required a substantial initial investment and employed a fairly large number of workers, the colonial iron plantation had certain characteristics which singled it out as atypical for the period and made it a legitimate precursor of the nineteenth-century industrial factory. Because iron production was a continuous-flow process, it demanded more labor discipline and regimentation than most colonial craftsmen were accustomed to. The ironworks had a small managerial class as well, for merchant investors usually hired a general superintendent and a founder to oversee daily operations. Yet because it was tied to a charcoal technology, relied almost exclusively on water power, and was situated in a rural environment, the colonial iron industry still retained a premodern character.

Although the Browns had a broader range of activities and greater involvement in manufacturing than other businessmen, the family's pattern of business behavior was duplicated on a smaller scale by hundreds of all-purpose merchants throughout the colonies. These merchants were often involved in a plethora of mercantile functions, ranging from importing to exporting and from retailing to wholesaling. They occasionally diverted funds into the production of intermediate and finished goods for local and distant markets.

No distinct manufacturing class existed. With few exceptions, there were only successful merchants who saw benefits in diversifying their business interests. For the most part, merchants personally managed their ancillary manufacturing enterprises. Iron production was, of course, an exception because of the large scale of operations and the technical knowledge required to oversee a successful furnace.

The volume of business activity and the accumulation of mercantile wealth was greatest in the major port cities. Until the 1740s, Boston was the leading commercial center in North America, and its merchant families were the most prosperous on the continent. But Boston's commercial and population growth stagnated in the mid-eighteenth century. The port lost much of its shipbuilding contracts and its export trade in fish to lesser rivals along the Massachusetts coast, such as Salem, Marblehead, and Gloucester. Meanwhile, Boston surrendered its dominance in the dry goods trade with England after increased European demand for American wheat from the middle colonies in the 1750s led to more direct trade between the mother country and New York and Philadephia. By the 1770s about one-half of the tonnage clearing the port of Boston was headed for other mainland locations.

By the late colonial period, Philadelphia had emerged as the most active port city. With over 30,000 residents, it was twice the size of Boston. On the basis of shipping tonnage cleared for overseas destinations, Philadelphia handled about 15 percent more foreign commerce than its older rival by 1770. The city had easy access to a heavily populated and highly productive agricultural hinterland in eastern Pennsylvania and western New Jersey. The mercantile community first developed an active grain trade with the Caribbean and southern Europe and then built up connections in England. Philadelphia became an entrepôt for finished goods, which the city's merchants sent out to storekeepers in nearby towns and villages. The city's merchants were among the wealthiest on the continent; in the period from 1746 to 1775, Gary Nash found only 3 Boston merchants who died leaving estates of more than £6,000 ($540,000), whereas Philadelphia had over 30 in that category.

In a recent book entitled *A Vigorous Spirit of Enterprise*, Thomas Doerflinger produced a richly detailed profile of the Philadelphia merchant community from 1750 until independence—and beyond. He argued that entry into the market was relatively open during this era, and many firms routinely entered and exited the wholesale sector of the economy. Entry was not difficult if a person had either capital, contacts overseas who could offer credit, or previous business experience; the minimum initial investment to enter the wholesale market was about £500 ($45,000). Although the risk of substantial losses was always present in this era of slow communication and transportation, so too were opportunities for enterprising men to earn substantial profits in just a few years. The social origins of budding merchants were diverse; among the new participants were former shopkeepers who had been strictly retailers, successful artisans expanding their horizons, and immigrants with overseas connections.

For every merchant who earned a great fortune, hundreds experienced more modest success. The typical Philadelphia merchant did not enjoy a standard of living significantly higher than skilled artisans. Many small merchants were not homeowners but rented dwelling space. Doerflinger estimates the median wealth of individuals involved in the wholesale sector in the 1770s at about £4,000 ($360,000). At the top of the scale, the city's most wealthy merchants possessed estates valued from £15,000 to £35,000 ($1.3 to $3.2 million). By comparison, wealthy Glasgow merchants had fortunes up to £150,000 ($13 million) and as high as £800,000 ($72 million) in London.

In the course of his analysis, Doerflinger challenged the conclusions of previous historians who had claimed that opportunities for employment and profit were declining for members of the lower and middling classes in Philadelphia in the 1760s and early 1770s. He believes that inferences about the degree of upward mobility based on trends in the concentration of wealth reflected in city tax rolls are misleading. Admittedly the ownership of land and housing fell increasingly into the hands of a few individuals, but extensive investments in real estate were not made by merchants still active in the business community. Investments in land and buildings were relatively safe and thus the favored earning assets of the city's idle rich; many were descendants of older mercantile families that had built past fortunes in trade, but had subsequently withdrawn from the risky and time-consuming world of international commerce.

Active merchants tended to keep their funds invested in merchandise, accounts receivable, ships, and cash—assets not listed on
the tax rolls and not subject to levies. For example, Robert Morris,
the very successful merchant who later served as the chief financier
for the Continental Congress in the early 1780s, owned real property
assessed for tax purposes at only £116 ($10,500) in 1774. While
conceding that some citizens did express increasing resentment
about the concentrated ownership of land and rental property, the
evidence also indicated that artisans and apprentices were prospering
along with enterprising merchants still involved in the commercial
life of the city. Generally speaking, Doerflinger concluded that
opportunities for entreprenuership and upward mobility were not
diminishing in Philadelphia in the last quarter-century of the colonial
era.

The third major port in the northern colonies was New York. Like
Boston, New York had been settled early in the seventeenth century,
although by the Dutch rather than the English. After the British
assumed control of the colony in 1664, the city's trade grew slowly
but steadily. Until the mid-eighteenth century, New York had been
a more active port than Philadelphia. Under the impetus of expanding grain exports, New York merchants developed an active commerce with outlying farmers and storekeepers along the Hudson
River and on Long Island. Wilkenfeld calculated that in 1764 the
tonnage departing from the port broke down geographically as follows: 48 percent to the West Indies; 27 percent to Great Britain; 11
percent to other countries in Europe; and 13 percent to other mainland ports along the Atlantic coast. Yet the pace of population growth
in the port's natural hinterland, while rapid in comparison with other
urban regions, nonetheless failed to match the spectacular rate of
increase in eastern Pennsylvania and western New Jersey after 1750.

The pattern of shipping in Rhode Island was much different than
elsewhere because there was so little direct trade with Great Britain.
Instead, English dry goods destined for the colony entered Boston
or New York and were transhipped to Rhode Island. On the eve of
independence, Newport had a population of just over 9,000, while
Providence boasted about 8,000 residents, which ranked them fourth
and fifth in relative size on the mainland. In the last few decades of
the colonial era, the coastal trade generated around 60 percent of

the commerce of these two ports. About 30 percent of their trade
was with the West Indies, while Africa accounted for the remainder.
Lynne Withey compiled a list of the ten most valuable exports and
their principal destinations between 1768 and 1772 (see table 5.2).

Rum was the colony's second most valuable export; Newport was
the only mainland port active in the exchange of alcohol, plus some
tobacco, for African slaves. In a careful examination of the port's
slave trade in the eighteenth century, Jay Coughtry pointed out that
Newport actually accounted for a very small percentage of the slaves
shipped in British ships—only 59,000 out of 2.5 million Africans, or
just over 2 percent of the total. This trading pattern was genuinely
triangular, involving Newport, Africa, and various southern ports in
the western hemisphere. Newport's slave traders sold 70 percent of
their human cargoes in the West Indies and South America. On the
mainland the largest markets were in Rhode Island itself, South
Carolina, Virginia, and Georgia. As late as 1775, slaves accounted
for nearly 15 percent of the population in Newport, the highest
percentage of black inhabitants in any northern city.

TABLE 5.2. Most Valuable Rhode Island Exports
and Their Principal Destinations, 1768–1772

	Total exported	Principal destination and its % of total	
Candles	£66,000	West Indies	95
Rum	55,000	Africa	98
Flour	48,000	West Indies	98
Fish	44,000	West Indies	98
Livestock	38,000	West Indies	100
Whale Oil	33,000	Britain	88
Lumber	28,000	West Indies	93
Beef/Pork	16,000	West Indies	94
Hoops	14,000	West Indies	100
Potash	12,000	Britain	100

SOURCE: Lynne Withey, *Urban Growth in Colonial Rhode Island: Newport and
Providence in the Eighteenth Century* (Albany: State University of New York Press,
1983).

The most important commercial center in the south was Charleston, South Carolina. Charleston's trading patterns and the organization of its mercantile community were distinctive. The strong European demand for rice and indigo led to an extensive bilateral trade with the mother country. As a result, much of the port's trade was handled not by Charleston merchants per se but rather by agents acting as representatives of mercantile firms based in London or Liverpool. The shipbuilding industry was also underdeveloped in comparison with northern ports, since much of Charleston's commerce was transported in English vessels. The city was therefore more of a "shipping point" than a genuine "commercial center," according to Jacob Price.

Nonetheless, Stuart Stumpf and Jennings Marshall identified over 500 separate mercantile firms in the period from 1735 to 1765 which were involved in trade distinct from the importation of British goods. In the last quarter-century before independence, from 80 to 120 merchants in any given year handled shipments to the West Indies, southern Europe, and other mainland ports. Gabriel Manigault was a wealthy Charleston merchant active in many markets before shifting his attention to his rice plantations in the 1750s. Manigault imported rum, sugar, wine, oil, textiles, and wheat flour; on outbound voyages he sent a long list of regional items, including rice, naval stores, lumber, shingles, leather, deerskins, corn, beef, peas, and pork.

Two southern cities with an expanding mercantile community in the late colonial period were Norfolk, Virginia, and Baltimore, Maryland. With a population of around 6,500, Norfolk was the mainland's sixth largest city in 1774, while Baltimore ranked seventh with just under 6,000 residents. Despite their location—the Chesapeake area—neither city was involved extensively in the tobacco trade. In a study of southern urbanization, Carville Earle and Ronald Hoffman argued that these port cities arose to serve primarily the grain trade to the West Indies and southern Europe. Grain was a bulky, heavy, and perishable product. For equivalent values of tobacco and grain, it took 10 times more shipping tonnage and 20 to 30 more ships to handle grain exports. Wheat generated more forward linkages in the marketing stage, and thus it supported a host of indigenous merchants. By the 1770s grain and other provisions accounted for about one-third of the value of Virginia's exports and a substantial share of Maryland's as well. Indeed, the rise of Norfolk and Baltimore and the growth of their mercantile communities reflected the surprising degree of agricultural diversification which had occurred in the Chesapeake region by the late colonial period.

In a continuation of his studies of the transatlantic commerce of the Chesapeake colonies, Jacob Price has focused recently on the "cargo" trade and the growing role of indigenous merchants in the local economy in the last fifteen years before independence. Three factors accounted for the increased entrepreneurship of native merchants. First, Price argues, the rising price of grain converted many previously small shippers of flour to the West Indies into much larger shippers of provisions to southern Europe, where they received payment through remittances, usually credits on London. Second, higher prices for tobacco gave planters more funds and encouraged them to branch out into mercantile ventures. The third factor was the easier and more generous credit terms offered by British merchants who decided to forego their previously passive stance for a more aggressive merchandising policy.

Under the cargo system, London merchants, upon the receipt of an order from a trusted Chesapeake trader, purchased goods valued as high as £5,000 ($450,000) and sent them out on the usual 12 months' credit. The London firms expected repayment either in tobacco or in good English funds, the latter normally being bills of exchange. Price asserted that the growth of independent indigenous merchants associated with the cargo system was among the most dynamic features of the Chesapeake economy between 1763 and 1774.

The influence of the shift toward grain production in the Chesapeake region is also revealed in the pattern of commerce in Alexandria, a small port in northern Virginia just across the Potomac River from the site that later became the new nation's permanent capital. Settled in the late 1740s, Alexandria had a mercantile community initially dominated by agents of British firms involved in the tobacco trade. In the early 1760s, however, the shipment of corn and wheat accelerated rapidly. By 1766 wheat had already superseded tobacco as the town's main export. According to Thomas Preisser, however, local merchants supplied little of the capital invested in outbound cargoes of provisions. Of the 25 traders operating in the port, only 3 were legitimate entrepreneurs willing to risk their own funds in overseas ventures. Preisser's analysis of conditions in this small but growing northern Virginia port seem incompatible with Price's evaluation of the increased role of native merchants in the region. Further investigation is therefore in order, and we must await the accumulation of more evidence before rendering any judgment.

Irrespective of location, individual merchants were often among the wealthiest men in colonial society and played an important role in the political affairs of the colonies, especially in the north. In Massachusetts, for example, the merchant class dominated the upper chamber of the legislature after the 1690s, and by the mid-eighteenth century, merchants provided half of the leadership in the lower assembly. Merchants were similarly involved in the political life of the other northern colonies, and they had a minor, yet increasing, role in southern governments. According to Peter Bergstrom, merchants constituted about 15 percent of the Virginia lower house in the 1770s.

This exercise of political power by the merchant class was another unique characteristic of the mainland colonies. Elsewhere around the world in the seventeenth and eighteenth centuries, large landowners were the social and economic elite, and they held a firm grasp on virtually all government offices. Even the accumulation of substantial wealth from mercantile activities would never buy respectability in most countries—not, for example, in France and Japan, two nations otherwise separated widely by geography, traditions, and culture. In England, merchants likewise ranked far below hereditary landowners, but upward social mobility was not completely restricted. With sufficient wealth, a British merchant could purchase a country estate and start down the path toward respectibility; he might later arrange to acquire a seat in the House of Commons, if not for himself, then perhaps eventually for one of his sons or grandsons.

In the mainland colonies, which had no domineering landholding class, merchants enjoyed high status from the outset. Moreover,

they were not required to become country gentlemen before exercising political power. Mobility was high too, for new mercantile
wealth frequently emerged and led to much turnover in leadership
positions. Merchants were normally esteemed members of the community, and the slow pace of business permitted them the leisure
time to pursue political careers vigorously. This factor explains, in
part, why outsiders have always perceived the United States as an
excessively business-oriented society, highly attuned to business
values; indeed, no other society possesses such a long tradition of
commercial leadership in its political system.

BIBLIOGRAPHICAL ESSAY

THE three sources which I relied on most heavily for merchants
were Stuart Bruchey, *The Colonial Merchant: Sources and Readings*
(New York: Harcourt, Brace & World, 1966); James Hedges, *The
Browns of Providence Plantation: The Colonial Years* (Cambridge,
Mass.: Harvard University Press, 1952); and Thomas Doerflinger,
*A Vigorous Spirit of Enterprise: Merchants and Economic Development
in Revolutionary Philadelphia* (Chapel Hill: University of North Carolina Press, 1986). Valuable information on frontier merchants is
found in Robert D. Mitchell, *Commercialism and Frontier: Perspectives on the Early Shenandoah Valley* (Charlottesville: University Press
of Virginia, 1977). On the rise of indigenous merchants in the Chesapeake, see Jacob Price, *Capital and Credit in British Overseas Trade:
The View from the Chesapeake, 1700–1776* (Cambridge, Mass.: Harvard University Press, 1980) and Peter Bergstrom, *Markets and Merchants: Economic Diversification in Colonial Virginia, 1700–1775*
(New York: Garland, 1985). Other valuable works on colonial merchants remain W. T. Baxter, *The House of Hancock: Business in
Boston, 1724–1775* (Cambridge, Mass.: Harvard University Press,
1945); Bernard Bailyn, *The New England Merchants in the Seventeenth
Century* (Cambridge, Mass.: Harvard University Press, 1955); and
Philip Hamer, George Rogers, et al., *The Papers of Henry Laurens*,
8 vols. (Columbia: University of South Carolina Press, 1968–).
    Three excellent articles on the port cities include Jacob Price,

"Economic Functions and Growth of American Port Towns in the Eighteenth Century," in Donald Fleming and Bernard Bailyn, eds., *Perspectives in American History*, (Cambridge, Mass.: Harvard University Press, 1974), 8:123–88; Carville Earle and Ronald Hoffman, "Staple Crops and Urban Development in the Eighteenth-Century South," *ibid.* (1976), 10:7–77; and G. B. Warden, "The Distribution of Property in Boston, 1692–1775," *ibid.*, 10:81–113.

Other important contributions include Thomas Doerflinger, "Commercial Specialization in Philadelphia's Merchant Community, 1750–1791," *Business History Review* (1983), 20–49; Stuart Stumpf and Jennings Marshall, "Leading Merchants in Charleston's First Golden Age," *Essays in Economic and Business History* (1986), 4:38–46; Maurice Crouse, "Gabriel Manigault, Charleston Merchant," *South Carolina Historical Magazine* (1967), pp. 220–31; and Thomas Preisser, "Alexandria and the Evolution of the Northern Virginia Economy, 1749–1776," *Virginia Magazine of History and Biography* (1981), pp. 282–93. The Rhode Island ports are covered in Lynne Withey, *Urban Growth in Colonial Rhode Island: Newport and Providence in the Eighteenth Century* (Albany: State University of New York Press, 1983), and Jay Coughtry, *The Notorious Triangle: Rhode Island and the Slave Trade* (Philadelphia: Temple University Press, 1981). For additional data on the slave trade, see Herbert Klein, *The Middle Passage: Comparative Studies in the Atlantic Slave Trade* (Princeton: Princeton University Press, 1978). For information on New York, see Philip White, *The Beekmans of New York in Politics and Commerce, 1647–1877* (New York: New York Historical Society, 1956) and Bruce Wilkenfeld, *The Social and Economic Structure of the City of New York, 1695–1796* (New York: Arno Press, 1978).

On the lives of workers and discussions of prevailing wages, see Stephen Innes, *Labor in a New Land: Economy and Society in Seventeenth-Century Springfield* (Princeton: Princeton University Press, 1983); Billy G. Smith, "The Material Lives of Laboring Philadelphians, 1750 to 1800," *William and Mary Quarterly* (1981), pp. 163–202; and Donald R. Adams, "Prices and Wages in Maryland, 1750–1850," *Journal of Economic History* (1986), pp. 625–45.

For information on artisans, a good starting point is Carl Bridenbaugh, *The Colonial Craftsman* (New York: New York University

Press, 1950). Also valuable are Richard Morris, *Government and Labor in Early America* (New York: Columbia University Press, 1946) and Blanche Hazard, *Organization of the Boot and Shoe Industry in Massachusetts Before 1875* (Cambridge, Mass.: Harvard University Press, 1921). More recent studies include Joseph A. Goldenberg, *Shipbuilding in Colonial America* (Charlottesville: University Press of Virginia, 1976) and Stephanie Wolf, *Urban Village: Population, Community, and Family Structure in Germantown, Pennsylvania, 1683–1800* (Princeton: Princeton University Press, 1976). Good data on rural artisans are found in James Lemon, *The Best Poor Man's Country* (Baltimore: Johns Hopkins University Press, 1972) and Paul Clemens and Lucy Simler, "Rural Labor and Farm Household in Chester County, Pennsylvania, 1750–1820," unpublished manuscript forthcoming in a collection of essays. The locations of iron furnaces and forges plus the geographic distribution of silversmiths are in Lester Cappon, ed., *Atlas of Early American History* (Princeton: Princeton University Press, 1976). For additional data on iron manufacture, see Paul Paskoff, *Industrial Evolution: Organization, Structure, and Growth in the Pennsylvania Iron Industry, 1750–1860* (Baltimore: Johns Hopkins University Press, 1983) and James Mulholland, *A History of Metals in Colonial America* (University: University of Alabama Press, 1981).

On the political activities of artisans in the 1760s and 1770s, see Charles Olton, *Artisans for Independence* (Syracuse, N.Y.: Syracuse University Press, 1975); Eric Foner, *Tom Paine and Revolutionary America* (New York: Oxford University Press, 1976); and the essays by Gary Nash, Eric Foner, and Dirk Hoerder in Alfred F. Young, ed., *The American Revolution: Explorations in the History of American Radicalism* (DeKalb: Northern Illinois University Press, 1976). Nash developed data on relative wealth in various ports in "Urban Wealth and Poverty in Pre-revolutionary America," *Journal of Interdisciplinary History* (1976), pp. 545–84. His book *The Urban Crucible: Social Change, Political Consciousness, and the Origins of the American Revolution* (Cambridge, Mass.: Harvard University Press, 1979), details further economic, social, and political issues in the major port cities. A rebuttal to the radical thesis is Hermann Wellenreuther, "Labor in the Era of the American Revolution: A Discussion of Recent Concepts and Theories," *Labor History* (1981), pp. 573–600.

CHAPTER VI

WOMEN IN THE
COLONIAL ECONOMY

T H E largest group of workers not fitting squarely into any of the broad occupational categories previously discussed were women—wives, daughters, and widows. With few exceptions, free women performed tasks planned to complement the activities of the male head-of-household, whether father or spouse. The work responsibilities of husband and wife were generally distinct and separate. Nonetheless, expectations about the proper work functions of the sexes periodically expanded. Gender roles on farms normally overlapped during certain critical periods in the growing cycle. In artisan families, a man's wife and children might assist him from time to time if his craft was normally practiced within the confines of the household—for example, shoemaking or weaving. Meanwhile, males occasionally participated in various types of domestic service such as child care, especially during the early years of marriage when incomes were still too low to afford hiring a young girl to help with routine household chores.

The main tasks of women everywhere were domestic service and the production of goods for household consumption or sale in the marketplace. Domestic service included cooking and serving family meals, creating the family's wardrobe from bolts of cloth, laundering, cleaning, and child care. Housewifery duties were more varied and included a host of possible activities; among them were milking cows, feeding swine, raising poultry, tending the vegetable garden, making butter and cheese, spinning woolen thread, knitting, and, in some areas, producing linen from flax. Over the course of the eighteenth century, housewifery production increased steadily as more families acquired the financial resources to make capital investments in the equipment required to facilitate production—especially butter churns and spinning wheels for flax and wool. Only wealthier households owned looms, however. Daughters assisted their mothers, or stepmothers, beginning around age 7; by age 12, they were full apprentices learning housewifery tasks. Most female work routines were performed on a daily or weekly schedule; they were less varied and more continuous throughout the year than typically male tasks, which were greatly affected by weather conditions and the seasonal demands of agriculture.

Colonial women were basically involved in household activities of one variety or another whether they performed unpaid work within their own family unit or received monetary compensation from others. Employment opportunities outside the home in both rural and more urban areas were overwhelmingly the performance of household and child care duties for neighboring families. Irrespective of class or status, a majority of girls earned modest wages from performing service work in another household before marriage. This stage of domestic service employment was normal in a female's life cycle; in this phase she became more acclimated to household work, earned extra income for the support of her parents and siblings, and saved a small dowry for her subsequent marriage. There was nothing demeaning or degrading about such employment since all considered it a strictly temporary arrangement ending by age 25 at the very latest. Most girls entered the domestic service workforce on at least a part-time basis soon after their fourteenth birthday. In most cases income earned by married women and by unmarried girls under 21 belonged legally to the male head of household.

Raising children was unquestionably a primary duty of colonial women, and it usually became a more burdensome task as the size of a family grew. About one-quarter of all children died before their fifth birthday, and only two-thirds survived to adulthood. Nonetheless, birthrates were so high that the typical women who married in her early twenties and survived multiple childbirth could anticipate managing a household of 6 to 8 persons by the time she had reached her early forties. Except in dire circumstances, such as desertion, a married woman with children did not have the option of seeking work beyond her own household on a permanent basis, with the exception of some married women in the largest port cities.

Colonial farm practices tended to follow patterns established in

England, where, unlike in many parts of Europe, women did not work regularly in the fields; most did, however, participate on a seasonal basis. According to Joan Jensen, women in the middle colonies usually helped with the easier tasks such as spreading hay cuttings to dry in the sun, gathering flax, digging potatoes and other root crops, and picking fruit. In wheat growing areas, women and children were expected to perform hard physical labor from sunrise to sunset along with males for several weeks during the harvest season. When wheat and other grain crops began to ripen, they had to be cut quickly or lost; thus every available hand was pressed into service.

In a study of women in seventeenth-century Maryland, Lois Green Carr and Lorena Walsh found the wives of some small to middling planters routinely spent part of the spring and summer months out in the tobacco fields. Tending tobacco plants was a task that required careful attention to detail but was not arduous work. Once a southern family could afford to acquire bonded workers, however, wives and daughters previously engaged in field work were usually transferred to strictly household tasks. In the slow winter months, males sometimes assisted women in household production designed to meet immediate family requirements or for sale in the marketplace.

Although women were not regularly engaged in field work, they were at least familiar with the skills necessary to operate a farm on a temporary basis. Home and workplace were not widely separated. When a husband became disabled or suddenly died, his wife was often called upon to manage the family farm. If the household had a number of teenage sons, a woman could make it on her own for several years; otherwise she sought out a new husband. As a rule, widows under 40 could usually count upon finding a recent widower seeking a new wife to assume management of his household and the duties of rearing his children. Our colonial ancestors were more practical about marital arrangements than their modern counterparts. Since few women could perform all the strenuous tasks associated with farming or had learned the skills required for artisanal work, and since few men had developed many household skills, the sexes were more dependent upon each other for mere survival than at present; marriage was not so much a matter of choice as a necessity.

At present we know less about the fate of older widows near the end of their childbearing years or beyond. Since women tended to marry older men more often than younger men, over half of the women married in their early twenties could anticipate becoming widowed. The possibility of remarriage for a woman over 40 was low, yet on average she could expect to live until about 70. Those women actually widowed in the forties usually faced nearly two decades without a husband. They looked to an inheritance and to their children for support. For many, widowhood brought poverty, however.

Irrespective of their feelings, few young women (or men) realistically aspired to remaining single. Unless a wealthy and generous parent left a young women property capable of generating an adequate yearly income, women did not have the option of complete independence. Even in those rare cases where financial resources were available, the social pressures on a woman in her twenties and thirties to marry and have children were enormous. The typical young woman reared in an average colonial household had no prospect of starting out on her own and having a successful career in any line of business or professional employment. Doctors, lawyers, government officials, and ministers (except Quakers in Pennsylvania) were never female.

In research on the domestic environment in England and the colonies, Carole Shammas argued that wives gained more authority over household activities over the course of the eighteenth century and that, as a result, more time and money was spent enhancing the quality of life in the home. In the seventeenth century one-pot meals were exceedingly common, and food was served and eaten with little ceremony. During the eighteenth century, however, mealtimes became more sociable occasions for family members. Knives and forks, table linen, glassware, and pottery appeared more often in estate inventories. Perhaps the most striking innovation was the spread of tea-drinking equipment—teapots, cups, kettles, and tea tables—through all strata of society. In probated estates in Virginia in the 1720s, only 3 percent contained evidence of tea drinking, yet by the 1770s nearly half of the estates in the Chesapeake had such equipment. Generally speaking, Shammas concluded that there was a greater emphasis on domestic work, and that this change probably improved the quality of life in colonial households.

In determining the shape of their lives, colonial women were never powerless, yet the range of choices were far, far less than today. Young women usually had some influence, if not final control, in the process of selecting a husband. This power was exercised most frequently in the southern colonies during the seventeenth and early eighteenth centuries, when females were proportionately less numerous than males and therefore in great demand as wives. At the same time, parental preferences always had to be considered, and especially in regard to assessing the income potential of any suitor, since parents looked to the households formed by their children as a prime source of financial support in old age. The younger daughter (or son) in a household sometimes had the option of delaying, or even foregoing marriage and caring for aging parents; in return, she received the promise of special consideration in the final settlement of the family estate. But her older sisters were expected to have made a match and formed their own households by the age of around 23 in the southern colonies and 25 in the north.

In a study of the courts in New York and Virginia, Joan Gunderson and Gwen Victor Gampel found that the legal rights of single women were, surprisingly, not substantially inferior to those enjoyed by males. Unmarried colonial women could hold property in their own name and manage it without male interference. Any income earned belonged exclusively to them. Although they were denied the privilege of serving on juries, they could bring suits and be sued in court. English law was much more liberal in this respect than in most other societies around the world. In most countries on the European continent, women were rarely allowed to hold property in their own name irrespective of marital status.

Once marriage occurred, however, the rights of colonial women under English common law were normally severely curtailed. Single women marrying for the first time generally lost complete control over all property brought to the marriage. Widows remarrying sometimes received more legal protection over the disposition of property brought to a new marriage, particularly when the children of a deceased husband (or husbands) still retained inheritance rights.

Still, there were exceptions to the normal rules. In a review of the colonial application of English equity law in South Carolina, which was administered by courts of chancery and functioned outside of the jurisdiction of common law, Marylynn Salmon discovered that married women were occasionally able to exercise a surprisingly high degree of control over their lives and property. These courts recognized and validated marriage settlements between prospective partners, or what today we call prenuptial agreements. Such settlements allowed married women full or partial managerial control over their property. Settlements could also be arranged after marriage if both parties consented. This system of law was used mainly by the wealthy; over 70 percent of 327 sample cases between 1730 and 1780 covered property valued at over £500 ($45,000). Yet smaller settlements were filed as well, with 10 percent for sums under £150 ($13,500).

In a survey of the legal status of women in New York under Dutch control in the seventeenth century, Linda Briggs Biemer discovered that single women also had the same legal rights regarding property as men. Moreover, in a system similar to the operation of English equity courts, a woman could wed under a Dutch-Roman version of "usus" law and thereby retain the power to control all her assets after marriage. She could retain her maiden surname, buy and sell both real and personal property, and operate a business without seeking the permission of her husband.

Margaret Hardenbroeck was one New Yorker cited by Biemer as an example of a Dutch woman who continued to acquire land and operate her own mercantile business following marriage in 1659. After the British assumed control of New York in 1664, the legal rights of Hardenbroeck and other married women were curtailed, however. She could no longer buy additional land in her own name, although she was permitted to retain and manage the enterprises and lands already in her possession. Twice widowed, Hardenbroeck remained a Dutch trader throughout her life; on her death in 1691, she left an estate that included 150,000 acres extending for over 20 miles along the east bank of the Hudson River.

In British America the women with substantial wealth in colonial society were invariably widows who failed to remarry. Various surveys of probated estates indicate that women possessed from 8 to 10 percent of total wealth; the figure is low mainly because women owned very little land. If we exclude land from the calculation and measure instead only holdings of livestock, slaves, inventories, financial assets, and household goods, women's share of the wealth on the eve of independence rises to 12 to 15 percent of all personal property.

Although poor women possessing only ambition and drive found the obstacles to self-fulfillment in the world of business or plantation agriculture virtually impossible to overcome, the same was not true of women who inherited or were given property originally accumulated by male relatives. In this instance, as Julie Matthaei points out in her overview of the economic status of women in American society over several centuries, colonial women faced a peculiar double standard. Women were given few, if any, opportunities to start from scratch and build formidable estates; but society recognized their efforts to preserve and expand a sizable estate once it came into their possession through male lineage, or if a husband or father was incapacitated or overburdened with responsibilities.

Or viewed another way, it was perfectly legitimate for a women with property to protect her family's assets and even to enhance them modestly, but her poorer counterparts could not aspire to acquire riches on their own initiative for their own self-advancement. Considered from still another angle, the preservation of inherited property was a respectable pursuit for both sexes, but acquisitiveness with the goal of financial independence was a behavior pattern reserved almost exclusively for males. In virtually every instance where a woman crossed over to exercise rights and powers within the male domain, society assumed she was merely acting as trustee, preserving the family's wealth for the ultimate benefit of male progeny.

The existence of these contradictory attitudes explains why historians can point to a few exceptional colonial women who experienced a considerable degree of success in the management of small artisan shops, mercantile firms, or large southern plantations. The

most notable woman in the last category remains Eliza Lucas, whose
achievement in adapting indigo plants to the South Carolina climate
was cited in an earlier chapter. Her father entrusted her with the
responsibility of managing three of his newly acquired plantations
at the age of 16, and she seized the opportunity and made the most
of it. Later, when husband Charles Pinckney widowed her in 1758,
she assumed managerial authority once again and exercised it for
three more decades. Similar instances of feminine business acumen
exhibited on a smaller scale were common throughout the colonies.
A review of advertisements in a prominent Boston newspaper in the
early 1770s indicates that about 10 percent of the port's mercantile
firms were headed by women. In most cases, the founder had been
a male relative.

Thus some women had an opportunity for limited participation
in the strata of society dominated by men. Through their control of
property, these women managed accumulated assets, hiring and
releasing their male employees (never other women). But business-
women rarely infringed on the everyday work territory of male
counterparts. Women who assumed control of artisan shops did not
practice the craft themselves; instead they hired male journeymen
to perform the work. Female store owners employed trusted clerks,
or used male relatives, to help in dealing with sexist customers and
the outside business world. Eliza Lucas did not manage workers in
the fields; instead she hired overseers who reported to her and who,
in turn, supervised the huge slave workforce. In sum, it was not
uncommon for women to manage the work of male employees but,
except for brief periods during the harvest season on family farms,
they rarely performed those work functions reserved, and preserved,
for males.

There were, however, exceptions to generalizations about the
absence of entrepreneurship among women. In some locations it
was possible for a married woman to start and operate a business
enterprise so long as her husband consented. In these instances a
married woman could conduct business as a "femme sole"; she
could enter into legal contracts, sue, and be sued. South Carolina
and Pennsylvania were the only colonies to enact legislation recog-
nizing the special status of married women operating business en-

terprises independent of their husbands, but the practice may have occurred elsewhere under the general guidelines in English common law. Married women whose husbands had deserted the family could also exercise more latitude in legal and business matters since they were functioning as "agents of necessity."

Colonial courts were protective of the rights of widows whatever the status of their husbands in society. The colonies had differing laws regarding inheritance, so it is impossible to make generalizations that will hold up in all cases. Irrespective of the instructions in a man's will, an angry or ungrateful husband could not prevent his widow from receiving a reasonable share of his remaining assets. The minimum inheritance was called a dower. Judges awarded, at a minimum, one-third of the husband's estate to the surviving spouse as her dower. When a man died intestate (without a will), probate courts followed the same rule, normally allotting at least one-third of the property to the widow—and one-half if there were no children. If the estate of an intestate man was small and the widow's limited share seemed inadequate for her immediate care, judges had the power to adjust temporarily the allocation of income generated by the deceased man's remaining assets. The aim was to provide a widow with sufficient financial resources for a minimal level of sustenance during the remainder of her lifetime or until she remarried. Property destined to be inherited by the deceased's surviving children could be tied up in a trust until they matured, with the income directed for the support of the widow. Variations of the trust device were used not only to provide support for surviving spouses but also to protect the inheritance rights of a man's minor children in the event his widow later remarried and his remaining assets came under the temporary control of stepfathers.

Fragmentary evidence indicates that living standards deemed sufficient for the support and comfort of widows rose over the colonial era. In New England, for example, Sarah McMahon found that the average annual meat allowance for widows, consisting of salted beef and pork, rose from 120 pounds at the beginning of the eighteenth century to 165 pounds by 1750, an increase of over one-third.

Divorces were extremely rare in an era when marriages were assumed to last until death, but they were occasionally granted to women married to abusive and dangerous men. In these cases the primacy of male responsibility for the financial needs of dependent women usually prevailed, and former husbands were required to pay continuing maintenance to support a separate residence for ex-spouses and children.

Employment opportunities for widows and deserted women were restricted, and the compensation was invariably low. Most of the work available to adult women seeking wages was in job areas traditionally segregated by sex. Domestic employment headed the list. In this market, older women competed directly with young girls employed temporarily before marriage. As Julie Matthaei explains: "A woman forced to supporting herself most commonly lived in another's home as a domestic, governess, seamstress, nurse (or new wife)." Few women were employed as teachers or tutors since, except for the daughters of the wealthy, their educations were normally rudimentary—like those of most men. In Philadelphia in the 1770s, women working in domestic service received about one-half the wages earned by unskilled males for day labor—or about £15 ($1,350) per year.

The second option for women seeking wages was piecework in the home. Under an arrangement called the "putting-out" system, male entrepreneurs with access to capital and credit supplied all the raw materials and sometimes the necessary tools. They recruited women to perform the labor required to produce intermediate and finished goods. All the work was done in the woman's household; if her children were old enough to contribute, they assisted. The types of activities included spinning woolen thread, knitting, sewing, button making, weaving, and leather work. The business organizers periodically visited the household and picked up the completed work. They paid a set rate for each finished item and left off more raw material for the next round of production.

The putting-out sytem had several advantages for workers and employers. Entrepreneurs were not required to maintain a place of employment, and labor costs were generally low. Why did organizers pay such low wages to workers? Was it simply because male businessmen discriminated against women and their children? Economists would argue no. The reason for low wage rates was that the number of women seeking employment in the home was large relative to the overall demand for their labor services. Or to put it another way: if organizers had had difficulty in recruiting workers, wages for home labor undoubtedly would have risen. Yet even under the best of circumstances, there was a distinct ceiling on how high wages could have climbed. At some marginally higher wage level, women workers would have priced themselves out of the labor market, and little production for outside markets would have occurred in colonial homes.

Meanwhile, the advantages of this type of employment for colonial women were twofold. First, their families had no financial investment in inventories and thus assumed little business risk. They supplied only the labor—nothing else. Second, women could combine piecework conducted at irregular times with the performance of household tasks and child rearing. Over the years, mothers could obtain an increasing amount of assistance from maturing children. Virtually no one, incidentally, advocated placing community restrictions on the conditions under which children worked in the home— no more than any group, except Quakers, believed servitude and slavery were immoral institutions and in need of reform.

The compatibility of child care with this form of economic activity was a consideration that made participation in the piecework market so attractive to some married women, especially in more commercial areas, as well as to the unattached. In a study of lower-class lives in Philadelphia in the third quarter of the eighteenth century, Billy Smith found that hundreds of married women in that urban environment augmented meager family incomes by performing piecework of all varieties in their homes.

Another group of women workers typically engaged in the performance of domestic duties were indentured servants arriving from Great Britain and later from Germany. Depending on dates and points of departure and disembarkation, females comprised from one-fifth to one-third of indentured migrants. Ambitious young women decided to emigrate because they hoped to serve out their terms, marry a local freedman, and eventually become a member of an independent household which owned the land it tilled. In short, their motives were roughly the same as the males who emigrated.

They were typically teenagers and women under the age of 25. Back in Europe, the vast majority of these young women could hope for little more than becoming the wife of a local tenant farmer, a man who had no real prospect of material and social advancement; or, alternatively, they might remain single and become stuck with the thankless task of caring for aging relatives. These adventuresome young women decided to take their chances in a new environment which possessed the opportunity for upward mobility in return for hard work and a bit of good luck.

Colonial buyers of the labor contracts of young, single immigrant women were mainly middling and upper-class families seeking to lighten the wife's burden in performing the tasks associated with maintaining a large household, which usually included several minor children and maybe an older relative or two. This type of domestic work provided a training ground and acclimation experience for immigrant women who, after 4 to 7 years of service, planned to marry a local resident and form their own households. The contracts of young women were typically shorter than for males throughout the colonial era because, on a comparative basis, the demand for household services performed by servants was greater relative to the supply of young women willing to travel across the ocean to an unknown future.

Youths subject to indenture were not merely immigrants, but some native-born children as well. Orphans and the offspring of the indigent and unfortunate were frequently placed in the families of nonrelatives by judges under various legal indenture contracts. A young girl who came under the authority of the courts might be bound out for terms typically running up to age 21.

This tradition of engaging the services of young women in colonial households was in conformity with practices in England and other parts of western Europe during the seventeenth and eighteenth centuries. English households were formed primarily on the basis of the nuclear family—just parents and their children—plus the periodic assistance of hired workers, male and female. These paid workers often lived on the premises and became members of the household, sharing bed and board. In eastern Europe, in contrast, the pattern of household formation was the extended family—parents, children, grandparents, cousins by blood or marriage, and other relatives. No hired workers were found in eastern European households except in those of the very wealthy. In western Europe the marriage age for women was typically delayed until the late twenties or early thirties, whereas in eastern areas marriage was arranged for youths in their late teens. The British colonies in North America adopted a mixture of western and eastern practices in terms of family formation and youth employment; they married early, in the eastern custom, but employed hired domestic workers within their households, in imitation of the norm in England.

A colonial widower left with minor children sometimes chose to acquire household services through the marketplace rather than risking a hasty marriage with whomever was available at the time. To tide the household over a family crisis, a man might acquire the contract of a female servant to perform household duties. If he later remarried and the servant's services were no longer required, he could sell the unexpired term of her contract to a third party. On the other hand, if he got along well with the servant, he might propose marriage, since there was no stigma associated with the status of temporary servitude. In other cases widowers went out and, for all practical purposes, bought a new wife; with the consent of a female servant in a neighboring household, he could purchase the remaining portion of her labor contract from the current owner and marry her. For some young women, this arrangement became the shortest and most advantageous route from servitude to freedom. Others, however, chose to serve out their terms and to exercise greater latitude in selecting a suitable mate. With freedom dues in hand, they usually had a small dowry and were thus good marriage prospects.

A fair number of female servants became pregnant during the term of their indenture. The vast majority of these women were in their very late teens and twenties, an age when sexual contact readily leads to conception in any society where contraception was rarely practiced. Approximately 20 percent of female servants gave birth to a child before the expiration of their contracts. What happened to a servant and her illegitimate child depended in large part upon who had impregnated her and whether he was willing and/or able to assume the duties of husband and father. If the man was another servant still obligated to future service, someone who had absconded, or a person unknown or unnamed, the errant woman normally had one or two years of service added to her existing indenture term. Judges imposed penalties partly to compensate the owner for time lost due to pregnancy and subsequent child care, partly to admonish the servant for her participation in the sin of fornication, and partly to impose sanctions on the servant for breaking the indenture contract, which typically specified chaste behavior for females. Except perhaps in some areas of Puritan New England, the economic and legal rationale took clear precedence over moral considerations in the assessment of penalties, however. If the father was acknowledged as a local man already married, judges might prescribe financial support for his illegitimate child plus payment to the servant's owner for the inconvenience of her pregnancy.

In other situations the impregnated servant experienced a different fate. If the father was an unmarried man with access to financial resources and was willing to face up to his responsibilities, he could buy out the unexpired time remaining on her contract and marry her. If the father was the servant's married owner, the outcome varied. The situation depended in part upon whether the servant was a willing participant, reluctantly cooperated under severe duress, or was the victim of outright rape. Some lustful owners unilaterally decided that the indenture contract implied the granting of sexual services in addition to the normal household duties. All servants had their economic freedom severely restricted, but they still retained their civil rights under English common law, including protection from rapists irrespective of their status in society.

When the courts determined that owner and servant had acted mutually and voluntarily, there was a tendency to mete out equal justice to both sinners. In Middlesex County, Virginia, according to Darrett and Anita Rutman, the expiration date of a servant's contract was usually lengthened one or two years and then sold to a third party. The sales proceeds went not to her sinful owner but instead benefited the local church. The servant was forced to work longer for her freedom and her master lost a valuable piece of human capital. When her indenture contract finally expired, the woman was on her own to eke out a living for herself and child; she hoped eventually to find a husband.

If the courts decided that an owner had forced himself upon an unwilling servant, judges were apt to shorten, or even void, her existing indenture and to stipulate continuing financial support for the illegitimate child. In most cases, the court's rulings were an effort to impose penalties reflecting the extent and degree of sexual abuse. Unlike today, individuals were not sentenced to long jail terms for crimes irrespective of their severity, because the public refused to bear the expense of maintaining prisoners. The death penalty was sometimes imposed for murder or for repeated offenses of a less serious nature. Criminals were sometimes branded on the face with a hot iron, or they suffered minor, but humiliating, mutilations such as clipped ears. In judicial cases involving the sexual misconduct of males, however, the main system of justice was financial compensation to the victim from the assets and future income of the transgressor.

In a study of adult females in two wards in the wealthier and poorer sections of Philadelphia in 1775, Carole Shammas discovered that the majority were not, as might have been supposed, married women sharing a household with their spouses. An even greater number of the 800 or so women covered in this study could be placed in one of six categories: female head-of-household, hired maid, indentured servant, slave, boarder, or an older child (over age 15) still living at home. One out of every five women who managed a household did so without the assistance of a spouse. The single-parent home was thus not uncommon in the colonial era.

Comparing her data with parallel evidence on adult males in these wards, Shammas was struck by the sharp difference in the instances of single persons listed as boarders. From 15 to 20 percent of all males were recorded as boarders whereas the number of women in that status was under 4 percent. In assessing the social and employment opportunities available to youths, Shammas concluded: "A young woman could not live on her own or even as a boarder, her options came down to domestic service as a daughter, maid, or wife."

A review of the occupational status of the 87 women in the two Philadelphia wards who qualified as head-of-household was likewise revealing. Most were widows. Nearly two-thirds had no occupational designation, and one-third had no visible means of support. The most frequently listed type of employment was as some form of retailer—a category which included shopkeepers, tavernkeepers, innkeepers, and street hucksters. About 20 percent of the pub and tavern licenses in Philadelphia in the 1770s went to women. Up to one-quarter of female heads-of-household received rental income either from boarders or from tenants in nearby properties. School-mistresses, washerwomen, and seamstresses headed about 10 percent of female households.

Although the amount of research on the lives of white women has increased steadily over the last decade, we still have less direct evidence about the economic lives of slave women, who comprised one-fifth of the total female population. Much of what we believe about this era is based on the assumption that colonial slavery resembled closely the system existing in the southern states during the first half of the nineteenth century. Most black women lived in nuclear families similar to the structures and patterns established by, and condoned by, their owners. Slave marriages were not recognized as legal contracts by government, but the informal unions sanctified by masters were generally enduring unless broken by death or the sale of a spouse to a distant owner.

Black women performed most of the same domestic and house-wifery tasks as their white counterparts. In northern homes, where they normally were house servants, black women cooked, washed and sewed clothing, fed the livestock, and assisted in child rearing as part of their routine duties. They periodically returned to slave quarters and performed similar tasks for their own families.

The vast majority of slave women lived on farms and plantations in the southern colonies. In the southern environment, their duties were broader and tended to vary over their life cycle. In their youth slaves were typically assigned to domestic service—laundry, kitchen work, and infant care. Later, however, they were expected to perform more arduous field work for most of their adult years. Most began walking to the fields in their teens and continued agricultural labor until aging or increased household responsibilities (their own or their owner's) altered their assignment. Older slave women were sometimes shifted back into the performance of domestic chores. The only workers who might conceivably avoid agricultural labor and remain in the same occupational category throughout their lives were cooks and washerwomen engaged in domestic service, plus thread spinners in the housewifery sector. Meanwhile, raising their own young children to maturity, and thereby permitting the perpetuation of the slave system without the necessity of constant forced immigration from Africa, was considered by their profit-oriented owners as one of the prime duties of all black women in the mainland colonies.

In recent research on the work of black women in Virginia in the eighteenth century, Carole Shammas discovered that the likelihood of finding females within the slave workforce rose as the size of plantation units increased. For example, most estates in the colony which included personal items worth under £200 ($18,000) reported two female slaves or less, whereas the larger personal estates typically listed more than five females. Shammas detected a clear shift in employment patterns after 1760; prior to that date only 15 percent of the female workforce was allocated to housewifery tasks, primarily spinning, but by the 1770s the nonagricultural sector contained up to one-quarter of all adult women. Robert Carter's plantation at Nomini Hall had 117 women workers divided as follows: 97 field hands; 6 domestics; 12 spinners, weavers, and seamstresses; one nurse; and one midwife. In fact, young girls trained to spin thread were rarely shifted into the tobacco fields during their adult years. By the last quarter of the century, slave artisans were teaching their children the skills of the family craft in a manner similar to patterns in free society.

When owners impregnated their female slaves, whether married or single, and irrespective of the circumstances under which sexual activity had occurred, the victims had no recourse whatsoever under the law. Any child born to a slave women was automatically considered legally black and became the absolute property of her owner. Unlike the case with indentured servants, owners assumed the right to sexual license with slaves, although instances of the abuse of that awesome power were probably less common than historians believed a generation ago. Maintaining the stability of slave family life was in the economic interest of owners, and most realized that incidents of sexual abuse were disruptive and counterproductive. Moreover, according to Allan Kulikoff, a white man's reputation among his peers could be ruined by fathering a mulatto child. The continued presence of obviously mulatto children on the farm or plantation was likewise a potential embarrassment for an owner's wife, his legal children, his extended family, and local residents in this race-conscious society. Regulating the actions of white overseers, usually single men in their twenties, on large plantations was probably a vastly greater problem for slaveholders than exercising self-control.

Frequently, the best solution to the presence of a visible mulatto youngster was to sell the woman and her offspring, and perhaps other members of her immediate family, to another owner in a distant county. Occasionally, a repentant owner left instructions in his last will and testament to grant freedom to illegitimate children born from his union with a slave women. Most did not, however, since they would have thereby deprived heirs of a valuable part of their expected inheritance.

When white women were discovered to have become sexually involved with male slaves, they faced serious consequences. In Virginia the woman was assessed a large fine, and if she could not raise the money, the court was authorized to place her into servitude for a term of up to five years. Mulatto children were likewise sold and remained slaves until age 31. Kulikoff found that, despite these penalties and the social stigma of miscegenation, in Prince George's county alone 16 white women gave birth to 25 mulatto children in the 1720s and 1730s. Twelve of these women were indentured servants newly arrived, who probably got their terms of service extended, and four were daughters of poor planters.

Sexism and racism were linked, and both were deeply ingrained in the attitudes and outlooks of colonial Americans.

BIBLIOGRAPHICAL ESSAY

SEVERAL articles focusing wholly or in part on the economic status of women have appeared within the last decade in *William and Mary Quarterly:* Lois Green Carr and Lorena Walsh, "The Planter's Wife: The Experience of White Women in Seventeenth-Century Maryland," (1977), pp. 542–71; Billy G. Smith, "The Material Lives of Laboring Philadelphians, 1750 to 1800," (1981), pp. 163–202; Joan R. Gunderson and Gwen Victor Gampel, "Married Women's Legal Status in Eighteenth-Century New York and Virginia," (1982), pp. 114–34; Marylynn Salmon, "Women and Property in South Carolina: The Evidence from Marriage Settlements, 1730 to 1830," (1982), pp. 655–85; and Sarah F. McMahon, "A Comfortable Subsistence: The Changing Composition of Diet in Rural New England," (1985), pp. 26–65. An important book recently published is Marylynn Salmon, *Women and the Law of Property in Early America* (Chapel Hill: University of North Carolina Press, 1986).

Other references on women include David Coon, "Eliza Lucas Pinckney and the Reintroduction of Indigo Culture in South Carolina," *Journal of Southern History* (1976), pp. 61–76; Carole Shammas, "The Domestic Environment in Early Modern England and America," *Journal of Social History* (1980), pp. 3–24; Shammas, "The Female Social Structure of Philadelphia in 1775," *Pennsylvania Magazine of History and Biography* (1983), pp. 69–83; Laurel Thatcher Ulrich, " 'A Friendly Neighbor': Social Dimensions of Daily Work in Northern Colonial New England," *Feminist Studies* (1980), pp. 392–405; Julie A. Matthaei, *An Economic History of Women in America: Women's Work, the Sexual Division of Labor, and the Development of Capitalism* (New York: Schocken Books, 1982), especially chapter 3, "Husbandless Women in the Colonial Economy: Women Working for Income"; Linda Briggs Biemer, *Women and Property in Colonial New York* (Ann Arbor: UMI Research Press, 1983); Darrett B. and Anita H. Rutman, *A Place in Time: Middlesex County, Virginia, 1650–1750* (New York: Norton, 1984); Mary M. Schweitzer, *Custom and Contract: Household, Government, and the Economy in Colonial Pennsylvania* (New York: Columbia University Press, 1987), chapter 2; and Joan Jensen, *Loosening the Bonds: Mid-Atlantic Farm Women, 1750–1850* (New Haven: Yale University Press, 1986). I also drew on William Sundstrom and Paul David, "Old-Age Security Motives, Labor Markets, and Farm Family Fertility in Antebellum America," Stanford University working paper, February 1986; and for comparative information on Europe, Robert Fogel and G. R. Elton, *Which Road to the Past? Two Views of the Past* (New Haven: Yale University Press, 1983).

For information on black women, see Carole Shammas, "Black Women's Work and the Evolution of Plantation Society," *Labor History* (1985), pp. 5–28, and Allan Kulikoff, *Tobacco and Slaves: The Development of Southern Cultures in the Chesapeake, 1680–1800* (Chapel Hill: University of North Carolina Press, 1986).

SECTION TWO

MONEY AND TAXES

 ROM the vantage point of the twentieth century, the colonial financial system was institutionally undeveloped. Absent entirely were specialized financial firms such as commercial banks, savings and loan associations, and dealers in stocks and bonds. Capital markets were thin, localized, and poorly organized. Demand deposits, savings accounts, bank loans, and stock certificates were unknown in the colonies. The money supply was composed of gold and silver coins, mostly of Spanish origin, plus paper currency issued by the various colonial legislatures.

Financial services were provided, however, by merchants and other traders who granted book credit to selected buyers in connection with the sale of merchandise. In addition, most colonial legislatures periodically loaned moderate sums to a broad spectrum of borrowers who could offer land or residences as collateral. Yet despite its institutional shortcomings by modern standards, the financial system functioned sufficiently well to support a rapidly expanding agricultural-commercial economy with high income levels. This performance was possible, in part, because the colonies were able to make indirect use, as Jacob Price has documented in a series of studies, of the financial services available in London, where money and capital markets were more fully developed.

The mainland colonies were unique by contemporary standards because they maintained an extremely low tax burden and because they were innovators in the sustained use of government-issue paper money. Moreover, these two unusual characteristics were linked. The lack of adequate tax revenues to finance a series of military campaigns against the French, Spanish, and Native American tribes on the frontier had been the prime stimulus leading colonial legislatures to experiment with the creation of paper currency to meet wartime expenses. Although the colonists often provided the initial funds for military campaigns aimed at expanding the British Empire, they expected Parliament to reimburse them at a later date for a large share of the associated costs. For decades, Parliament, and British taxpayers, had accepted willingly that financial burden plus the continuing costs of defending all the territories already acquired from any foreign attack.

Over the last two decades of the colonial era, however, the king's ministers adopted new policies designed to shift more of the tax burden for defending North America and the Atlantic shipping lanes to the colonies themselves and to restrict, and perhaps even outlaw, the use of paper money. These two issues of contention—paper money and especially new taxes—were in the forefront of the economic and political dispute between Britain and the colonies in the decade and one-half before the final decision for independence.

CHAPTER VII

MONEY AND POLITICS

IRRESPECTIVE of the controversy over paper currency, coins were a major component of the colonial money stock. In part because Parliament did not allow the export of English coin from the British Isles, and because it refused to grant permission for the establishment of a separate mint overseas (except for a brief experiment in Massachusetts in the 1650s), the colonies relied primarily on silver coins from Spain's New World mines for everyday monetary transactions and a store of value. To assist her colonies in attracting and retaining foreign monies, the mother country, in 1705, permitted them to overvalue by one-third foreign coins relative to English money in domestic transactions. The official rate for "lawful money," or proclamation money, on the mainland thus became 133 colonial "pounds" for every foreign coin valued at 100 pounds in England. The thirteen colonies eventually adopted their own individual proclamation values, which ranged from 125 to 180 percent of monetary values in England.

Even with the overvaluation of foreign coins, the colonists complained almost constantly about a dearth of specie. Although sales of foodstuffs to the West Indies and southern Europe produced a steady inflow of silver coins, contemporaries cited the persistent trade deficits with England and claimed that purchases of British imports caused an excessive drain of specie to the mother country. Commonplace in the seventeenth and eighteenth centuries were merchants' grumblings about the stagnation of colonial commerce, coupled with predictions of continued hard times, all because of allegedly insufficient quantities of hard money in circulation.

It is difficult to accept the colonists' complaints at face value, however. There is no firm evidence suggesting that the colonies were plagued by a severe and persistent shortage of specie. Merchants and farmers in England were voicing similar complaints about the monetary stock. Yet according to colonial rhetoric, it was to England that specie was constantly being "drained."

Aggregate data on price levels point toward another conclusion. In the eighteenth century, sterling prices in the colonies rose slowly but steadily. Since we have no evidence of a change in the velocity of money, the price data suggest that the world money stock was growing at a slightly faster pace than the production of goods and services. Had world specie supplies been genuinely short, then prices over this era would undoubtedly have fallen—a phenomenon which the U.S. economy actually experienced during the deflationary years from 1866 to 1896, when the stock of money expanded at a slower pace than the growth of goods and services. During the colonial period, the outpouring of specie from Latin American mines was rapidly distributed throughout the Atlantic economies, including the mainland English colonies. The supply of specie was not deficient in the North Atlantic economies.

Another factor often overlooked in discussions of the size of specie stocks in a given economy is the domestic demand for money. As Dennis Flynn has recently argued in an analysis of sixteenth-century Spain, the composition of that nation's monetary stock was a reflection not only of the supply of specie available but also the aggregate demand for it. Despite a century-long influx of specie from Latin America, Spain contained virtually no gold or silver coins at the end of the sixteenth century. To serve as a medium of domestic exchange, the Spanish government introduced copper coins into the monetary system, and the volume was large enough to accommodate the domestic demand for money. Specie went abroad to acquire foreign goods and services. The Spanish population required just so much money to accommodate the level of domestic economic activity, and this aggregate demand was met mostly by copper coins. The excess money in the financial system, namely specie, was spent in the international market.

In the thirteen English colonies, the size of the specie stock was likewise influenced by local demand. If the colonists had genuinely wished to increase the availability of gold and silver coins over the long run, they had the option of reducing the volume of imports and of foregoing entirely the use of domestic money substitutes such as paper currency and commodity money. Overall, the colonists held about as much gold and silver coins and other forms of money as they demanded.

To be sure, specie shortages of sufficient magnitude to dampen trade were periodically experienced in the colonies, but it was not a chronic condition. Ron Michener argues that contemporaries were generally unable to distinguish between "causes" and "effects" in assessing economic and monetary disturbances. An economic contraction was usually triggered by some other independent event, often of foreign origin, and completely unrelated to domestic monetary conditions. For example, the contraction of credit by foreign merchants and curtailed colonial exports might, in combination, lead to reduced inflows of specie and sterling bills of exchange and eventually result in transitory shortages of money. Since disruptions in normal patterns of overseas trade and shortages of specie were usually simultaneous occurrences, contemporaries frequently assumed that the former—the recession, or a prolonged period of weak demand—had been caused by the latter—a shortage of money. But in actuality, the reverse was equally plausible, namely that the lack of specie was merely a side effect of the slowdown in trading activity.

Meanwhile, in less volatile periods, shifting prices for sterling bills of exchange (claims on British monies) were the main factor keeping the monetary system in equilibrium over the long run. The mechanism functioned briefly as follows: from the sales of goods in overseas markets and the provision of shipping services, the colonists generated inflows of sterling bills of exchange; these bills, in turn, were sold to local importers who had debts payable in London. Although foreign exchange markets were strictly local in scope and institutionally immature, this system operated smoothly so long as overseas earnings and the expenditures on imports were roughly equal. During certain years, however, and especially late in the era, imports ran consistently ahead of earnings from exports and shipping services. When the imbalance persisted, the colonies were faced with an accumulation of debts and a growing balance-of-payments deficit vis-à-vis the mother country.

Normally, these payments deficits were financed through the

voluntary extension of credit to colonial buyers by English merchants. In London, unlike the colonies, large amounts of capital were readily available at modest interest rates, and merchants and manufacturers drew upon those funds to finance their overseas sales. At times, however, colonial debts temporarily exceeded the ability or the willingness of English merchants to carry their customers. The subsequent efforts of colonial debtors to cover, almost simultaneously, their deficit accounts drove the price of foreign exchange so high that many found it less costly to forego the acquisition of sterling bills completely and instead remit specie to England. When this chain of events affected the inhabitants of a given colony, its specie stock was usually sharply reduced, and domestic trade was hampered somewhat by the shortage of a convenient means of payment.

Fortunately, these monetary disturbances were self-correcting. The high sterling rates raised the effective prices of British goods and led to a curtailment in a colony's imports. The reduced purchases of British merchandise translated into a lowered demand for sterling bills in the ensuing months, and the exchange rate began to fall. Specie exports to England automatically ceased. Meanwhile, trade with the Caribbean area and southern Europe continued to produce a regular inflow of gold and silver coins, and the colony's money stock was eventually replenished.

In sum, the colonies were full participants in an emerging international financial system, with gold and silver at its base. Since the flow of specie from nation to nation and to their colonies was not unduly restricted, the distribution of the total money stock was never heavily skewed in favor of one region or to the disadvantage of another. Cycles of specie contraction followed by replenishment were frequent in the colonies and elsewhere. Fundamental market forces were at work responding to relative prices for internationally traded products and fluctuations in foreign exchange rates.

In addition to the use of coin, the colonists found other means of expediting domestic transactions. Wampum, the polished shells valued by Native Americans, was accepted as lawful money for a short time in the seventeenth century. The ageless system of direct barter was exceedingly common, especially in frontier areas remote from active markets. Within the mercantile community, the extension of book credit in anticipation of the receipt of a return shipment of similarly valued goods or subsequent monetary payment was routine. Merchants, large and small, at home and abroad, exchanged goods with other merchants and local consumers through the convenient medium of bookkeeping entries.

Although modern economic analysis excludes book credit in the measurement of the money supply, several scholars of colonial finance believe that twentieth-century monetary theories may be too narrow for an understanding of eighteenth-century finance. Joseph Ernst in his influential study of money and politics from 1755 to 1775 concluded that the inclusion of book credit in the definition of the colonial money supply was extremely beneficial in explaining movements in foreign exchange rates. In subsequent research, Robert Craig West has also called for more serious consideration of book credit in the financial system. He hypothesized that book credit may have played a role analogous to demand deposits in the modern economy. In the more advanced commercial areas, Ernst and West suggest that it served as the most common medium of domestic exchange. The validity of this approach remains unproven, however; Winifred Rothenberg, Bruce Smith, and Ron Michener are among those financial historians who have questioned its usefulness in discussing the monetary stock, in part because measuring the volume of outstanding book credit has proven impossible.

In some colonies, valuable commodities resistant to spoilage were designated as legal tender in the payment of debts and the fulfillment of contracts. Tobacco is the best example. In Virginia and Maryland, this form of commodity money was an important component of the monetary system during certain periods. Taxes, duties, court fees, and the salaries of clergymen were sometimes payable in tobacco. To expedite even further this medium of exchange, Virginia established official storehouses where the depositors of tobacco received warehouse receipts which then circulated conveniently as money. The main drawbacks of commodity money were that it fluctuated in value, moving in unison with the market price of tobacco, and its volume was limited to the amount of tobacco in local warehouses.

The colonial legislatures also experimented with the issuance of paper currency. Paper money was intended to supplement specie in the monetary system. By 1755, after the Virginia assembly had finally acted, every colony had emitted some variant of paper money. At present, scholars are divided about whether this form of payment eventually superseded specie as the main component of the money stock in some regions. Roger Weiss argued that paper money rarely approached one-half of any colony's total money stock, except for certain periods in Pennsylvania, New York, and Virginia. On the other hand, several monetary historians have accepted as reasonably accurate an estimate made by Alexander Hamilton in the 1780s that paper constituted three-fourths of the total colonial money supply on the eve of independence.

The North American colonies were among the earliest political units in modern history to test the viability of paper currency as a medium of exchange and to persist in its use. The Chinese had preceded the colonies in issuing sizable volumes of paper notes, but they abandoned the practice in the fifteenth century. No European state had previously authorized the issuance of paper money on a vast scale. In the mother country, the Bank of England and the government Treasury issued notes and Exchequer bills in the eighteenth century, but these instruments were never made legal tender in the payment of private debts. The high denominations of these notes and bills, a £20 ($1,800) minimum for the Bank of England and a £100 ($9,000) minimum for the Treasury after 1709, effectively prevented them from circulating widely and becoming an everyday medium of exchange.

Most economic and political leaders in England strongly favored an exclusively specie system. They viewed paper currency as, at best, a novel aberration. For some, it was a matter of deep-seated principle: paper money violated a presumed economic axiom; it was inherently unsound and probably corrupt. Since it had no underlying base, paper currency was certain to depreciate in value and disrupt, if not destroy, any economy. Most of the king's ministers associated with the administration of colonial affairs were prejudiced in varying degrees against paper money, although they frequently condoned its issuance as a temporary expedient.

In the colonies, on the other hand, paper currency was widely supported—by merchants as well as farmers—as a legitimate feature of the financial system. The focus of colonial leadership was on practicalities rather than abstract monetary principles. The relative degree of consensus was surprising, given the very controversial course of American monetary history in the nineteenth century. With the possible exception of political battles in New England, few irreconcilable arguments broke out between hard money diehards and paper-money advocates. Indeed, the colonial paper-money issue defies easy class analysis, as Leslie Brock argued in a penetrating dissertation written in 1941, but only recently published. Although paper normally depreciated to the detriment of creditors, it was enthusiastically endorsed by most members of the elite economic classes who dominated colonial legislatures and were often creditors in domestic transactions.

The various colonial legislatures had a mixed record in terms of the general management of their currency issues. As Elmus Wicker has observed, we must make a sharp distinction between some of the earlier questionable practices and the much more responsible policies which prevailed over the last quarter of the colonial era. During the first half of the eighteenth century, several colonies, most notably South Carolina, Rhode Island, and Massachusetts, performed poorly as judged on the basis of high rates of depreciation and price instability. After 1750, however, no evidence exists that any colony managed its paper money ineptly.

The initial emission of paper currency came in Massachusetts in 1690, and the circumstances of its issuance set a pattern that was repeated in colony after colony. An underfinanced military campaign against French Quebec failed, and the returning soldiers who had not been paid the promised wages were on the verge of mutiny. The colony's treasury was almost empty, and with no banks or other private sources of loanable funds, the Massachusetts legislature fell upon the expedient of creating and issuing £7,000 ($630,000) in paper bills of credit. In an effort to uphold the value of the bills, they were made legal tender in the payment of provincial taxes, and after 1691 at a 5 percent advance over the face amount. Upon their receipt at the Treasury, the bills were to be promptly destroyed. Thus, this detour from established financial practices was designed to be temporary and self-liquidating. In this first instance, the paper bills were retired in due course, and the monetary experiment was deemed a huge success.

In later years in Massachusetts and elsewhere, new emergencies continually arose, and colonial legislatures resorted to printing and issuing paper money to finance government expenditures. Usually a financial crisis had military origins, and the imperial officials in London reluctantly approved (invariably after the fact) fresh emissions of paper.

Since this system functioned so effectively from the colonists' standpoint, legislatures discovered other reasons for authorizing new emissions. In some cases, especially Pennsylvania in the 1720s, the justification was the stimulation of lethargic trade; in other cases—for example, Maryland in 1733—the explanation was merely the convenience of the inhabitants because of a shortage of specie and commodity money for daily transactions. As time passed, the expiration dates of the individual issues lengthened from merely two or three years to ten or more years; old bills received in tax payments were not always burned, but occasionally reissued; and a colony's various emissions began to overlap one another in time. When a colony's paper depreciated heavily, as happened in New England and South Carolina during the first half of the eighteenth century, the legislature often authorized an exchange of "new" tenor bills for the outstanding "old" tenor bills at some fixed ratio. In short, the perpetuation of a long series of temporary emissions gave many colonies de facto a permanent system of paper currency to supplement the local supply of specie and commodity money.

The terms of currency issues differed in all thirteen colonies, which makes generalization difficult. Variations existed in the backing for the bills, the length of issue, the method of retirement, interest-rate features, and legal-tender provisions. For our purposes, the issues can be divided in two broad categories, with the source of funds for retirement, whether public tax revenues or loan repayments by private citizens, the distinguishing characteristic. In most colonies both types were outstanding at the same time.

Given the universally modest level of taxation and the correspondingly small accumulation of specie in almost every colony's treasury, legislatures frequently authorized the emission of paper currency to pay pressing military expenses and other outstanding government debts. The economic consequences were twofold. This action meant that those who accepted the paper bills in payment had actually been forced to make involuntary loans to the colonial government. Simultaneously, it postponed until the assigned retirement date of the bills the collection of taxes for ongoing expenses, which explains in large part why such legislative acts were popular, since, given the option, most individuals—then and now—preferred to delay taxes rather than pay them currently.

In some instances, the paper bills carried no interest rate, and thus became a "free" loan for the colonial government. (The greenback dollars issued during the Civil War, some of which were never retired from circulation, remain with us today as examples of an interest-free loan forced upon holders by government.) On other occasions, even within the same colony, the terms of issue provided for the acceptance of the bills in the payment of future taxes at some stated premium, often 5 percent. In yet another variation, the interest associated with a given issue of currency compounded during the years it remained outstanding.

In addition to the fairness of compensating noteholders for accepting paper in lieu of specie, the interest-rate feature served to hold up the value of the currency and diminish or even prevent its depreciation. The only drawback was that many individuals began to view the bills as investments rather than everyday money as the retirement date approached. When citizens hoarded interest-bearing paper currency for its investment qualities, they prevented its wide circulation and denied the colony the convenience of an expanded money supply. Michener has questioned whether issues held extensively for investment purposes should be counted as part of the money stock because of low transactions velocity.

Not every issue was the result of a financial crisis or emergency; some legislatures simply voted to increase the local money supply in the hope of stimulating domestic trade and attracting more foreign commerce. Richard Lester has written extensively about new currency issues in Pennsylvania in 1723 and 1729 which were intended to boost economic activity and overcome mild recessions. According to Lester, the emissions were very successful, and the legislature largely achieved its goals.

Convinced of the beneficial effects of an increased money supply in New York and Pennsylvania, the Maryland legislature, in 1733, decided to test the usefulness of paper as a medium of exchange. Much of the Pennsylvania paper had already spilled over the Maryland border and was readily accepted in local trade. The Maryland currency was distributed throughout the colony on a per capita basis to all persons subject to taxation. Every taxable individual was given 30 shillings ($135), with the amounts allocated for taxable indentured servants and slaves turned over to their masters.

In all the cases cited above, the legislatures relied solely on provincial tax revenues to provide sufficient funds to retire the currency issues. As a rule, special taxes were imposed for this purpose. Two common sources of revenue were property taxes and head taxes. But there were also other systems of retirement. In the Chesapeake colonies an export tax on tobacco shipments went toward retiring the outstanding paper. Maryland, for example, built up a substantial sinking fund from the collection of export taxes on tobacco; the colony's tax revenues were transmitted to London and invested in the stock of the Bank of England. As a result, that colony had the most secure currency system on the mainland if measured in terms of the likelihood of redeeming its currency at face value. In other instances, legislatures voted a special tax assessment only in the last year or two before scheduled retirement. The impending implementation of plans to collect special taxes led many legislatures to consider favorably alternative proposals to reissue the old currency or replace it with a fresh emission of paper bills.

In a second broad category of currency issues, colonial legislatures established loan offices which loaned funds to resident property holders with land and improvements as security. They were commonly called "land banks" in the eighteenth century; that term would be institutionally inappropriate today because these government offices accepted no deposits and negotiated only real-estate loans. Every colony except Virginia created loan offices in the eighteenth century.

To guarantee a fairly wide distribution of the paper money, limits were usually placed on the sums available to individuals. In 1737, for example, the New York legislature authorized loans ranging from £25 ($1,270) to £100 ($5,085) at 5 percent interest for 12 years against mortgages on properties valued at twice the amount of the loan. In Salem County, New Jersey, the median loan was £32 ($1,750) in 1738, according to research by Thomas Purvis. In Pennsylvania the average loan was £65 ($3,525); between 1724 and 1756 about 3,500 individuals borrowed money to improve the total output of their lands and business firms. In this primarily agricultural economy, land was the safest security for most financial obligations, and the only asset widely held by the white residents. Under these loan arrangements, the original borrowers, not taxpayers, were individually responsible for repaying their loans and ultimately retiring the note issue.

This lending mechanism for the issuance of paper bills was advantageous in several respects. The colony's circulating medium was enlarged, which pleased most citizens because transactions became easier to negotiate. The availability of loans in an economy chronically short of capital encouraged new investment in productive resources by thousands of individuals. Loans were made at interest rates typically between 5 and 8 percent, a figure well below the going rates for the limited funds available from wealthy merchants and planters. In the absence of private intermediaries, the government loan offices performed a legitimate and important financial function.

Meanwhile, the interest revenue accruing to the colony's treasury contributed significantly to the cost of maintaining government services. The burden on taxpayers was correspondingly lightened. In Massachusetts in the 1720s, the towns administered the currency loans and kept the interest revenue for their own benefit. In Pennsylvania and New York, James Ferguson has shown that interest revenues alone were sometimes sufficient to cover most of those two colonies' nonmilitary expenses—a figure often no higher than £5,000 ($265,000) per year.

In terms of the colonies' relationship with the mother country, the most controversial features of the paper-money emissions were the legal-tender provisions. In an effort to generate a steady demand for the paper bills, most colonies made them legal tender in the payment of public fees and taxes and in the repayment of loans at government offices. The acceptance of the bills at full face value in public transactions was an important factor supporting the market value of paper currency relative to specie and foreign bills of exchange.

Over the years, pressure mounted in some colonies to make paper currency legal tender in private transactions as well. Many legislators felt that this added feature aided in maintaining the value of the currency and simultaneously encouraged economic activity. At times, legislatures asserted that such features were absolutely essential, and they incorporated legal-tender provisions in acts authorizing fresh emissions.

Difficulties arose, however, when debtors attempted to pay off old obligations with paper that had depreciated during the intervening months or years. In these situations, creditors often demanded specie or expressed a willingness to accept paper money only at its current market value. Many disputes over the proper settlement of old debts in colonies with heavily depreciated paper eventually ended up in the colonial courts for adjudication.

One group deeply concerned about the danger of court-ordered debt settlements in depreciated currency were British merchants with extensive sales on credit. These merchants feared that anticipated profits on transactions in goods would be reduced and might even be converted into losses if they were forced to accept in payment a form of money worth less, in relation to specie and British sterling, than it had been worth on the original sales date. This group felt exceedingly vulnerable to potential abuse in the colonial court system, which was thousands of miles across the ocean.

Based largely in London, these merchants were in a favorable position to exert varying degrees of political influence over British colonial policy. In negotiations with the Board of Trade and parliamentary ministers, London merchants first tried to seek the disallowance of all colonial acts with provisions that made paper currency lawful money in private transactions. But faced with the intransigence of some legislatures and the generally casual attitude of crown officials toward colonial affairs before the 1760s, English merchants later accelerated their demands and asked increasingly for a complete ban on all legal tender provisions, public as well as private. In some colonies where depreciation was viewed as a constant threat, they advocated the elimination of paper currency altogether.

Responding to the direct pressure from English merchants, while at the same time moving toward a general plan for greater administrative control over the mainland colonies, Parliament passed two separate acts, in 1751 and 1764, relating to paper money. The first act was aimed at the New England colonies, where, besides South Carolina, depreciation had been heaviest. It restricted the life of new emissions in Rhode Island, Connecticut, Massachusetts, and New Hampshire to just two years, and it prohibited the designation of the bills as legal tender in private transactions.

The path for this legislation had been cleared somewhat in 1747, when Parliament voted to reimburse the four New England colonies for their expenses in connection with the military campaign against Louisburg, in French Canada, in 1745. Massachusetts used its £183,649 share ($16.5 million) to retire all the outstanding paper money then in circulation and thereby return to a specie standard. The Act of 1751 was not, therefore, punitive. Moreover, during the next quarter-century, the four northern colonies used all the leeway in the law to issue substantial amounts of the permissible two-year paper, which was not lawful money in private transactions. These were high-value interest-bearing notes—the lowest denomination was £6 ($400) and the most common was £100 ($6,770)—and they did not circulate widely. For the most part, specie was used as the everyday medium of exchange in New England after midcentury, and the controversy over paper currency shifted southward.

During the parliamentary debate in 1751, the possibility of extending the act to all the mainland colonies was raised, but a split in the ranks of London merchants temporarily diverted that proposal. The depreciation rates of currencies emitted in Pennsylvania, New York, New Jersey, Delaware, and Maryland were modest in comparison to the record established in New England in the 1740s. The agents representing these colonies' interests in London argued for an exemption from the act, and they gained momentarily the support of English merchants trading heavily in those provinces. Except in

South Carolina, which had been singled out earlier and denied permission to declare any new emissions of legal-tender currency for private debts after 1731, English merchants had not been exposed to excessive currency risks outside New England, and they were willing to follow a wait-and-see policy toward the other colonies.

By the early 1760s, however, attitudes in England had altered. Virginia, the colony with the largest bilateral trade with Britain, had issued its first paper money in 1755, with full legal-tender provisions. Consequently, an increased number of London merchants faced greater exposure to currency risks. More complaints arose about the alleged inequities of settlements in colonial courts, especially in comparison to the situation in New England, where all private debts were strictly on a specie basis. Although specific instances of actual losses were few, except perhaps in North Carolina, the vacillating London merchants had concluded by 1764 that, on balance, the extension of the restriction on legal-tender provisions to all the mainland colonies was in their best interest.

Meanwhile, the crown and Parliament had grown more interested in exerting control over colonial affairs generally. Under consideration inside the ministry headed by George Grenville was one proposal, supported, incidentally, by Benjamin Franklin, to create a comprehensive currency system for all the mainland colonies under the supervision of the British government; the paper was to be secured by a special fund generated from the revenues of a proposed stamp tax. But a strong bias against all forms of paper money prevailed in the Grenville ministry. Finally, all links between proposals for currency reform and new taxes were dissolved.

The Currency Act of 1764 applied only to the colonies outside New England. The law expanded the previous ban on legal-tender provisions to include not only private debts but inexplicably public obligations as well, at least as interpreted by members of the Board of Trade. Whereas the four northern provinces had adjusted readily to the earlier act, the remaining colonies were in a more combative mood by 1764, and they resisted. Colonies like New York and Pennsylvania, which had managed paper-money systems for decades with only slight depreciation, felt the new regulations were unjustified and unreasonable. In those two colonies, paper money comprised a substantial percentage of the money stock in 1764.

In defiance, legislatures continued to authorize new paper emissions with legal-tender features and then coerced their governors into submitting the laws to British officials for approval. In some instances, colonial acts were summarily disallowed, but in other cases irregularities were overlooked. British officials rejected, for example, two South Carolina acts in 1770 and 1772 and one from New York in 1769 because of unacceptable legal-tender clauses. Yet, crown ministers in 1770 let stand a Pennsylvania act which made the new bills legal tender at the colony's loan office.

After 1764, the colonies sought revisions in the rules pertaining to the lawfulness of paper currency in meeting public obligations. In 1770, New York's agents and their London allies lobbied hard for a special act giving the colony permission to make its paper legal tender for all public purposes, and Parliament granted New York an exemption from the 1764 law. Other colonies asked for similar consideration. Finally, in 1773, Parliament revised the law and permitted the colonies to declare their currency issues legal tender in all public payments. The ban on paper-money settlements of private debts remained in force. There the matter rested until the outbreak of the war.

After decades of wrangling, the question was largely resolved to the general satisfaction of the colonies and the British overseas merchants. The latter received protection from the risk of losses stemming from the depreciation of colonial paper, and the legislatures retained the authority to emit new currency in anticipation of taxes and through provincial loan offices.

Why this currency matter proved so difficult to reconcile has perplexed historians. Joseph Ernst has pointed to a link between the shifting views of the English merchant class and the level of foreign exchange rates for sterling bills. The indecision of British officials reflected, Ernst argues, the vacillating outlook of London merchants. When a colony's debts were weighty and the exchange rate for sterling bills rose far above par, the merchants became especially fearful that colonial courts might settle old debts in depreciated paper. If a currency act came before the Board of Trade while sterling rates in a given colony were high, the merchants were almost certain to oppose it. On the other hand, when sales in a given colony were slack and sterling rates were near par or lower, the same merchants were likely to revise their position and favor the emission of new paper because they hoped it might stimulate commerce and increase their lagging exports. In sum, Ernst suggests that fluctuations in British attitudes about the merits of paper money can be explained in large part by fluctuations in colonial indebtedness and sterling rates.

The British merchant class was not the only group to damn the consequences of currency depreciation; a century later most professional economists and historians viewed colonial monetary practices even more harshly. By the late nineteenth and early twentieth centuries, depreciation was condemned as representing not merely irresponsible economics but moral corruption as well. As happens so often, these scholars had their eye focused almost exclusively on current events, and in looking for "lessons" from the past, they foisted their hard-money biases on their defenseless ancestors. Beginning with the pioneering studies of Richard Lester in the 1930s through those of E. James Ferguson in the early 1950s and the contributions of Elmus Wicker, Ron Michener, and Bruce Smith in the 1980s, the older, doctrinaire outlook has undergone steady modification. The modern judgment is more benign and tolerant, even positive in most respects.

Paper money was neither as harmful as its critics alleged nor as essential as its proponents asserted. Fluctuations in its volume and value may have influenced the rhythm of economic activity over the short run, but there is no reason to believe that its existence or absence had more than the slightest impact on income levels in the colonies over the long term. Paper currency was merely one feature of the financial system, and in some colonies at certain times it constituted only a fraction of the real money stock. Virginia is an example of a colony that prospered and maintained a viable financial system without paper currency until the first emission in 1755. The New England colonies were largely on a specie standard after midcentury. Thus, the argument advanced by many colonial legislatures in their negotiations with the mother country after 1760, that paper currency was essential for their economic survival, must be discounted heavily. The underlying issue here was political control, not economic necessity.

On the other hand, the contention of the colonial legislators that paper currency was convenient, useful, and produced few ill effects had considerable merit. Currency maintained a market value relative to specie, and irrespective of its level of depreciation, paper remained in circulation and fulfilled in varying degrees its function as a medium of exchange. Moreover, its drop in value was rarely precipitous but extended over months or years. Colonists seeking a monetary store of wealth could always hold silver and gold in bars, coins, or expensive tableware. To the extent that wealth in the form of mortgages and other debts was eroded somewhat by depreciation, urban residents, who were more deeply involved in financial transactions, probably felt the effects more than farmers.

The depreciation of currencies can also be viewed as an alternate method of taxation. Legislatures frequently issued new paper in financial emergencies to avoid a sharp hike in current taxes. To the extent that the currency depreciated and was never fully redeemed, the real tax burden fell on all those who held the paper over the years. In many ways, this became a relatively painless tax system, for the incidence was spread out over a long period of time. The recipient of paper merely lost a few percentage points in the value of the money when the next transaction occurred. The net effect was analogous to a modern excise tax.

When sales were made on credit, however, merchants became more vulnerable the longer an account remained unpaid. English merchants, who had debts strung out for long periods of time across an ocean, increasingly lobbied Parliament for ironclad protection against currency risks. In truth, colonial courts generally sought equity in their proceedings and usually took into account the changing market value of paper currency in settling debts. English creditors may have fared somewhat worse than local ones in colonial courtrooms, but the London merchants' fears of grossly unfair treatment were based on isolated cases and were much overdrawn.

Until fairly recently, scholars had assumed a close link between the volume of paper money in circulation and changes in price levels in the various colonies. Yet, when Robert Craig West ran a series of regressions to measure the correlation between the issuance of currency and the rate of inflation in Boston, Philadelphia, New York, and Charleston from 1700 to 1764, his results were mostly negative. Only in Boston during the period from 1720 to 1749, when the volume of paper in circulation in New England was extremely high and no specie was present, did the data reveal a significant statistical correlation. In the other three cities, the volume of currency in circulation was unrelated to changes in commodity prices and movements in exchange rates for sterling bills.

Subsequently, Bruce Smith and Elmus Wicker conducted more research on related issues and reached similar conclusions. In a study of money and prices from 1755 to 1768, which covers the Seven Years' War (French and Indian War), Wicker observed that, although several colonial legislatures injected thousands of pounds of paper currency into the economy at a very rapid pace to finance the war effort, exchange rates were remarkably stable. Meanwhile, Smith noted that Pennsylvania had increased its per capita issue of paper money by 278 percent between 1755 and 1760, yet prices rose only 17 percent. Later, New York reduced its per capita paper circulation by 86 percent in the 1760s, but prices dropped a mere 2 percent.

Despite persistent attacks on the usefulness of the quantity theory of money in explaining price movements throughout the era, this analytical tool has retained academic defenders. Indeed, in the late 1980s a sharp scholarly debate was ongoing over exactly what mechanism actually did determine the rates of inflation and deflation for the various colonial currencies. The contending sides were in agreement on certain issues; both acknowledged that the quantity theory of money provided a good explanation of price movements in New England from 1720 to 1750. For other colonies and other periods, however, disagreement prevails about why some currency issues failed to depreciate significantly. Smith has argued that currency values were linked to the strength, or weakness, of their "backing," meaning that, irrespective of the volume of paper placed in circulation, issues which the public perceived as likely to be redeemed and retired from circulation, as a result of either taxation or individual repayment of outstanding loans, suffered little depreciation.

Michener dissents. First, he finds the evidence for the backing theory unconvincing. He believes instead that currency issues tended to maintain purchasing power because of the existence of de facto fixed rates governing the exchange of specie and paper money. Where fixed exchange rates prevailed, Michener contends, specie exports offset most of the increases in paper money, leaving the size of the money stock (specie plus currency) only slightly larger than its previous level. As a result, prices climbed only modestly, rising in unison with the size of the aggregate money stock. Later, when currency issues contracted, specie flowed back into the colony to prevent deflation. Only in instances where floating (not fixed) exchange rates were in effect, such as in New England prior to 1749 when the volume of currency placed in circulation exceeded greatly the original size of specie stocks, was depreciation a serious problem according to Michener. But Wicker challenges the existence of sufficient empirical evidence for this alleged substitution effect.

Perhaps in the years ahead, monetary historians will be able to reach greater consensus about the fundamental forces at work in determining changes in the value of colonial currency issues. At present, however, the question remains controversial and unresolved. To permit more thorough analysis, specialists sorely need more accurate data on the actual size of the *total* money stock for individual colonies.

In many colonies the mechanism of distributing new currency was probably of greater significance than the volume of paper issued. The government land offices, as was mentioned earlier, provided loans to a large number of farmers, and some artisans and merchants, at very moderate interest rates, usually 6 percent or lower. Alternative sources of loanable funds, in the absence of private financial institutions, were not available at comparable interest rates. For an economy almost as short of capital as it was of labor, these mortgage loans encouraged the colonists to expand the productive base of their economy more rapidly, and thereby encouraged economic development.

The denominational structure of paper-currency issues was also designed to make monetary transactions convenient for the general public. Four colonies issued currency in sums as low as one shilling ($4.15). John Hanson reviewed the denominational structure of the currency in Pennsylvania, New York, Maryland, Rhode Island, New Jersey, and Virginia, and found that the volume of bills issued in amounts under 5 shillings ($20.75) ranged from a low of 40 percent in New York to a high of 81 percent in Rhode Island. Because of the relatively large number of small notes in circulation, transaction costs were probably lower in the colonies than in the mother country, where low- and medium-value coins were scarce, and this factor may have contributed slightly to the growth in per capita incomes.

Finally, there remains the proposition that paper money was an important factor in overcoming economic slowdowns in some colonies. The fresh emission of paper created an immediate surge in demand for goods, and, according to this hypothesis, the revival of commerce was normally sustained. On the basis of his detailed examination of Pennsylvania in the 1720s, Richard Lester advanced this argument in the 1930s. In this instance the sample size has unfortunately remained too small to determine whether the issue of fresh paper was a major cause of colonial economic recoveries or whether it merely coincided with them. Nonetheless, the issuance of paper currency and the sudden increase in the size of the money stock in Pennsylvania and elsewhere in certain years probably contributed somewhat to increased economic activity. Mary Schweitzer has recently cited the positive influence of currency issues on the Pennsylvania economy, especially in western counties and other remote areas. Over the entire colonial era, however, it remains questionable whether paper currency had a major role in determining the overall level of output or any great influence on per capita incomes.

During the last twenty-five years of the colonial era, the paper-money controversy was, nonetheless, responsible for much of the turmoil in Anglo-American relations. By the 1760s, more than just economics was at stake; compromise solutions were readily available, but neither side was in a mood to give them serious consideration.

Unlike their strategies in developing the earlier navigation acts, the British never developed a comprehensive plan for a colonial monetary system. The use of currency evolved piecemeal on a colony-by-colony basis, with provincial legislatures providing the initiative. The record of the Board of Trade and parliamentary ministers regarding colonial monetary acts was contradictory and discriminatory; their rulings depended on the personalities holding office at home and abroad, the efforts of colonial agents in London, the previous financial performance of the colonies in question, and the prevailing attitude of wavering London merchants. The Currency Act of 1764 was poorly drafted, for it implied that colonial paper could no longer become legal tender in public or private transactions. Thereafter, in discussions about possible revisions, British officials failed to heed the advice of Benjamin Franklin, who recommended a simple ban on legal-tender status for paper in all foreign debts, which would have resolved the one point of contention between the legislatures and the London merchants.

By the same token, the argument of some colonial legislatures that legal-tender status for paper in all private transactions was essential cannot be accepted as valid. In numerous instances, and in New England by statue after 1751, colonies found it advantageous to issue paper which was lawful money only in public transactions. Except in Maryland, where a reserve fund of sterling and Bank of England stock provided security, the main support for the value of currency was the steady public demand to settle accounts, exchange goods, repay mortgage loans, and discharge taxes. No correlation exists between the inclusion of private legal-tender provisions and the maintenance of par values for colonial currencies.

In 1773, when Parliament finally agreed to permit the emission of legal-tender currency for public debts in every mainland colony, the issue was largely settled. It was not a major grievance on the eve of independence. The one unresolved economic question remained the extent and manner of colonial contributions to the tax revenues of the British empire.

BIBLIOGRAPHICAL ESSAY

SOME important books on colonial finance are Curtis Nettels, *Money Supply of the American Colonies Before 1720* (Madison: University of Wisconsin Press, 1934); Leslie Brock's printed 1941 dissertation, *The Currency System of the American Colonies, 1704–1764* (New York: Arno Press, 1975); Joseph Ernst, *Money and Politics in America, 1755–1775* (Chapel Hill: University of North Carolina

Press, 1973); Thomas L. Purvis, *Proprietors, Patronage, and Paper Money: Legislative Politics in New Jersey, 1703–1776* (New Brunswick: Rutgers University Press, 1986); and Jacob Price, *Capital and Credit in British Overseas Trade: The View from the Chesapeake, 1700–1776* (Cambridge, Mass.: Harvard University Press, 1980).

A contemporary analysis of the currency issue was Benjamin Franklin's "Remarks and Facts Relative to the American Paper Money," written in 1767, and published in Benjamin Labaree, ed., *The Papers of Benjamin Franklin* (New Haven: Yale University Press, 1970), 14:76–87. Other volumes with colonial sources are Andrew M. Davis, ed., *Colonial Currency Reprints, 1682–1751* (New York: Kelley, 1964) and Herman Krooss, ed., *Documentary History of Banking and Currency in the United States* (New York: McGraw-Hill, 1969). For information on paper money in China and England, see Lien-sheng Yang, *Money and Credit in China: A Short History* (Cambridge, Mass.: Harvard University Press, 1952); John Clapham, *The Bank of England: A History*, 2 vols. (Cambridge: Cambridge University Press, 1945); and Emanuel Coppieteis, *English Bank Note Circulation, 1694–1954* (The Hague: Louvain Institute, 1955).

Among the recent assessments of colonial finance are Elmus Wicker, "Colonial Monetary Standards Contrasted: Evidence from the Seven Years' War," *Journal of Economic History* (1985), pp. 869–84; Bruce Smith, "American Colonial Monetary Regimes: The Failure of the Quantity Theory and Some Evidence in Favor of an Alternate View," *Canadian Journal of Economics* (1985), pp. 531–65; Smith, "Some Colonial Evidence on Two Theories of Money: Maryland and the Carolinas," *Journal of Political Economy* (1985), pp. 1178–1211; Ron Michener, "Shortages of Money in Colonial New England: An Explanation," unpublished manuscript, 1983; and Michener, "Fixed Exchange Rates and the Quantity Theory in Colonial America," manuscript prepared in 1986 for Carnegie-Rochester conference on monetary economics and scheduled for publication in an upcoming proceedings volume. See also pertinent chapters in Mary Schweitzer, *Custom and Contract: Household, Government, and the Economy in Colonial Pennsylvania* (New York: Columbia University Press, 1987).

Paper money is assessed in Roger Weiss, "The Issue of Paper

Money in the American Colonies, 1720–1774," *Journal of Economic History* (1970), pp. 770–85; Weiss, "The Colonial Monetary Standard of Massachusetts," *Economic History Review*, (1974), pp. 577–92; E. James Ferguson, "Currency Finance: An Interpretation of the Colonial Monetary Practices," *William and Mary Quarterly* (1953), pp. 153–80; M. L. Burstein, "Colonial Currency and Contemporary Monetary Theory: A Review Article," *Explorations in Entrepreneurial History* (1966), pp. 220–33; and John McCusker, "Colonial Paper Money," in Eric Newman and Richard Doty, eds., *Studies on Money in Early America* (New York: American Numismatic Society, 1976). Two studies which focus on the origin of paper-money emissions are Andrew Davis, *Currency and Banking in the Providence of Massachusetts Bay* (New York: Macmillan, 1901) and Richard Lester, "Currency Issues to Overcome Depressions in Pennsylvania, 1723 and 1729," *Journal of Political Economy* (1938), pp. 324–75. An older but still useful review of land banks is Theodore Thayer, "The Land Bank System in the American Colonies," *Journal of Economic History* (1953), pp. 145–59.

Several articles focus on the Currency Act of 1764; see Jack P. Greene and Richard Jellison, "The Currency Act of 1764 in Imperial-Colonial Relations, 1764–1776," *William and Mary Quarterly* (1961), pp. 485–518; Joseph Ernst, "The Currency Act Repeal Movement: A Study of Imperial Politics and Revolutionary Crisis, 1764–1769," *ibid.* (1968), pp. 177–211; and Robert Weir, "North Carolina's Reaction to the Currency Act of 1764," *North Carolina Historical Review* (1963), pp. 183–99. Another valuable article on a later period is Richard Sheridan, "The British Credit Crisis of 1772 and the American Colonies," *Journal of Economic History* (1960), pp. 161–86. Other articles focusing on the colonial monetary system include Robert Craig West, "Money in the Colonial American Economy," *Economic Inquiry* (1978), pp. 1–15; and John R. Hanson, "Money in the Colonial American Economy: An Extension," *ibid.* (1979), pp. 281–86. Winifred Rothenberg makes a contribution to colonial financial history in "The Emergence of a Capital Market in Rural Massachusetts, 1730–1838," *Journal of Economic History* (1985), pp. 781–808.

For an analysis of the demand for money in sixteenth-century

Spain, see Dennis Flynn, "A New Perspective on the Spanish Price Revolution: The Monetary Approach to the Balance of Payments," *Explorations in Economic History* (1978), pp. 388–406, and Flynn, "Fiscal Crisis and the Decline of Spain (Castile)," *Journal of Economic History* (1982), pp. 139–47.

Extensive data on the relative values of colonial monies are presented in John McCusker, *Money and Exchange in Europe and America, 1600–1775* (Chapel Hill: University of North Carolina Press, 1978). Data on prices in two colonies are found in Winifred Rothenberg, "A Price Index for Rural Massachusetts, 1750–1855," *Journal of Economic History* (1979), pp. 975–1001, and Donald R. Adams, "Prices and Wages in Maryland, 1750–1850," *ibid.* (1986), pp. 625–45.

CHAPTER VIII

TAXES AND POLITICS

T HE level of taxation in the colonies was extremely low. The rates rarely, and then only periodically, approached 50 percent of those prevailing in England. Few organized governments taxed their people so lightly in the seventeenth and eighteenth centuries. The colonists soon became accustomed to minimal taxation, and by the late colonial period they viewed low taxes as almost a birthright. Until 1764, the British had inadvertently encouraged this attitude, for Parliament had not only asked for little colonial revenue for over one hundred years, it had also regularly sent substantial sums from the pockets of English taxpayers overseas to finance a series of military campaigns on the North American continent. With their defense costs subsidized in large part by the mother country, and without a sitting monarch, an idle aristocracy, or a large court establishment to support, the colonies incurred modest governmental expenses at the provincial level. Since the overall financial arrangements were quite favorable to the thirteen colonies, it is easy to understand why, after 1760, they attempted to maintain the status quo in Anglo-American relations.

Whether the independence movement had fundamentally economic or political origins has been the subject of scholarly debate for generations. The emphasis has shifted between interpretations, depending upon the outlook of our most respected historians and the mode of historical analysis in vogue. The aim here is not to mediate that debate, although one side of the argument is tested and a tentative judgment offered. Because this chapter focuses almost exclusively on economic factors, many readers might reasonably assume at the outset that the author leans heavily toward an economic interpretation. That, however, is not the case; indeed, my review of the financial evidence had led me to play down, but not eliminate, the importance of economic factors relative to the role of ideological conviction and the quest for political autonomy.

Many historians, however, are not so willing to dismiss economic forces and the issue of taxation. Several scholars argue that the rising rate of domestic taxation in the larger cities over the course of the eighteenth century was a source of urban discontent and may have contributed to the political activism of artisans and common laborers in the 1760s and 1770s. In *The Urban Crucible,* Gary B. Nash points out that the amount of taxes paid by individual taxpayers during the Seven Years War rose rapidly; from 1750–54 to 1760–64 the tax burden increased 70 percent in New York, 80 percent in Boston, and 250 percent in Philadelphia. Although the tax burden had dropped back to prewar levels in Boston and New York by the 1770s, it failed to decline in Philadelphia. Nash believes that the rising level of taxes in northern cities, the increasing incidence of poverty, and the stagnation of incomes for many artisans were, in combination, an important part of the calculations by which the colonists embarked upon a dual revolution to sever the colonial connection and internally reform their societies. Although I do not find this general argument persuasive, it nonetheless represents an alternative viewpoint on a crucial issue.

In a recent research project on the Philadelphia mercantile community from 1760 to 1775, Thomas Doerflinger reached radically different conclusions about economic conditions in the city. He concluded that this period had been generally prosperous, with only a slight downturn between 1764 and 1768. For the most part, Philadelphia's merchants were not in a revolutionary mood, and they gave only lukewarm support to those groups opposed to the stamp tax and subsequent import duties. Complaints about the British were not strongly articulated—at least not until 1773, when some merchants expressed resentment at being denied equal opportunity to participate in the lucrative tea trade.

In a separate study of the origins of the independence movement in Virginia, Marc Egnal dismissed the most commonly cited economic explanations governing the behavior of the planter elite and substituted a new hypothesis of his own. The colonists were not seeking to escape payment of debts due British creditors, according to Egnal, and their opposition to import duties was so weak that it ceased altogether after 1771. The motive of Virginia's leaders was expansionism; they wanted easy access to the rich lands to the west where they envisioned a bountiful future. The British policy of creating a fixed and militarily fortified frontier between the colonies and various Indian tribes was an obstacle to those ambitions. Virginia planters wanted neither liberty nor freedom from taxation as much as they prized opportunities to acquire land grants in the western territories. Gaining access to western lands had been the main purpose for supporting the French and Indian War; yet following the departure of the French from the continent, Parliament was inexplicably seeking to thwart further expansion westward. The British had become obstructionists, according to Egnal's analysis, blocking the path to economic advancement.

In the brief volume of essays which serves as an introduction to his massive study on the migration of peoples to North America, Bernard Bailyn emphasizes the importance of land speculation, both by Europeans and by native-born Americans, in recruiting migrants and settling many thinly populated regions. Bailyn never points to speculative activity as a possible cause of the break with Britain, but his presentation is at least reasonably compatible with Egnal's general line of argument about the motives of Virginians.

In an independent review of the underlying causes of separation from the mother country, Jack P. Greene observed recently how the end of the French and Indian War sent expectations about future developments "veering off in opposite directions." Parliament viewed the outcome as a new opportunity to proceed with a broad program of colonial reform. The colonies, in contrast, anticipated that greater security from outside attack would lead to greater prosperity and more autonomy; but they received instead a constant series of threats to their traditional freedoms. This divergence between expected rewards and actual treatment led to a sense of betrayal and deep bitterness on the part of many Americans.

Echoing the theme of betrayal, T. H. Breen has recently emphasized the strongly negative feelings of great planters in Virginia's tidewater tobacco region about the consequences of mounting debts owed British merchants who marketed their crops. The credit crisis of 1772, which led to a curtailment in credit facilities and in some cases demands for a swift settlement of accounts, angered many wealthy planters because they had viewed debts as personal obligations rather than as strictly business transactions. Moreover, some came to believe that British merchants were involved in a "conspiracy" to use indebtedness to deprive them of their estates and properties. The credit crisis, according to Breen, was the unifying force which rallied a coalition of politically active planters who had become extremely suspicious of almost everything British in origin by the mid-1770s.

Irrespective of their views about underlying causation, most historians have agreed that the movement for independence was precipitated by economic factors. The strongly negative reaction to a proposed series of increases in imperial taxes, with further rises anticipated, was the catalyst that unified and mobilized a diverse group of mainland colonies.

In normal years, colonial legislatures voted taxes for a very limited number of government services. Salaries for the appointed governor, for a few judges, and in some provinces for the recognized clergy, plus compensation for their own legislative expenses, were typically major items in the annual budget. In colonies with outstanding government debts in the form of circulating paper money, a partial retirement sometimes made a heavy claim on revenues. In Massachusetts from 1765 to 1774, the average yearly expenditures were only £27,000 ($1.8 million), while New Hampshire spent just £2,000 ($13,500) in 1772. The costs of road maintenance, poor relief, and other incidentals were generally left to the counties and towns. Although the data remain sketchy, tax collections at the local level may have rivaled or exceeded provincial taxes in many areas.

By the late colonial era, per capita taxes at the provincial level generally ranged from 2 to 4 shillings, with 3 shillings ($13.50) a rough average. These taxes represented no more than 1.5 percent of estimated per capita incomes. In England, by comparison, the national tax rate ranged from 12 to 18 shillings ($54–$81) and represented from 4 to 7 percent of per capita incomes.

Each colony employed differing methods of taxing its inhabitants, and over the decades legislatures frequently shifted the emphasis from one tax to another. In the only comprehensive study of provincial taxes, Robert Becker demonstrated the great variety of colonial revenue systems in the period after 1763. Except for poll (head) taxes and import taxes on slaves, the methods of taxation are familiar today. As shown in table 8.1, taxes were applied to land, livestock, inventories, liquor, imports and exports, and mercantile profits, including interest income.

The colonies possessed a mix of progressive and regressive taxes. In this era, property holding was considered a reliable indicator of yearly income. As a consequence, taxes based on assessed values of land, improvements, personal property, and inventories were relatively progressive, because they normally reflected a person's ability to pay. One method assessors used to determine land values was to make estimates on the basis of the rents paid by tenants on comparable plots in the same region. In England, land taxes were stated as a percentage of each £100 in actual rents or the potential rental income. In the colonies, the most progressive tax systems included levies on unimproved, wilderness tracts held for speculation; while

TABLE 8.1. Types of Domestic Taxes, 1763–1775

Land—unimproved	Rhode Island, Pennsylvania
Land—assessed value	Massachusetts, Rhode Island, Connecticut, Pennsylvania, New Jersey
Land—per acre	Virginia, Maryland, South Carolina, Georgia
Other property—assessed	Massachusetts, New Jersey, South Carolina
Excise—liquor, etc.	New Hampshire, New York, Maryland, Virginia, North Carolina
Merchant profits	Massachusetts, New Hampshire, Pennsylvania, Connecticut, Rhode Island, South Carolina
Import—finished goods	Pennsylvania, New York, Georgia
Import—slaves	New York, Maryland, South Carolina
Export—tobacco	Maryland, Virginia
Poll—flat	Maryland, Virginia, North Carolina
Poll—linked to wealth	Connecticut, Massachusetts, Rhode Island
Poll—discriminatory toward free blacks	South Carolina, Georgia

SOURCE: Robert A. Becker, *Revolution, Reform, and the Politics of American Taxation, 1763–1783* (Baton Rouge: Louisiana State University Press, 1980).

the more regressive systems, all in the south, taxed farmland strictly by the acre, irrespective of its productive value.

Poll taxes applied to males over a certain age, often 16, fell most heavily on families with low incomes. Their regressive impact was often modified, however, by increasing the poll tax rate in line with the value of other taxable property, which was the system followed in Connecticut and Rhode Island. In the upper south, a greater share of the burden was borne by slaveholders, since they usually became liable for additional head taxes on all slaves and servants over 12, including females as well as males. Georgia and South Carolina used poll taxes for purposes of racial discrimination; they imposed them exclusively on free blacks.

Other items produced tax revenues. Several colonies taxed the vices, assessing import duties on rum and wine plus excise taxes on domestic liquors. In the Chesapeake region, export taxes on tobacco were an important source of revenue, with those growers shipping the largest number of hogsheads progressively incurring the largest share of taxes. In some provinces, legislators sought tax revenue from business "faculties," by which they meant the incomes of merchants from trade and moneylending. In Massachusetts, the tax rate on incomes from business activities was set at 5 percent in 1773. Finally, as discussed in the last chapter, some colonies imposed taxes in a disguised manner by forcing the holders of paper currency to suffer steady depreciation.

The New England colonies generally had the most progressive tax rates. Land and property taxes were based on assessed values, which were higher in more commercial areas. Northern merchants were usually subject to income levies; and poll taxes, when applied, were often linked to property holding. Perhaps because South Carolina also had a major port city in Charleston, Becker found it was the one southern colony with a tax system similar to New England's. The only colony with a consistently regressive tax structure in the eighteenth century was North Carolina, where the legislature relied heavily on flat poll taxes, plus excise taxes on liquor, for revenue. The other southern and middle colonies employed a mixture of taxes with progressive and regressive features.

In a study of the Pennsylvania economy in the eighteenth century,

Mary Schweitzer examined the system of government services at the provincial, county, and township levels. These entities were in competition for tax dollars, and until midcentury local governments were generally much more successful. The counties taxed wealth— improved land and livestock—at rates ranging from 0.4 to 1.2 percent of assessed value, with the funds spent largely on poor relief and workhouses. Townships, with some help from counties, were responsible for building and maintaining roads wide enough to permit the transport of carts laden with wheat and other provisions to larger markets, particularly Philadelphia. Local governments had little difficulty in collecting taxes, or making labor requisitions, for projects benefiting local residents, but the tax collectors commissioned by the provincial legislature were often less successful. Provincial collectors encountered so much opposition from the populace early in the century that Pennsylvania suspended completely the direct taxation of individuals for over 40 years. From 1711 to 1755 the province collected no head or property taxes whatsoever; the only sources of revenue for the legislature were import duties on alcohol plus interest earnings from the operations of the government loan office.

Despite the paucity of revenue, Pennsylvania sponsored a fairly extensive system of public services for its citizens. These services were financed by allowing public agencies to collect self-sustaining user fees and commissions. According to Schweitzer, the entire court and jail system was run on a fee basis, with even innocent parties forced to contribute to the support of judges and court officials. The recording of land purchases and property transfers required special fees high enough to cover the costs of providing this vital public service. In an effort to enhance the reputation of the colony's flour in overseas markets, and thereby raise its price, Pennsylvania enacted a law requiring strict inspection of all flour exports. The official inspector received one pence per cask from all persons subject to regulation; in some years his earnings totaled more than the governor's salary. In Philadelphia the city treasurer kept 5 percent of all incoming revenues from fines and fees, plus he received another 5 percent commission on all city expenditures—in total, 10 percent of the city budget.

In colonies with major port cities, legislative battles over the assignment of regional tax quotas were frequent. It was common practice to assign counties and towns the responsibility for collecting a fixed portion of a colony's revenues. Boston, Providence, New York, Philadelphia, and Charleston complained constantly that they bore a disproportionate share of provincial taxes. Usually under-represented in the legislatures, the ports' residents often fought to prevent the assessment of their property at values closer to market prices than corresponding assessments in rural areas. Philadelphia paid 43 percent of provincial property taxes between 1763 and 1775. In South Carolina, the only place where land taxes were assessed ad valorem rather than per acre was in Charleston.

The port cities also sought tax relief because of the relatively high cost of government services at the local level. Poor relief had become a large item in city budgets by the late colonial era. In the 1760s, Boston allocated up to 60 percent of its local taxes for charity; the city spent £3,057 ($205,000) on poor relief in 1769 and £3,355 ($225,000) in 1773. Charleston's representatives complained con-stantly about the number of indigents who flocked into the city, and they badgered the province to assume greater responsibility for poor relief. The belief, widespread today, that modern American cities, under the strong influence of sympathetic liberals, were the first to allocate a substantial portion of their tax funds for various welfare programs is contradicted by the performance of the colonial port cities.

Although the legislative contests between rural and urban resi-dents were sometimes lengthy and acrimonious, the maneuvering for advantage and the rhetoric displayed in debates over tax policies at the provincial level should not obscure the point that, for the most part, little money was really at stake. Domestic tax rates were so low in all the colonies that no class or region was unduly burdened. In a study of the family budgets of common laborers in Philadelphia in the 1770s, Billy Smith estimated that taxes accounted for about 5 percent of annual income. In the 1980s, U.S. citizens commonly pay up to 30 percent of their income in taxes for government services. By modern standards, colonial taxes were almost unbelievably light.

As for imperial taxes, leaving aside all constitutional questions and the institutional mechanism for colonial representation in Parliament, from a financial standpoint one can readily empathize with the exchequers of the British Treasury in their quest for an American tax revenue. At the close of the Seven Years War (French and Indian) in 1763, Britain had accumulated an enormous national debt of more than £135 million ($12 billion) plus continuing defense costs in newly won Canada, along the midwestern frontier, and at sea in the North Atlantic. The expense of maintaining these military forces overseas was over £350,000 ($31.5 million) annually. Tax rates in England had been high in 1755 and went higher during the war; the land tax jumped from 10 percent of assessed value to 20 percent, and excise taxes were raised across the board. Lance Davis and Robert Huttenback estimated that British national taxes yielded about £1 ($90) per capita from 1770 to 1775, or about 8 percent of per capita income. British tax rates were almost certainly the highest in the Western world. Meanwhile, after 1764, the colonial contribution to meeting defense costs in North America was virtually nil.

Until the 1760s, Parliament had reserved the right to disallow the acts of the colonial legislatures, but it had failed to seek a steady tax revenue from the mainland colonies. Only the Virginians, who continued to pay quitrents, an old form of feudal dues, in amounts up to £5,000 ($450,000) annually until independence, made any regular contributions to the imperial coffers, and those sums were trifling. Maryland's quitrents went to the proprietor, Lord Baltimore, rather than to Parliament. Quitrents due in other colonies were rarely collected.

The Navigation Acts applied to colonial trade after 1650 had placed duties on the importation of certain foreign products, but the aim was to constrain the pattern of commerce, not to generate revenues. Thomas Barrow estimated that the cost of collecting these duties on the mainland often exceeded the amounts received. The Molasses Act of 1733 raised the duty on imports from the French and Spanish islands in the Caribbean to 6 pence ($2.25) per gallon; the intention was to halt or significantly curtail the foreign molasses trade. Instead, the colonists evaded the royal customs collectors or settled with them for a fraction of the total due; in Boston, one-tenth was reportedly the standard rate for looking the other way.

When these duties were established, no one in the colonies had raised the issue about the absence of colonial representation in Parliament. Until the mid-eighteenth century, the legislatures were still relatively inexperienced at running their own affairs and were less bold in asserting their political autonomy.

The Navigation Acts had, of course, placed a burden on the colonial economy. But it came in the form of lost opportunities for additional profits—especially the direct sale of enumerated goods to the European continent. As was discussed at greater length in chapter 2, the indirect burden on the colonies was probably slightly more than the benefits accruing to them from British defense spending in the late colonial period. Few contemporaries were in a position to make even tentative estimates of these opportunity costs associated with membership in the British empire, however. In the colonies, Daniel Dulaney, a Maryland lawyer and ardent pamphleteer, calculated that restrictions on the tobacco trade alone reduced grower's profits by about £270,000 ($24.3 million) in 1765. Dulaney's calculations were fairly accurate and erred, if at all, on the conservative side. Such arguments fell on deaf ears in the Exchequer, for even if they were true, the hypothetical "costs" made no tangible contribution to imperial tax revenues.

The colonists were not merely successful in avoiding direct imperial taxation; they also succeeded in gaining substantial reimbursements from Parliament for funds expended on military campaigns against French and Spanish outposts or settlements. Until 1763, the British, the latecomers to the New World, were engaged in a struggle for empire on the North American continent with European rivals. Julian Gwyn puts British spending in North America from 1740 to 1775 at £450,000 ($40.5 million) annually, with over 85 percent devoted to military activities. The colonies were intelligent enough to use this British thirst for military and political empire to their own advantage. In return for firm promises from Parliament to reimburse them fully or partially at a later date, the colonies frequently agreed to recruit soldiers locally and to supply them throughout a military campaign. In many colonies, the governors and their legislative allies were anxious to volunteer aid under these favorable conditions, or even instigate hostilities, since the profits from war contracts were one of the few financially rewarding opportunities available to government officials and their friends and relatives.

The system was doubly advantageous because in the long run the English taxpayer footed a substantial share of the bill. Parliamentary ministers were not familiar with the financial capabilities of the colonies, and acquiring accurate information from overseas was slow and difficult. When the colonists grieved about their own allegedly high taxes and limited resources, crown ministers, ignorant of the real situation, felt they had little choice but to acquiesce in demands for reimbursement, since the possible expansion of the empire and the defeat of a rival power took precedent over financial considerations.

Parliament sent £1.1 million ($100 million) to the thirteen colonies to reimburse them for expenses incurred during the victorious French and Indian War. This sum covered over 40 percent of the colonies' expenditures. The legislatures used this largesse to reduce debts and lower provincial tax rates, which fell everywhere between 1765 and 1775. By 1770, most of the colonies were virtually free of war debts, while English taxpayers remained saddled with interest payments of £5 million ($450 million) annually to service a swollen national debt. Ironically, by fulfilling its earlier pledges of reimbursement, Parliament had unwittingly reinforced the colonists' belief in their general immunity to high taxes.

When the English government, after decades of indifference and neglect, finally began to reassess its colonial policies in the early 1760s, the costs of maintaining a militarily secure North American empire were uppermost in the minds of crown ministers. Parliament was resigned to accepting expenditures during the past war as a "sunk" cost, irretrievable and now irrelevant, but the continuing peacetime expenses were viewed much differently. Primarily on the basis of advice from the British military commander in North America, Lord Jeffrey Amherst, the government had decided to station about 10,000 troops in North America.

The costs of colonial defense soon rose to over £350,000 ($31.5 million) a year. Excluding interest payments on the national debt, these sums accounted for about 12 percent of Parliament's operating budget and were more than twice the amounts spent on North

American defense before 1755. The thirteen mainland colonies, the ministry assumed, were the prime beneficiaries of this British military presence; but, as in the past, they were contributing little to its upkeep. Colonial revenue to offset at least some of these expenses therefore seemed in order. British officials estimated colonial population in the 1760s at 1.6 to 1.7 million (a very good estimate and only slightly below the probable figure), yet the colonists paid only £64,000 ($5.8 million) in imperial taxes, or 9.5 pence ($3.50) per capita.

The first act designed specifically to raise a colonial revenue actually lowered the duty on foreign molasses and wine. The prohibitive duty of 6 pence ($2.25) per gallon on molasses imported from the French and Spanish islands in the Caribbean dropped to only 3 pence ($1.125) per gallon. The rate on wine shipped through Britain came down too. This 1764 law signaled a major shift away from the strategy of using high duties for protectionism—with the beneficiaries to date having been influential British investors in the Caribbean. The new policy called for more modest rates that, given an enlarged volume of trade, might generate larger tax revenues. In 1766, the molasses duty was lowered again to merely one pence ($0.375) per gallon, but it now applied to all molasses entering the colonies, British as well as foreign. The two reductions in duties on molasses were expected to reduce the incidence of smuggling, previously rampant, and to stimulate more trade.

To handle the anticipated larger volume of commerce and to tighten the enforcement of imperial regulations in general, Parliament also decided in 1764 to reorganize and upgrade the colonial customs service. Except for the royal governors and a few high-ranking military officers, these poorly paid customs officers were the only visible representatives of the British civil government in the colonies. While some colonial leaders were apprehensive about the language in the preamble of the tariff revision act, which proclaimed forthrightly the goal of raising an overseas revenue, and others were suspicious about the greater degree of imperial control, they were in no position to protest too loudly. Duties on imports clearly fell within the scope of the long-standing navigation laws. Moreover, the tax rates on wine and molasses had been lowered rather than raised, which left few grounds for complaint.

The ministry headed by George Grenville thus made an auspicious start toward producing a steady colonial revenue in 1764. The precedent for taxing foreign commerce was well established in the colonies. Collected from merchants when goods entered port, the tax burden was passed along to consumers indirectly in the form of higher prices. The tax revenues anticipated from this alteration in the duty on molasses were largely realized. In the period from 1768 to 1771, for example, around 3.5 million gallons of molasses entered through the customs houses annually and generated annual duties of £14,000 ($1.26 million). These amounts alone were sufficient to convert the operations of the customs service on the mainland, even after its expansion, from a perennial financial loser into a slightly profitable government bureau. But the net revenues from the molasses and wine duties combined covered a small fraction of the military budget for North America.

Seeking additional sources of revenue, the Grenville ministry settled on a stamp tax in 1765. A common feature of the English tax system, stamp duties applied to a host of legal and government documents, including wills, licenses, and deeds, to name a few, plus miscellaneous items like newspaper advertisements, playing cards, and dice. In his recent book on Grenville and the genesis of the stamp tax, John Bullion points out that this form of taxation was selected in part because its incidence was expected to fall equally on the residents of every colony. The stated aim was to raise roughly £40,000 ($3.6 million) in the colonies or about 10 percent of the yearly costs of defense. Privately, however, Grenville hoped the volume of transactions would raise £100,000 ($9 million).

The Stamp Act marked a significant departure from previous parliamentary behavior, and it produced a loud outcry in the colonies. Unlike the duties on imports, stamp levies were not hidden in the prices of consumer goods. Atypical in the colonies, they were highly visible taxes, certain to catch the attention of the average citizen.

Internal taxes were also unprecedented in imperial relations. Many legislative leaders in the colonies called them plainly unconstitutional, because their enactment violated the British political principle of no taxation without the presence of adequate representation in Parliament to affirm the consent of the voters. Some legislators in 1765 distinguished between Parliament's prerogative to

vote external taxes and the alleged illegality of internal taxes, but
the majority were becoming increasingly opposed to any imperial
taxation whatsoever, or at least to any increases in existing levels.
Few Americans bothered to consider that implementation of the
Stamp Act threatened to cost the average taxpayer no more than an
extra 5 pence ($1.85) a year, or less than 0.2 percent of per capita
income.

Instead they organized a protest movement. The colonists terror-
ized or intimidated the appointed tax collectors and forced them
either to resign their positions or to agree not to perform their
assigned duties. Nine of the thirteen colonies sent representatives
to a hastily called Congress in New York to coordinate strategies.
The Congress issued a declaration protesting the passage of the
Stamp Act, in particular, and the enactment of tax laws without
representation, in general. A principle was now at stake; it was more
than just a battle over money.

An intense American lobbying effort was directed at English
merchants trading extensively with the colonies. These merchants
were expected to assist in a coordinated movement to repeal the
stamp tax, for if that movement failed, the colonies threatened to
continue indefinitely an organized boycott of English imports. The
colonists soon discovered that an economic boycott could be a powerful political tool.

Faced with such extreme, completely unexpected hostility and
with the surprising cohesiveness of the colonial opposition, Parliament backed down and repealed the Stamp Act in 1766. The way
was eased when Benjamin Franklin explicitly assured the House of
Commons, in person, that his countrymen objected solely to internal
taxes and not to traditional methods of raising revenue such as
external taxes on imports. Whether Franklin was badly misinformed
or deliberately misled Parliament to gain temporary advantage is
uncertain, but his expression of colonial sentiments was grossly
inaccurate, according to Edmund and Helen Morgan in their brilliant
analysis of the Stamp Act controversy. In a recent article, however,
Thomas Slaughter has defended Franklin somewhat, claiming that
the American spokesman told Parliament simply that his fellow
citizens could avoid paying external duties by refusing to purchase

foreign imports whereas stamp taxes would be impossible to avoid in the normal conduct of business and personal affairs.

Determined to reassert its legislative superiority and convinced that the colonists had no constitutional objections to further increases in import duties, Parliament looked about for other revenue opportunities. A change of ministries brought Charles Townshend into office as Chancellor of the Exchequer. A former member of the colonial Board of Trade, Townshend was much more familiar with overseas affairs than his predecessors.

His experience suggested that the colonial governors were generally much too dependent on the goodwill of their supposedly subordinate legislatures. This happened, he reasoned, because legislatures normally had control over their governors' salaries. The governors' divided allegiance on so many vital issues was thus easy to understand. Parliament's failure to assume the financial responsibility for these salaries—and thereby to give the governors some independence from local political pressure—had been, in Townshend's estimation, a major blunder in imperial affairs, a prime example of a false economy. He planned that a portion of any new overseas revenues would go to pay the salaries of the royal governors. The cost was relatively modest, probably less than £20,000 ($1.8 million). Given the realities of colonial politics, however, this was one expense the legislatures did not wish to surrender.

In late 1766 and early 1767, Townshend reviewed a series of new tax proposals for the colonies. Meanwhile, the vote in Parliament to lower the English land tax by 25 percent, a bill he had opposed, cost the Exchequer about £500,000 ($45 million) and made the search for alternative sources of revenue even more compelling. For a time, Townshend considered a plan for creating a land-bank office for all the colonies, with the interest income accruing to the imperial coffers. The plan had circulated in London for years and had been recommended by Benjamin Franklin and other colonial agents as an alternative to the stamp tax in 1765. The proposal appeared to have considerable merit, since the colonies were simultaneously pressing for a liberalization in the terms of the Currency Act of 1764. Proponents argued that the issuance of paper money through parliamentary loan offices might even be welcomed overseas. It might be the ideal solution for two outstanding colonial issues: money and taxes.

But for a combination of reasons, Townshend decided to lay aside the loan-office proposal and to concentrate instead on raising duties on other American imports. Several factors probably influenced his decision. A parliamentary land bank and a single paper-currency system would link the economies of the thirteen colonies more closely, yet the outcome of the coordinated protest against the stamp tax had revealed that greater economic unity might have serious political dangers. Second, many members of Parliament still had reservations about the propriety of paper money. After passing a series of acts restricting its usage, the most recent in 1764, Parliament might feel reluctant to reverse policy so suddenly. Finally, Townshend may have feared that the colonists would interpret the collection of interest income as a form of internal taxation and respond with another protest movement. On the basis of Franklin's assurances to Parliament, new taxes on imports seemed less controversial and therefore the safer choice.

Townshend finally recommended new duties on glass, paint lead, paper, and tea. The aim was to generate about £40,000 ($3.6 million)—the same figure as the earlier stamp tax—in new revenues immediately, with other increases planned in subsequent years. The amount represented about 10 percent of British defense expenditures in North America. The bill passed Parliament with hardly a dissent, not even from the colonies' staunchest allies in the constitutional battle over the stamp tax.

The reaction in the colonies to the new Townshend duties was comparable to the response to the stamp tax. Having challenged and successfully undermined the most recent British attempt to increase taxes, the colonists were predisposed to try again. The arguments about the absence of representation in Parliament were revived—with no distinctions between internal and external taxes, Franklin's remarks notwithstanding. The constitutional issue was in the forefront of colonial minds, and it had escalated into queries about the power of Parliament over colonial affairs in general.

To combat the Townshend duties, the colonies relied most heavily on the proven tactic of economic coercion. A boycott of all English imports was quickly organized, and watchdog committees of citizens kept merchants in the larger cities from circumventing its terms. Since few British goods were necessities, the boycott meant only inconveniences for some consumers. Few colonists lost their liveli-hood or suffered declines in income, except a few merchants in the major ports. The Americans were, by this point, an aroused and determined people.

The volume of business lost by British merchants closely associ-ated with the colonial trade was staggering. In 1768 and 1769 com-bined, the figure rose to over £1 million ($90 million) in sales fore-gone. The sum dwarfed the meager amount of £2,700 ($243,000) collected from the Townshend duties in 1770. The economic real-ities of the boycott again dictated that Parliament knuckle under, and it finally conceded defeat by rescinding all the Townshend duties—except one. The tax on tea was retained as a symbol of parliamentary authority. But for all practical purposes, Parliament had given up the cause in 1770. The effort to establish a permanent colonial revenue to offset a major portion of the costs of defending North America had failed. In short, the one economic issue driving a wedge between the mother country and her mainland colonies had been largely resolved. Only the matter of political autonomy re-mained outstanding.

The colonists resented the continuation of the tax on tea, but they grudgingly paid it. After falling to a low of 108,600 pounds in 1770, tea imports rebounded sharply in 1771 to 359,000 pounds and re-mained steady over the next two years. In the period from 1771 to 1773, the customs service collected duties of £34,000 ($3 million) yearly, mainly on molasses, wine, sugar, and tea. These sums amply covered the expenses of operating the customs houses and provided funds to pay the salaries of the governors of Massachusetts and New York, judges of the Admiralty Courts, and a few other imperial officials. Some of the monies even became available to supply the royal navy patrolling in the North Atlantic.

The final episode linked to the tea tax occurred in late 1773. The East India Company, a large English trading firm closely tied to the government, found itself in serious financial difficulties because of matters completely unrelated to the American market. The firm had enormous holdings of tea in its English warehouses, and in an effort to save the company from bankruptcy, Parliament granted it a monopoly on tea sales to the colonies. Hoping to forestall a possible charge of financial exploitation, Parliament adjusted the tea regulations and tax rates in England so that tea prices overseas would drop, even after the payment of the existing colonial tea duty.

This effort to rescue the East India Company and to give colonial consumers the benefit of lower prices went awry, however. A small group of militant colonists, still angered by the tea tax, seized this opportunity to inflame public opinion. They focused on the monopoly issue in particular, with unsupported claims that the East India Company had plans to undermine the entire mercantile community and obtain exclusive rights to all colonial commerce, not merely tea. Thomas Doerflinger has shown that the monopoly issue made a serious impact on Philadelphia merchants, for example. Circulars asserted that the real motive behind the whole scheme was to force the colonies to recognize the legitimacy of the existing tea tax. Since Americans had been paying that tax for over two years, the latter charge was overblown. But in the politically charged colonial atmosphere, the economic logic of the situation was totally lost.

On the night of December 16, 1773, the Boston Tea Party took place. Tea valued at £9,000 ($810,000) was destroyed by 30 to 40 men in a well-executed, three-hour operation. Parliament promptly closed the port of Boston. The First Continental Congress met in September 1774; fighting erupted at Lexington and Concord in April 1775; and the final movement for independence was under way.

How important were economic forces in causing the American revolt? In the five years before the signing of the Declaration of Independence, the British imposed no new taxes. Parliament gave little serious consideration to alternative revenue proposals for the colonies. The retention of the tea tax in 1770 was strictly a face-saving device. The colonies had demonstrated twice within a five-year period the power of the boycott. Parliament was ready to settle for the status quo, including the assumption of over 90 percent of defense expenditures in North America.

The remaining imperial taxes were hardly burdensome. The Virginia quitrents contributed around £4,000 ($36,000) yearly, and customs duties grossed £34,000 ($3 million), but they netted only £18,000 ($1.6 million) after expenses. The imperial tax burden was 4 pence ($1.50) per capita—a negligible portion of family income even in the eighteenth century, no more than 0.1 percent. Meanwhile, domestic tax rates continued to decline after 1765; by the 1770s, provincial taxes had fallen below 2 shillings ($9.00) per head or just under 1 percent of per capita income in some colonies. The colonial rhetoric about the heavy burden of existing taxes was mostly that—rhetoric with little substance.

Taxes were a major unresolved issue in Anglo-American relations only in the period from 1765 to 1770. They were the surface topic around which most political and constitutional arguments centered. Doubting the sincerity of colonial statements about the necessity of representation in the taxation process, historians have often noted the colonies' acceptance of the revision of the molasses duty in 1764. The molasses tax was, however, a special situation. This tax on molasses imports had been in effect for over a century, and the adjustment was downward to one-half and later one-sixth of the former rate. No American representatives in Parliament, had they existed, could have objected strongly to that form of tax revision.

The stamp tax and later Townshend duties were different matters altogether, because they proposed to increase colonial tax rates. Although designed to raise only 10 to 15 percent of Parliament's annual defense budget in North America, many contemporaries and subsequent scholars have argued that these new taxes were only a start. John Bullion claims that Grenville never envisioned the Stamp Act as opening the door for higher taxation at a later date because the minister did not want to diminish the region's financial ability to purchase an increasing volume of English goods. But Townshend clearly intimated in subsequent speeches to the House of Commons that more revenue acts were likely to follow. Some believe that colonial tax revenues might soon have approached per capita levels in England and thereafter exceeded them. Within a few years, the colonies could potentially become major contributors to the allegedly bloated and corrupt British government, headed by a lavish monarch who maintained a host of pensioners and other parasites. To avoid this outcome, revolt was justified and, moreover, easily explained.

The hypothesis that the political separation had economic origins rests heavily, then, on the estimate of what was likely to happen at some undetermined point in the future. The alleged intent of Parliament to raise taxes higher and higher provides the main evidence. In other circumstances, historians have considered such speculative evidence extremely weak, but in the context of American independence it seems to have survived and thrived.

In this case, the economic argument is doubly suspect, because it is questionable on its own terms. Even if such predictions had proved accurate and tax increases had become a reality in subsequent decades, political separation in the 1760s on the basis of anticipated future costs would have been financially premature. Furthermore, even if the burden associated with the Navigation Acts is included in the calculations, the overall cost of participation in the British Empire was no more than 5 shillings ($22.50) per head. Colonial taxes would have had to triple to reach a comparable per capita rate with England. Borrowing from modern business techniques for appraising investment alternatives, we can also calculate that the "present value" of any future tax payments, using a modest discount rate of 8 percent, were very low in 1765, when based on the steady implementation of British tax policy over a twenty-year period. Long before the development of sophisticated investment analysis techniques, the colonists knew very well that a tax dollar avoided in 1765 was worth considerably more than the same amount paid, if at all, at some indefinite date in the future. The independence movement came, in sum, a generation too early for an economic explanation of its origins to account for its emergence.

Numerous scholars have analyzed imperial affairs in the last quarter-century before the outbreak of hostilities and pointed to grievous errors in British assessments of the overall economic, political, and military situation in North America. We have only limited space to sample a few representative studies. In a book written over a quarter-century ago, John Alden questioned the basic premise that Parliament needed to maintain a large military establishment on the continent after 1765 and thus incur such continuing defense expenditures. Before the French and Indian War, Parliament had never kept as many as 1,000 Redcoats in the colonies. After achieving

victory, however, British military leaders insisted on stationing six-
teen regiments in North America—about 8,000 troops on paper, but
since units were usually at two-thirds strength during peacetime,
the actual numbers were around 6,000. This standing army was
unnecessarily large, Alden concluded, and indeed its presence was
"actually a menace to British power in the Thirteen Colonies." The
policy of maintaining such a large military establishment was "a
proposition arguable in 1763, dubious in 1765, very doubtful in 1768,
and indefensible after 1770." In short, the most effective and sensible method of trimming the huge financial deficits in the colonies
was by a drastic reduction in expenses rather than by seeking additional revenues to support an expensive, counterproductive, and
ultimately disastrous policy. But as happens all too often in human
affairs, one of the most logical solutions was never given more than
slight consideration by decision makers on either side of the Atlantic.

In a more recent analysis of the politics surrounding the breakup
of the British Empire in North America, Robert Tucker and David
Hendrickson raised similar questions about the wisdom of maintaining a large standing army. The initial decision was made on the basis
of good intentions; Parliament had come to realize by the 1760s that
the thirteen colonies were by far Britain's most valuable overseas
assets (the West Indies had been number one in the seventeenth
century), and it sincerely wanted to provide adequate protection.
Almost inadvertently, this new focus of attention brought to the
surface the previously ignored issue of political sovereignty, and,
mistakenly, the king's ministers became convinced that, without
complete sovereignty, all other interests, tangible and intangible,
would be lost. Tucker and Hendrickson noted that few political
leaders had the foresight to realize that British prosperity was based
primarily on improvements in agricultural methods, transportation
and communication networks, and industrial machinery, not on the
possession of far-flung colonies. Few people at the time took seriously the advice offered by Josiah Tucker in an essay published in
Gloucester in 1774 entitled *The True Interest of Great Britain Set
Forth in Regard to the Colonies*. Tucker recommended granting the
colonies complete freedom and concentrating on the growth of bilateral trade.

As one part of their research on the economic costs and benefits associated with modern political empires, Lance Davis and Robert Huttenback examined the British experience in North America after 1750. They found that the course of events in the thirteen colonies was consistent with the normal pattern elsewhere; few colonial ventures by the western European nations proved financially beneficial to taxpayers in the mother country. With the possible exception of the colonization of India, British overseas ventures consistently cost more to defend and administer than they were worth to the nation's taxpayers as a whole. The maintenance of an empire in North America during the eighteenth century saddled the English taxpayers with an enormous burden of war debts and escalating defense expenditures. From a purely economic standpoint, Davis and Huttenback speculated that Britain was probably a "victor" in defeat, for, after independence, U.S. taxes rose precipitously. From 1792 to 1811, U.S. per capita tax rates were over 10 times higher than the imperial taxes levied by the British from 1765 to 1775.

The economic tactics used by the Americans from 1765 to 1770 had significant implications for future political action as well. The colonies had become a large market for English manufactured goods over the course of the eighteenth century. The extent of British dependency on American markets was revealed in its vulnerability to the trade boycott. The colonies had found a powerful economic and political weapon to use against a nation heavily reliant on international commerce for its prosperity. Almost forty years later, Presidents Thomas Jefferson and James Madison adopted a similar strategy of economic coercion in the years preceding the War of 1812. The trade embargo was less successful in the first decade of the nineteenth century, but its potential nonetheless remained. In the 1970s, the Arab nations imposed an oil embargo against the United States, and the tactic was widely deplored. Ironically, a leader in the innovative use of economic coercion had become its chief victim almost two centuries later.

When the crown ministers tried in the early 1760s to increase colonial taxes severalfold and to generate a revenue to offset somewhat the high cost of defending North America, the colonies protested strongly. The rate of increase was very rapid, given the very low base of imperial taxation in prior decades. The British aimed initially at raising from 10 to 15 percent of their defense expenditures in North America. But the colonists found these new taxes unacceptable in practice and in principle. The confrontation over imperial taxes quickly escalated into debates over constitutional issues like representation in Parliament and the future role of the colonies in the empire.

In conclusion, we have tested the hypothesis that underlying economic differences between the colonies and the mother country were largely responsible for the final political separation in the 1770s. It is not a convincing argument. The degree of economic regulation and the level of imperial taxation were not sufficient causes of the War for Independence, for they had little real financial impact on the colonies. Having discounted heavily hypotheses about the economic origins of the independence movement, we must look to other explanations—ideological, political, social—to determine the motivations behind the independence movement.

BIBLIOGRAPHICAL ESSAY

THE best source on domestic taxation is Robert A. Becker, *Revolution, Reform, and the Politics of American Taxation, 1763–1783* (Baton Rouge: Louisiana State University Press, 1980). Becker also published "Revolution and Reform: An Interpretation of Southern Taxation, 1763 to 1783," *William and Mary Quarterly* (1975), pp. 417–42. An excellent account of tax collection and expenditures at the local and provincial levels is found in Mary Schweitzer, *Custom and Contract: Household, Government, and the Economy in Colonial Pennsylvania* (New York: Columbia University Press, 1987).

The collection of imperial taxes is covered in Thomas Barrow, *Trade and Empire: The British Customs Service in Colonial America, 1660–1775* (Cambridge, Mass.: Harvard University Press, 1967). Pertinent articles in one major journal include Alan P. Watson, "The Quitrent System in Royal South Carolina," *William and Mary Quarterly* (1976), pp. 183–211; Marvin Kay, "The Payment of Provincial and Local Taxes in North Carolina, 1748–1771," *ibid.* (1983), pp.

197–226; and Thomas Slaughter, "The Tax Man Cometh: Ideological Opposition to Internal Taxes, 1760–1790," *ibid.* (1984), pp. 566–91.

For information on taxation in England and on the continent, see Stephen Dowell, *A History of Taxation and Taxes in England*, 6 vols. (1884; reprint, New York: Kelley, 1965); and Carlo Cippola, *Before the Industrial Revolution: European Society and Economy, 1000–1700* (New York: Norton, 1976), p. 47.

On the tax revisions and political controversies during the last quarter-century before the break with Britain, see Bernhard Knollenberg, *Origin of the American Revolution, 1759–1766* (New York: Free Press, 1965); Knollenberg, *Growth of the American Revolution, 1776–1775* (New York: Free Press, 1975); Edmund and Helen Morgan, *The Stamp Act Crisis: Prologue to Revolution* (Chapel Hill: University of North Carolina Press, 1953); John R. Alden, *The South in the Revolution, 1763–1789* (Baton Rouge: Louisiana State University Press, 1957); Jack P. Greene, *The Quest for Power: The Lower Houses of Assembly in the Southern Royal Colonies, 1689–1776* (Chapel Hill: University of North Carolina Press, 1963); John Bullion, *A Great and Necessary Measure: George Grenville and the Genesis of the Stamp Act, 1763–1765* (Columbia: University of Missouri Press, 1982); and Alison Olson, "The London Mercantile Lobby and the Coming of the American Revolution," *Journal of American History* (1982), pp. 21–41.

The events after 1766 are covered in P.D.G. Thomas, "Charles Townshend and American Taxation in 1767," *English Historical Review* (1968), pp. 33–51; Robert Chaffin, "The Townshend Acts of 1767," *William and Mary Quarterly* (1970), pp. 90–121; and Benjamin Labaree, *The Boston Tea Party* (New York: Oxford University Press, 1964).

For a different interpretation of the importance of economic forces, see Joseph Reid, Jr., "Economic Burden: Spark to the American Revolution," *Journal of Economic History* (1978), pp. 81–100; Marc Egnal and Joseph Ernst, "An Economic Interpretation of the American Revolution," *William and Mary Quarterly* (1972), pp. 3–32; Marc Egnal, "The Origins of the Revolution in Virginia: A Reinterpretation," *ibid.* (1980), pp. 401–28; and Gary Nash, *The Urban Crucible* (Cambridge, Mass.: Harvard University Press, 1979).

Two valuable essays are found in Peter Marshall and Glyn Williams, eds., *The British Atlantic Empire Before the American Revolution* (London: F. Cass, 1980): see Jack P. Greene, "The Seven Years' War and the American Revolution: The Causal Relationship Reconsidered," pp. 85–105, and Julian Gwyn, "British Government Spending and the North American Colonies, 1740–1775," pp. 74–84. Another essay by Jack P. Greene is "An Uneasy Connection: An Analysis of Preconditions of the American Revolution," in Stephen Kurtz and James Hutson, eds., *Essays on the American Revolution* (Chapel Hill: University of North Carolina Press, 1973), pp. 32–80.

For a broad analysis of events in this era, see Robert W. Tucker and David Hendrickson, *The Fall of the First British Empire: Origins of the War of American Independence* (Baltimore: John Hopkins University Press, 1982), and W. A. Speck, "The International and Imperial Context," in Jack P. Greene and J. R. Pole, eds., *Colonial British America: Essays in the New History of the Early Modern Era* (Baltimore: John Hopkins University Press, 1984). Lance Davis and Robert Huttenback likewise place events in North America in a comparative perspective in a paper drafted at the California Institute of Technology in the late 1970s.

CHAPTER IX

LIVING STANDARDS AND INCOME GROWTH

T HE material standard of living enjoyed by the typical white family unit in the thirteen mainland colonies was almost certainly the highest in the world by the 1770s. Leaving aside regional variations, I have estimated median income per capita at around £10 ($900), and a mean income figure of £12 ($1,080). By comparison, for white Americans in 1985 the median income was $11,700. The incomes of slaves—measured in food, clothing, housing, medical care, and other maintenance costs— were probably around £7 ($630) per person. Two centuries later for black Americans the median income was $6,900 in 1985. Income levels for whites and blacks in North America have thus risen by multiples of approximately 11 to 13 times over the last two centuries, increasing at annual rates somewhere between 1 and 1.3 percent.

Pretax incomes in the mother country in the same period were probably about the same, or only slightly below, the figure for the free colonial population. The colonists had higher disposable incomes for the purchase of private goods and services, however, because taxes in the colonies, local to imperial, were normally around 75 percent below the rates prevailing in Great Britain. As a result, the typical colonial family maintained a material standard of living at least 10 percent above its counterpart across the Atlantic Ocean. In a careful study of the Maryland economy on the eastern shore, Paul Clemens estimated that local farmers usually had up to one-third more cash available at the end of the annual harvest to purchase goods and services than comparable farmers in England. Research by Carole Shammas on household consumption patterns indicates that colonial families spent over £3 ($270) per person, or one-quarter of their income, on products imported from outside their colony of residence in the decades before independence, which likewise suggests a surprising degree of market activity for people living in the eighteenth century. Angus Maddison has estimated that income levels in Britain and its North American colonies were about twice as high as those in most of the rest of the world in this era.

The accepted view of what level of income constitutes wealth or poverty in North America has changed radically over time. Colonial incomes, high by the standards of the time, were about 70 percent below the official poverty line established by the U.S. government for a family of four in 1985. Indeed, colonial incomes were roughly the same as the food stamp benefits available to qualifying families in large metropolitan areas in the early 1980s. Poverty and wealth, beyond a minimal subsistence figure of perhaps $250 a year, have become relative concepts over time and between cultures.

Despite their meagerness by current U.S. standards, colonial incomes were higher than those in a group of countries that, in combination, hold over one-half of the world's population today. Nations with mean incomes under $500 per head in 1980 included India (with 15 percent of global population), Pakistan, Bangladesh, Vietnam, Haiti, and Ethiopia. A sample of countries with mean per capita incomes between $500 and $900 in 1980 included mainland China (with 20 percent of global population), Indonesia, the Philippines, Egypt, Nigeria, and Sudan. In short, over two hundred years ago, our colonial ancestors enjoyed living standards, however spare, that remain the aspirations of a majority of people inhabiting this globe in the 1980s. On a relative and comparative basis, therefore, North America has been an affluent society for over 300 years.

The quality of life was high in the colonies as well. Land was abundant, and population densities were low. Except in some areas of New England, farms were usually over 75 acres; in Europe plots of 20 acres or less were common. Water was rarely polluted; thus a person could normally drink safely from a river or stream. Air pollution was not a problem. The absence of crowding meant that communicable diseases, which often ravaged Europe, spread much more slowly in North America. Indeed, the colonies were almost plague resistant. The overall health of the inhabitants, free and slave, was unrivaled in the eighteenth century if measured on the basis of low infant mortality and adult death rates.

Since food was everywhere plentiful, famine was never, as in most other countries, considered a serious threat. After 1630 extensive crop failures were rare, and the colonists felt economically secure. Birthrates were very high, near the biological maximum, in large part because parents were confident about future food supplies for their offspring. Unemployment rates were low in this land of labor scarcity, and incidences of abject poverty were slight for a free population of 1.8 million in 1775.

In research on the so-called strolling poor in Massachusetts, Douglas Jones pinpointed an increasing number of transients during the eighteenth century. About an equal number of men and women were "warned out" of towns in an effort to avoid the cost of poor relief; many women were unwed mothers with children in tow. Ex–indentured servants were common among wandering vagabonds. But the data do not indicate that the rate of transiency was climbing as fast as the size of the total population in New England.

Energy sources were also abundant for a preindustrial society. Wood for cooking and heating was bountiful in most areas, and the cost was low compared to England. In New England the typical household burned 30 to 40 cords annually, or the firewood yielded by about one acre of forest. Colonial homes were tolerably, and sometimes even comfortably, heated during the winter months. Warmer houses led to improved personal health. Because wood was less expensive in the colonies, families could divert more of their income to buy other goods. Abundant and affordable energy contributed to the relatively high living standards in North America. Indeed, the natural environment was generally attractive and healthful, excepting only the swampy southern coastal areas.

The quality of life was immeasurably enhanced too by the many opportunities for middle-class and lower-middle-class farmers to acquire their own land. The ownership of land was the prime economic goal of virtually all preindustrial peoples, since land was the main source of wealth and income. In the colonies, ownership meant not only economic independence from haughty landlords but the privilege of participating in the political life of the society as well. The average white farmer owned at least a 40-acre plot, which guaranteed males the right to vote according to British tradition and law. Perhaps as much, or more, than any other tangible evidence of the quality of life, widespread land ownership made the colonies a genuine country of opportunity for thousands of British and northern European immigrants.

One of the surest signs of colonial well-being was revealed in diets. The typical family allocated around one-third of its income for the consumption of basic foodstuffs such as grains and vegetables. A portion of surplus grain was fed to livestock; in some regions, the amount of grain allocated to producing meat was as much as 20 percent of total output. High meat consumption is generally considered an indication of relative wealth, since one characteristic of subsistence living standards, in the past and today, is a low percentage of protein in diets. The colonists ate large quantities of pork and beef plus dairy products. In some areas the adult consumption was half a pound of protein-rich meat per day.

The food supplies available in the port cities were normally ample and varied. In a study of eighteenth-century Boston, Karen Friedman found a surprisingly efficient system of food accumulation and distribution. Many city residents bought their bread from local bakers and willingly paid prices from 35 to 85 percent higher for wheat loaves than for corn or rye breads. Cattle arrived in town from area farms on foot, and the business of butchers flourished. Friedman estimated that Bostonians drank milk at two meals every day. For the most part, city residents lived on nutritionally sound diets, except perhaps during the winter months when the selection of food was limited. The typical urban family spent up to 50 percent of its income on food, with sizable meat portions and dairy products included in that total. Today, the average American family spends about 17 percent of its after-tax income on groceries; elsewhere the inhabitants of the world's poorest nations frequently devote up to 70 percent of their meager earnings to maintain an unvaried and almost meatless diet.

In related research on comparative diets in England during the eighteenth century, Carole Shammas calculated that the populace normally allocated about 70 percent of household expenditure to food. Moreover, she discovered a surprising degree of elasticity in spending patterns; indeed, as income rose, families over the decades spent a higher proportion of their budgets on food and drink, not a lower proportion as most economic historians had previously hypothesized. In this era, the English poor actually devoted less income to diet than the middling classes. Ironically, Shammas concluded, despite greater expenditures, diets deteriorated over the century because a large portion of the extra purchases went for sugar, coffee, tea, and tobacco. These items were tasty to many palates but poor nutritionally.

A new methodology for estimating the nutritional status of the white population comes from an analysis of the average height of males entering the military in the eighteenth century. Kenneth Sokoloff and Georgia Villaflor studied the muster rolls of soldiers recruited to fight in the French and Indian War (1756–63) and the War for Independence (1775–83). They discovered that native-born Americans were surprisingly tall; indeed, the native-born group had nearly reached modern heights—now an average of about 5'9" for males. Scientific research has proven a direct correlation between the general level of nutrition, the consumption of protein, and the final heights of individuals. Sokoloff and Villaflor's findings corroborate other evidence indicating that the colonials were avid meat eaters. In an analysis of the occupations listed by recruits, they found no significant difference in heights among farmers, artisans, common laborers, or social classes generally, which suggests that the diet of the lower classes in the colonies was nutritionally sound.

Sokoloff and Villaflor also found that colonial soldiers were normally two inches taller than recruits entering the service of the British Royal Marines. The existence of this differential suggests that colonial diets were more ample and varied than across the Atlantic. Since large meat consumption is typically a sign of high incomes in a developing economy, this factor reinforces the argument that living standards were higher in the colonies than in the mother country in the mid-eighteenth century.

This methodology of assessing the composition of diets on the basis of height measurements has also been applied to the slave population in an article by Richard Steckel. Unfortunately, the data analyzed are from the nineteenth century rather than the colonial era; but, if we assume that later experience was mirrored in an earlier period, which seems probable, then Steckel's conclusions are useful in this context. His findings were paradoxical. Slave children in their unproductive years ate very inadequate diets, and their growth was normally stunted. By their teenage years, when they began to enter the workforce, the quality of diets changed dramatically. Slave heights spurted between ages 10 and 20. Likewise, the mortality rates for slaves under the age of 10 was twice the figure for the white population. After age 20, however, no significant differences in the mortality rate for blacks and whites existed. Steckel concluded that slaves were "poorly fed as children but extraordinarily well-fed as workers."

In research on the living standards of the lower classes in Philadelphia in the mid-eighteenth century, Billy Smith drew up a household budget covering food, rent, wood, and clothing for various occupations: tailors, cordwainers (shoemakers), common laborers, and sailors. For the typical family of four (2 adults, 2 children) in these categories, the annual cost of food, including a half-pound of meat daily for adults plus milk, was around £16 ($1,440); rent varied from a low of £6 ($540) for laborers up to £13 ($1,170) for cordwainers and tailors; firewood for heating and cooking ran about £3 ($270); and clothing—including a pair of shoes, two shirts, one pair of pants or a skirt, and a cloth coat for each family member—cost around £5 ($450). Taxes added another £1.5 ($135) to £2 ($180). The normal budget for a lower-class family in Philadelphia was approximately £35 ($3,150), or £9 ($810) per capita.

By eliminating meat from the diet, a family could cut its food budget in half, but it was still difficult to survive on an income much less than £21 ($1,900) to £24 ($2,160) per year. Fully employed males in various occupation groups could earn up to the following amounts: day laborer—£36 ($3,240); sailor—£30 ($2,700); journeyman shoemaker—£35 ($3,150); master shoemaker—£45 ($4,050); journeyman tailor—£38 ($3,420); and master tailor—£60 ($5,400). Because of irregular employment patterns in these occupations, however, many families were pressed to maintain living standards without extra income from the part-time employment of wives and older children. (Ironically, many American families today claim to be in a similar position, despite mean after-tax family incomes of over $23,000 in 1985.)

Smith characterized the lower classes in Philadelphia as living in

very circumscribed material conditions and constantly threatened by
the unpredictability of illness, seasonal unemployment, and general
economic slowdowns. Despite the meagerness of their family incomes and the degree of vulnerability from a twentieth-century
perspective, the colonial urban worker, nonetheless, experienced an
unusually high standard of living for the eighteenth century and one
near the global median in 1985.

Differences in income and wealth levels existed among regions
and between rural and urban areas. Alice Hanson Jones produced a
series of masterful quantitative studies of colonial wealth based on
a sample of probated estates drawn from throughout the colonies in
the year 1774. Critics have pointed to deficiencies in the sample
data, such as underestimating death rates in urban areas and parts
of the southern colonies, failing to include subregions like the Shenandoah Valley and the southern backcountry, and weighting too
heavily Charleston in the overall averages. She also faced the problem of reducing all the various paper currencies to a common value.
Despite probable error, Jones's study nonetheless remains the most
comprehensive survey to date of colonial wealth, and its data and
conclusions continue to be cited by scholars as reasonably accurate
reflections, and certainly the best available at present, of the economic status of the colonists in the early 1770s.

Jones's numbers indicated that New England had the lowest levels
of per capita wealth and income, probably because of its rocky soils.
The mean physical wealth of free adult wealth-holders in the region
was £161 ($15,000). Median wealth, a figure more accurate for the
population as a whole, was £74 ($6,650). The top 20 percent of New
England estates held about two-thirds of the region's entire wealth
(table 9.1). Mean incomes in the four northernmost colonies were
probably close to £10.5 ($945) per person, or about the same level
as in England.

The middle colonies had the least concentrated distribution of
wealth. Median wealth was 80 percent of the mean figure of £189
($17,000). The top 20 percent of all estates held only one-half of
the region's wealth. Mean incomes in the middle colonies were
approximately £11.5 ($1,035), a number lying between the estimates
for the free population in the other two sections.

The southern colonies, with a large slave population, had the most unusual pattern of wealth and income distribution. Slaves held no wealth except perhaps clothing and a few personal items; meanwhile they were human assets owned by one segment of the white population. In the early 1770s, adult male slaves were valued at from £55 ($5,000) to £70 ($6,300) in Virginia. Slaves did have incomes, however, as measured by food consumption, clothing and housing allocations, wood burned for cooking and heating, medical services received, and minor incidentals. My estimate of slave incomes at £7 ($630) represents 50 percent of the mean income of free whites in the region. The typical slaveholder by expropriating roughly one-half of the output of two slaves could raise family income by 15 to 20 percent. Even without the advantage of slaveownership, however, white incomes in the south were higher than in the northern colonies.

The southern colonies claimed the largest share of colonial wealth,

TABLE 9.1. Total Physical Wealth, 1774:
Estate Sizes and Composition for Free Wealth-Holders
(in £ sterling)

	All Colonies	New England	Middle Colonies	South
Mean average	£252.0	£161.2	£189.2	£394.7
Median average	108.7	74.4	152.5	144.5
Distribution				
Bottom 20%	0.8%	1.0%	1.2%	0.7%
Top 20%	67.3%	65.9%	52.7%	69.6%
Composition				
Land	53.0%	71.4%	60.5%	45.9%
Slaves and servants	22.1%	0.5%	4.1%	33.6%
Livestock	9.2%	7.5%	11.3%	8.8%
Consumer-personal	6.7%	11.2%	8.4%	5.1%

SOURCE: Alice Hanson Jones, *American Colonial Wealth: Documents and Methods*, 2d ed., 3 vols. (New York: Arno Press, 1978). Tables in vol. 3.

followed by the middle colonies and New England. Table 9.2 reveals that the south held 55 percent of the total physical wealth in probated estates in 1774. When slave wealth is excluded from the calculations, the ranking of the three regions remains the same. The south held 45 percent of nonhuman physical wealth, although the existence of slavery in the region may have contributed to increasing the value of other assets, especially land. By comparison, the New England colonies had the lowest wealth totals whether measured in nonhuman terms (25 percent) or total physical wealth (20 percent).

The distribution of regional economic output also favored the southern colonies. The south generated 46 percent of aggregate colonial output. The inclusion of slave incomes in the calculations lowers the region's share of aggregate output nearly 10 percentage points below its share of total physical wealth. Table 9.3 reveals that the middle colonies accounted for 29 percent of aggregate colonial output, while New England trailed with a share of only 25 percent. The mean income for the free population, which was 99.2 percent white, was around £12 ($1,080); the inclusion of slaves and indentured servants in the calculations reduces the mean average to £10.7 ($960).*

The value of estates shows that the largest number of very wealthy men lived in the south. The average value of estates for the top 1 percent of southern wealth-holders was £2,646 ($238,000), a figure over twice the size of the largest estates in the northern colonies. The first American millionaires had already emerged by the eighteenth century; the largest probated estate in the Jones sample belonged to Peter Manigault, a South Carolina planter and lawyer, who listed total assets of £27,958 ($2.5 million). Even with slaves excluded, Manigault still possessed the largest estate, since his nonhuman assets alone were recorded at £16,108 ($1.5 million). Indeed, 9 of the 15 largest colonial estates, on the basis solely of *nonhuman*

---

* Readers should not be confused just because these mean averages are higher than the median estimates used earlier in the chapter to describe the living standards of the *typical* white family; the figures are not inconsistent, merely two different types of averages. These figures were extraordinarily high for a preindustrial society.

TABLE 9.2. Regional Distribution
of Physical Wealth, 1774 (in millions of £ sterling)

	Free Population	Nonhuman[a] Wealth	%	Total Wealth	%
Southern Colonies	652,585	£40.2	45.6	£60.5	55.3
Middle Colonies	585,149	25.8	29.3	26.8	24.4
New England	582,285	22.1	25.1	22.2	20.3
Total	1,820,019	£88.1	100.0	£109.5	100.0

[a]Nonhuman wealth does not include value of slaves and indentured servants in probated estates.
SOURCE: Data derived from table 3.7 in Alice Hanson Jones, *Wealth of a Nation to Be: The American Colonies on the Eve of the Revolution* (New York: Columbia University Press, 1980).

TABLE 9.3. Regional Distribution
of Economic Output, 1774 (in £ sterling)

	Total Population	Mean per Capita Output[a]	Aggregate Regional Economic Output	%
South	1,105,500	£10.4	£11,500,000	45.6
Middle Colonies	640,700	11.5	7,350,000	29.3
New England	607,800	10.4	6,300,000	25.1
Total	2,354,000	£10.7	£25,150,000	100.0

[a]Per capita income figure estimated on basis of nonhuman physical wealth for total population and a capital-to-income ratio of 3.5 to 1.
SOURCE: Data based on information in tables 3.5, 3.6, 3.7 in Jones, *Wealth of Nation to Be.*

assets, were from the south in the Jones sample, and 8 of the 9 were in South Carolina.

The percentage of wealth-holders in the free population was fairly uniform in all three regions, ranging from 23.5 to 24.5 percent. Women constituted from 8 to 10 percent of wealth-holders, but the mean value of their estates was about one-half the male figure, largely because women rarely owned land. The richest woman in the Jones sample was Abigail Townsend, who lived outside Charleston and listed assets of £2,559 ($230,000).

The composition of estates varied according to size and region. Land was most the important asset in most colonial households. In New England, it accounted for 71 percent of wealth, and in the middle colonies for 60 percent (table 9.1). In the southern colonies, Jones's minimal figure for land is 46 percent, while slaves represented around 34 percent of wealth. In the north, land and personal items were the two most important assets in small estates (under £100 [$9,000]), but land as a percentage of wealth rose steadily as the size of the estate increased. In the south, livestock (30%) and personal items (21%) were the most valuable assets in small estates. Land (42%) outranked slaves (28%) in medium-sized estates (£100–£399); in the largest southern estates (over £400 [$36,000]), land (48%) and slaves (35%) combined for over four-fifths of total assets.

The wealthiest occupational group in the thirteen colonies was "esquires, gentleman, and officials," with mean asset holdings of £572 ($52,000). Table 9.4 reveals that merchants were the second most prosperous group, followed by farmers with ancillary income (i.e., southern great planters); professionals such as doctors, lawyers, and ministers; farmers with no outside income plus fisherman; shopkeepers and innkeepers; and artisans and chandlers. The middle colonies displayed no significant deviations from the general pattern, but New England and the south revealed some differences. Merchants ranked first in New England, while the inclusion of fishermen in category 3 with farmers may help explain why that group fared so poorly in the New England standings.

In the south, in contrast, farmers with ancillary incomes—great planters—were the second wealthiest group after "esquires, gentlemen, and officials." Southern merchants dropped to fifth place in that region's occupational rankings, reflecting the small role of urban areas in the southern economy. For the thirteen colonies overall, it is notable that the mean wealth for all wealth-holders, at £252 ($22,680), and for farmers and small planters, at £262 ($23,580), were almost identical. The data reinforce once again our image of average northerners as family farmers and southerners as nonslave-holding households.

The data on the relationship between urban and rural wealth-holding are subject to different interpretations. From one standpoint, urban wealth appears to be higher; but from another, rural wealth comes out on top. When wealth is measured strictly on a *regional* basis, urban dwellers uniformly held more wealth than rural residents. In New England, urban wealth-holders held assets of £191 ($17,200), compared to only £151 ($13,600) for rural wealth-holders; in the middle colonies, the comparable figures were £287 ($25,800) for urban and £173 ($15,600) for rural wealth-holders; and for the south, they were £641 ($57,700) for urban and £392 ($35,300) for

TABLE 9.4. Mean Value of Physical Wealth Held by
Socioeconomic Groups, 1774 (in £ sterling)

Wealth-Holder Group	Thirteen Colonies	New England	Middle Colonies	South
All wealth-holders	£252.0	£161.2	£186.8	£394.7
1. Esquires, gentlemen, and officials	572.4	313.4	1,233.0	1,281.3
2. Merchants	497.1	563.1	858.0	314.0
3. Farmers with ancillary income plus fishermen	410.5	144.2	257.3	801.7
4. Professionals	341.0	270.6	240.6	512.2
5. Farmers and small planters with no outside income	262.3	155.3	179.8	396.1
6. Shopkeepers, innkeepers	204.3	219.0	221.7	194.7
7. Artisans, chandlers	122.5	114.5	144.5	137.8

SOURCE: Compiled from data in table 7.5 in Jones, *Wealth of a Nation to Be.*

rural wealth-holders. On the basis of this analysis of wealth-holders in each section, urban dwellers appear to have held more assets.

Yet, when we aggregate the wealth data for the entire thirteen colonies, surprisingly rural wealth at £255 ($22,950) has a slight edge over urban wealth at £232 ($20,900). How could the outcome for the whole thirteen colonies appear to contradict the results in all three individual regions? There is a logical explanation: the rural wealth-holding figure for free southerners is so high, at £392 ($35,300), that it actually exceeds the wealth-holding of urban residents in the northern colonies. Because the south had the largest rural population, the southern figure had the greatest influence over the final average for the thirteen colonies. At the same time, the urban figure for the south exerted little influence upon the overall urban average, since the northern colonies held the vast majority of the continent's urban residents. Again, the wealth figure for northern urban dwellers was significantly lower than the comparable figures for rural southerners. As a result, when all the data are aggregated, rural residents held 90 percent of the wealth in the colonies and urban dwellers only 10 percent; on a per family basis, rural wealth-holders averaged about 9 percent more assets than their urban counterparts. Generally speaking, we must be careful in defining whether we are discussing rural versus urban wealth-holding on a regional or continental basis before rendering judgments.

Wealth was concentrated in the hands of the elite classes throughout the thirteen colonies. One measure of the degree of concentration is the percentage of wealth held by the top 20 percent of wealth-holders. For the colonies overall, this group held 68 percent of total assets. The regional breakdown was as follows: middle colonies—53 percent; New England—66 percent; and the southern colonies—70 percent (table 9.1). The pattern of concentration usually emerged fairly rapidly after initial settlement. In one study of New England, Bruce Daniels found that wealth was largely in the hands of an elite class in most towns within forty years of their establishment. In Boston, for example, the concentration of wealth was about the same in the 1770s as it had been in 1700, with the upper 30 percent of wealth-holders owning from 85 to 90 percent of all taxable property.

Despite the existence of widespread slavery in the southern colonies, the pattern of wealth distribution was not significantly different in the south than in New England, where slaves were few in number. Southern wealth-holders in the top 20 percent claimed only 4 percent more of their region's assets than their counterparts in New England. Slavery was then only one of many factors accounting for the skewed distribution of wealth in the south; and indeed, even in its absence, the pattern of concentration might not have changed significantly. In the middle colonies, which had the widest distribution of wealth, the top 20 percent of wealth-holders still claimed just over one-half of all assets. Meanwhile, although one-fifth of wealth-holders owned over two-thirds of the total physical assets in the mainland colonies, this pattern of concentration was no impediment to the realization of the highest income levels in the contemporary world for the typical white family.

Over the last two decades, scholars have debated whether a trend toward greater inequality in wealth distribution emerged during the eighteenth century. The initial research, based on an analysis of tax lists in major port cities, indicated that the upper classes had succeeded in accumulating a larger share of community assets as the decades passed. Later, however, Gerard Warden and William Pincok discovered flaws in the application of the tax-list methodology in Boston, primarily because of inconsistencies in the valuation of taxable assets over time. After recalculating the Boston figures to reflect the differences in valuation procedures, Warden argued that wealth concentration had changed very little in the eighteenth century; in 1681, the top 10 percent of wealth-holders owned 42 percent of taxable assets, while in 1771 their share had increased to only 47.5 percent. The difference was too small to establish a clear-cut trend.

In research on the social and economic structure of New York City during the early eighteenth century, Bruce Wilkenfeld discovered no significant change in the distribution of taxable property between 1701 and 1730; the top 10 percent of wealth-holders owned about 45 percent of local real estate. Over these same three decades, the share owned by the lower half of all taxpayers actually climbed slightly from 10.5 to 12.7 percent of all property.

In their broad survey of long-term trends in the distribution of wealth in the United States, Jeffrey Williamson and Peter Lindert discovered that the distribution of wealth remained surprisingly stable over the entire colonial era. They focused mainly on the interior towns and countries, rather than on the major port cities and the densely settled regions along the coast. These interior areas contained over 90 percent of the total population. Williamson and Lindert found that the constant opening up of new frontier regions, where wealth distribution was invariably more equitable, generally offset any movement toward greater concentration in the most heavily urban areas. While conceding that wealth shares of the elite merchant class might have risen in a few isolated locations such as Philadelphia and Worchester County, Massachusetts, and might conceivably have triggered demands for revolution and social change, they emphasized that these areas were atypical. Indeed, urban residents declined as a percentage of colonial population after 1700. In sharp contrast to the increasing rate of wealth inequality clearly evident in the nineteenth century, Williamson and Lindert concluded, the overall distribution of wealth showed no measurable trend for society as a whole in the colonial period.

The careful measurement of wealth levels over the entire life cycle of individuals ranks among the most elucidating new perspectives to emerge on colonial society in the last decade. Jackson Turner Main has been at the forefront of this mode of analysis, and the data he assembled on Connecticut in the seventeenth and eighteenth centuries reveal the potential benefits of this methodological approach. Most earlier studies of wealth based on tax rolls or estates had indicated that up to one-third of the population possessed few assets and therefore might be assumed to form the core of an impoverished lower class. Main argued forcefully, however, that most males in this category were single persons under the age of 30 who, despite their lack of tangible assets, were not, in fact, permanent members of a poor underclass. Rather they were, typically, still quasi-dependents within their parents' or relatives' households; these youths worked the family farm and performed unskilled labor of all varieties for neighboring farmers, and some artisans, for modest daily wages until the date of marriage. Even these low wage rates provided about twice the minimal income necessary for survival for single men, according to Main.

After marriage, couples used personal savings plus inheritances and gifts from relatives to acquire sufficient land to support a growing family. Indeed, marriage usually led immediately to a tripling of household wealth. As men in these households advanced in age, their wealth and income correspondingly increased, reaching its height around the age of 50, when most of their children had reached adolescence and were therefore able to contribute substantially to the labor requirements of the farm and household. Men who survived into their sixties and seventies normally relinquished a share of their accumulated assets, particularly land, to younger members of their families.

Only that small segment of the male population who never married were likely to flirt with poverty throughout their lives. The number of adult men with wives and children living at subsistence levels represented no more than 6 percent of all families. Main purposely excluded women from the scope of his study, but many unmarried widows probably lived at close to poverty levels as well. Nonetheless, in assessing economic conditions in Connecticut over a period of a century and a half, Main characterized the colony as "a land of plenty for some and of sufficiency for most."

In her study of the economy of Pennsylvania in the eighteenth century, Mary Schweitzer discovered essentially the same life-cycle patterns prevailing. The typical youth in the colonies, with little net worth at 25, looked confidently to more comfort in the years ahead and perhaps even a little luxury in old age; these aspirations and anticipated earning patterns over an entire lifetime are not markedly different from American youths in the twentieth century.

Living space in the typical colonial home with five members was cramped by modern U.S. standards. The typical farmhouse in Maryland in the late seventeenth century contained less than 400 square feet of living space, according to Gloria Main; it had two rooms and a dirt floor. In Philadelphia in the 1770s, Sam Bass Warner found that the average artisan or shopkeeper lived in a narrow, story-and-a-half structure with about 800 square feet of space. The owner usually used the larger front room as a work area. In Germantown, Pennsylvania, Stephanie Wolf discovered about the same total living space available in most houses, although these small-town artisans

normally worked outside the home in separate buildings. Generally
speaking, urban residences in Pennsylvania typically contained four
separate rooms with fairly specialized functions, whereas rural homes
had three rooms for more general use, according to the studies of
Jack Michel.

Houses did not have indoor plumbing, and a fireplace provided
all the cooking and heating facilities. A few beds, chairs, stools, and
cabinets were the usual furnishings. In slave quarters, which accounted for about 20 percent of family living units by the 1770s,
houses were furnished with straw bedding and barrels for chairs.
Candles and whale-oil lamps provided the lighting. The only methods of preserving food were salting, smoking, and drying. In urban
areas, water was drawn from shallow wells, which were occasionally
contaminated, since no town had water pipes or sewage lines.

The personal property of the typical colonist was limited. A few
items of handmade clothing, including one or two wool garments
for winter, and a pair of shoes were the basic wardrobe. The lower
classes frequently ate from wooden bowls. One-pot cooking was
common in the seventeenth century. By the eighteenth century,
most middle-class families owned earthenware, bed and table linen,
knives, forks, and a Bible. A family with income above the median
might possess a few fancy clothes, a watch, china plates, fine furniture, some silver items, and other small amenities. The wealthy
might possess fine clothes and furniture, exquisite china and silverware, nonreligious books, a man's wig, artwork, a carriage, and a
large volume of luxury goods. The wealthy in all sections usually
purchased servants or slaves to perform routine household tasks.

Although the picture of colonial living standards on the eve of
independence has now come into sharper focus, it remains less clear
how much those standards changed during the seventeenth and
eighteenth centuries, and precisely when improvements in incomes
might have occurred. A quarter-century ago, when scholars began
thinking more seriously about American economic growth before
industrialization, most economic historians doubted that personal
incomes had risen very much, if at all, before 1840.

That view of stagnation has undergone substantial modification
in the last several decades. Initially, scholars such as George Rogers

Taylor, Robert Gallman, Robert Fogel, and Paul David pushed back the onset of per capita growth to the 1820s and 1830s; they and others also hypothesized that some growth might actually have occurred during the colonial era after all. The data remain fragmentary, but the best guess now is that colonial incomes climbed steadily, and at a rate of 4 to 6 percent per decade over the entire 150-year period. In recent years estimates of the pace of advancement have tended to drift toward the high end of the scale; in their wide-ranging assessment of the status of scholarship on colonial economic history, published in 1985, John McCusker and Russell Menard settled on 6 percent per decade. This number is much lower than the growth rates experienced by the most successful economies in the twentieth century, but in the context of the seventeenth and eighteenth centuries, the colonial performance was laudatory. In England, for example, McCusker and Menard estimated the rate of per capita growth at only one-half the colonial figure, while Peter Lindert argues that real wages stagnated after 1725. Elsewhere, most of the counties in Europe, and around the globe, realized no increases at all in living standards during this era.

The beginning of income growth in the colonies can be traced back to the seventeenth century, according to separate studies by Terry Anderson and Menard. From 1650 to 1710, Anderson argued, average incomes in New England rose at a rate perhaps as high as 1.6 percent per annum, with 1 percent the absolute minimum. The average value of estates rose one-third over the second half of the century, with the largest percentage increases in the 1670s. Anderson's data suggest that living standards in New England in 1700 were more than 75 percent of the level attained in the 1770s, which translates in a per capita mean income of about £8.5 ($765) at the beginning of the century.

In the eighteenth century, in contrast, Anderson cited evidence indicating that the rate of income growth per capita slowed appreciably. In a detailed analysis of Hampshire County, Massachusetts, from 1700 to 1779, he discovered that a population boom offset much of the rise in aggregate output and held the increase in living standards to no more than 3 percent a decade. The size of the typical household in Hampshire climbed from 4.6 members in 1691–1715 to 6.4 members in 1761–80. The relatively weaker performance of the economy in this region reinforced Anderson's view that New England had experienced greater gains in productivity per capita during the previous century.

Meanwhile, Russell Menard's research on the Chesapeake region revealed that individual incomes rose rapidly in the 1630s, progressed gradually in the period from 1640 to 1670, and then remained steady over the remainder of the century. Productivity increased continuously in tobacco farming, with the number of plants one man could cultivate jumping threefold from 1630 to 1700. The introduction of standardized shipping containers aided in reducing freight costs by one-half in the late 1620s and early 1630s, while the expense of marketing tobacco in England fell from 10 percent to 2.5 percent of the sales proceeds by the end of the century. Per capita incomes failed to move upward at the same rate after 1640, however, because of a sharp rise in the dependency ratio—which is the ratio of total population to taxables (adult males). Males increasingly shared their property and income with wives, children, and relatives; simultaneous increases in productivity and the dependency ratio generally offset one another and kept living standards in the tobacco regions at about the same level from 1670 to 1720.

The accumulation of evidence pointing to a continued rise in incomes over the eighteenth century is also varied but fairly persuasive when considered jointly. At the more abstract quantitative level, a comparison of the mean values of New England estates calculated by Alice Jones for 1774 with the same figures generated by Terry Anderson for 1700 are consistent with the hypothesis that per capita wealth rose at a rate of over 3 percent a decade at a minimum. Since Bruce Daniels has argued that the concentration of wealth did not change significantly over the eighteenth century, the conclusion that the incomes of the typical New Englander increased at about the same rate as wealth accumulation appears reasonable.

Some of the most persuasive evidence of rising incomes arose from the research of Duane Ball and Gary Walton on agricultural productivity in the middle colonies. An assessment of productivity changes in the agricultural sector is critical, because farming accounted for the lion's share of colonial output. Based on a detailed study of Chester County, Pennsylvania, located southwest of Philadelphia, Ball and Walton estimated that agricultural productivity rose about 2 percent a decade in the eighteenth century and complementary nonagricultural activities added perhaps another 1 percent to the total. Indeed, few scholars now support growth figures any lower than Ball and Walton's calculation of a minimum of 3 percent increase per decade in living standards.

Efforts to identify broad periods of income growth are complicated by the fact that the thirteen colonies were settled at widely varying dates. Nonetheless, McCusker and Menard have recently outlined three general cycles in the colonial economy. The first phase centered around the middle of the seventeenth century in New England and the Chesapeake; it was characterized by very rapid income growth fueled by high rates of saving and much capital formation. Late in the seventeenth century, stagnation became the rule, in large part because of increased family size and a rising dependency ratio. Sometime after 1740, McCusker and Menard argued, living standards rose again—this time in response to rising overseas demand for colonial exports plus the development of wider markets at home.

That pattern of income growth seems reasonably compatible with movements in individual colonies, although the dates of an initial spurt, stagnation, rebirth, and perhaps another retrenchment varied in each case. For example, Jackson Turner Main described the Connecticut economy as declining in the 1730s and 1740s, enjoying a rejuvenation from 1750 to 1765, and then tailing off in the last decade before independence. Mary Schweitzer depicted Pennsylvania as experiencing little growth in the decade and one half after 1715, but the economy boomed between 1730 and 1750. By the latter period, Schweitzer accorded high marks to the Pennsylvania economy on the basis of three performance criteria: rising living standards, equity in the distribution of income and wealth, and the efficiency of markets. In a survey of economic growth in the Chesapeake colonies from 1704 to 1776, Allan Kulikoff found slow growth in the tobacco regions until midcentury, but rapid acceleration from 1755 to 1775.

In a study of the changing asset composition of estates in St. Mary's County, Maryland, between the seventeenth and eighteenth centuries, Lois Green Carr and Lorena Walsh discovered clear signs of improving living standards. In the seventeenth century, the typical family owned little furniture and few personal items. Over the next century, however, the number of amenities in estate inventories went up. Carr and Walsh made a list of 12 common amenities and traced their frequency in two periods—1658–1702 and 1703–77. Whereas the typical estate before 1702 listed only 2 to 3 of these amenities, after that date the number was 4 to 6. In the seventeenth century, the only two items listed in one-half of all estates were earthenware and linen, but after 1703 the list had expanded to include knives, forks, and religious books as well. In the largest estates, spices, secular books, clocks and watches, and maps turned up much more often in the eighteenth century. The median value of estates in St. Mary's County more than doubled from 1703–15 to 1755–77.

In a separate article on consumer behavior in the Chesapeake, Walsh argued that, by the mid-eighteenth century, the range of domestic goods that the typical farmer found desirable had "exploded." Before 1730 only the rich purchased such items as matched china place settings, mahogany chairs, buffets, and bookcases; from that date forward, "items of comfort and convenience were no longer luxuries, but rather were becoming essential to life in middling households." Paul Clemens described these developments as examples of "nascent consumerism."

Several scholars have sought to identify areas of increasing productivity which might have accounted for eighteenth-century income growth. James Shepherd and Gary Walton concentrated on improvements in transportation and distribution. The suppression of piracy in colonial waters eliminated the need for space-consuming armaments and larger crews. Insurance costs likewise fell. They also found that raw materials were handled and processed more efficiently; for example, the tighter compression of tobacco in packing boosted the weight of a hogshead by one-third. The increased volume of trade reduced the number of idle days that ships spent in port collecting cargoes. The cost of borrowing to buy imported goods from England declined as well; interest rates in London fell during the eighteenth century, and American consumers were among the beneficiaries. In the refining of iron ore, Paul Paskoff cited increases in labor productivity and the more efficient use of charcoal energy as factors leading to lower unit costs.

Marc Egnal has also argued that, in addition to increased agricultural productivity, the colonies gained from a favorable shift in the terms of trade. First, the introduction of the "cradle" scythe around 1750 permitted farmers to harvest more grain than formerly. More important, however, the market prices of agricultural products, which were the colonies' main exports, climbed steadily after 1760, while the prices of English manufactured goods remained roughly the same. In the 1740s, 100 bushels of colonial wheat could be exchanged for 150 yards of woolen cloth, but by the early 1760s, Egnal observed, an identical 100 bushels bought 250 yards of the same material, a two-thirds increase. Per capita colonial imports rose from £0.65 ($58) in 1743–47 to £1.49 ($134) in 1758–62. As the prices of exported foodstuffs rose in relation to the prices of the foreign manufactured goods, colonial living standards went up. Yet, because foreign trade involved only 10 to 13 percent of colonial output, the contribution to overall living standards was fairly limited. John Hanson estimates a gain of perhaps 0.5 percent annually in the period from 1745 to 1760.

Finally, we have the estimates of Alice Hanson Jones. On the assumption that the growth in incomes corresponded closely with increases in the size of probated estates, she calculated annual growth rates for three distinct periods: 1650 to 1725—0.3 percent; 1725 to 1750—0.4 percent; and 1750 to 1775—0.5 percent. Jones concluded in *Wealth of a Nation To Be* that "despite possible local or regional spurts or lags or even actual declines in some subperiods, there was from 1650 on an overall fairly steady rate of intensive growth for all regions combined." Significantly, her data indicate that living standards advanced more slowly in the seventeenth century. Only New England appears to have experienced a possible slowing in productivity during the eighteenth century; in this respect, her findings are generally compatible with those of Terry Anderson and Bruce Daniels. Most important, however, Jones estimated that not only were

per capita incomes rising but that the rate of growth was accelerating
during the half-century before independence.

In sum, the overall performance of the colonial economy in terms
of extensive growth and the standard of living achieved for the white
population was unmatched anywhere in the eighteenth century.
England and Holland may have been experiencing modest per capita
growth, but neither was absorbing the same rate of population increase as the thirteen colonies. The highest average incomes in the
world for the free population combined with growth rates on a par
or higher than its only two rivals, and all in the face of a population
boom at close to the reproductive maximum for the species—these
were among the unique colonial characteristics.

By the mid-1770s, the colonial gross product was around £25
million ($2.25 billion) annually. It was nearly one-third the figure
for the mother country. Moreover, the colonies were rapidly gaining
on Great Britain, for just three-quarters of a century earlier, in 1700,
their gross product had been a trifling 4 percent of Britain's. Parliament was surely right when it determined that the thirteen North
American colonies were financially strong enough to incur additional
taxes for their own defense. On the other hand, the colonies also
had ample economic resources to steer an independent course.

BIBLIOGRAPHICAL ESSAY

THE best sources of data on colonial wealth remain the scholarly
works of Alice Hanson Jones; see her *American Colonial Wealth:
Documents and Methods*, 3 vols., 2d ed. (New York: Arno Press,
1978)—the second edition has the revised southern figures in a
special appendix—and her analysis of the accumulated data in *Wealth
of a Nation to Be: The American Colonies on the Eve of the Revolution*
(New York: Columbia University Press, 1980). For critical reviews
of her work, see Allan Kulikoff, *William and Mary Quarterly* (1982),
pp. 359–65, and Maris Vinovskis, *Journal of Economic History* (1981),
pp. 415–20. Other studies of the distribution of wealth are Bruce
Daniels, "Long Range Trends of Wealth Distribution in Eighteenth-Century New England," *Explorations in Economic History*

(1973–74), pp. 123–35, and Jeffrey Williamson and Peter Lindert, *American Inequality: A Macroeconomic History* (New York: Academic Press, 1980).

Two books describing the middle-class status of colonial Americans by Jackson Turner Main are *The Social Structure of Revolutionary America* (Princeton: Princeton University Press, 1965) and *Society and Economy in Colonial Connecticut* (Princeton: Princeton University Press, 1985); see also his "Standard of Living and Life Cycle in Colonial Connecticut," *Journal of Economic History* (1983), pp. 159–65. Gloria Main has also produced some valuable contributions; see her "The Standard of Living in Colonial Massachusetts, *ibid.*, pp. 101–8, and *Tobacco Colony: Life in Early Maryland* (Princeton: Princeton University Press, 1982). For additional information on living standards in the north, I used Sam Bass Warner, *The Private City: Philadelphia in Three Periods of Its Growth* (Philadelphia: University of Pennsylvania Press, 1968); Stephanie Wolf, *Urban Village: Population, Community, and Family Structure in Germantown, Pennsylvania, 1683–1800* (Princeton: Princeton University Press, 1976); Jack Michel, "In a Manner and Fashion Suitable to Their Degree: A Preliminary Investigation of the Material Culture of Early Pennsylvania," in Glenn Porter and William Mulligan, eds., *Working Papers* (Wilmington, Delaware: Hagley Museum, 1981), 1–83. Stephen Innes, *Labor in a New Land: Economy and Society in Seventeenth-Century Springfield* (Princeton: Princeton University Press, 1983); Douglas L. Jones, "The Strolling Poor: Transiency in Eighteenth-Century Massachusetts," *Journal of Social History* (1975), pp. 28–54; William Pencak, "The Social Structure of Revolutionary Boston: Evidence from the Great Fire of 1760," *Journal of Interdisciplinary History* (1979), pp. 267–78; Billy Smith, "The Material Lives of Laboring Philadelphians, 1750 to 1800," *William and Mary Quarterly* (1981), pp. 163–202; and Smith, "Inequality in Late Colonial Philadelphia: A Note on Its Nature and Growth," *ibid.* (1984), pp. 629–45. A contrary view is presented in Thomas Doerflinger, *A Vigorous Spirit of Enterprise: Merchants and Economic Development in Revolutionary Philadelphia* (Chapel Hill: University of North Carolina Press, 1986). I also consulted Mary Schweitzer, *Custom and Contract: Household, Government, and the Economy in Colonial Pennsylvania*

(New York: Columbia University Press, 1987); James Lemon, "Household Consumption in Eighteenth-Century America and Its Relationship to Production and Trade: The Situation Among Farmers in Southeastern Pennsylvania," *Agricultural History* (1967), pp. 59–70; and Bruce Wilkenfeld, *Social and Economic Structure of the City of New York, 1695–1796* (New York: Arno Press, 1978). On food and diet, see Karen Friedmann, "Victualling Colonial Boston," *Agricultural History* (1973), pp. 189–205.

For the south, see Aubrey C. Land, "Economic Base and Social Structure: The Northern Chesapeake in the Eighteenth Century," *Journal of Economic History* (1965), pp. 639–54, and Paul Clemens, *The Atlantic Economy and Colonial Maryland's Eastern Shore: From Tobacco to Grain* (Ithaca: Cornell University Press, 1980). The data on height and nutrition is from Kenneth Sokoloff and Georgia Villaflor, "Colonial and Revolutionary Muster Rolls: Some New Evidence on Nutrition and Migration in Early America," Working Paper No. 374, National Bureau of Economic Research (Cambridge, Mass.: NBER, 1979); see also Richard Steckel, "A Peculiar Population: The Nutrition, Health, and Mortality of American Slaves from Childhood to Maturity," *Journal of Economic History* (1986), pp. 721–42.

For an introduction to the controversy about the rate of growth in per capita incomes in the colonies, see George Rogers Taylor, "American Economic Growth Before 1840: An Exploratory Essay," *Journal of Economic History* (1964), pp. 427–44; Paul David, "The Growth of Real Product in the United States Before 1840: New Evidence and Controlled Conjectures," *ibid.* (1967), pp. 151–97; and Robert Gallman, "The Pace and Pattern of American Economic Growth," in Lance Davis et al., *American Economic Growth: An Economist's History of the United States* (New York: Harper & Row, 1972). For data on England, see Phyllis Deane and W. A. Cole, *British Economic Growth, 1688–1959*, 2d ed. (Cambridge: Cambridge University Press, 1967); Peter Lindert, "English Living Standards, Population Growth, and Wrigley-Schofield," *Explorations in Economic History* (1983), pp. 131–55; Carole Shammas, "Food Expenditures and Economic Well-Being in Early Modern England," *Journal of Economic History* (1983), pp. 89–100; and

Shammas, "The Eighteenth-Century English Diet and Economic Change," *Explorations in Economic History* (1984), pp. 254–69. Comparative data are presented in Angus Maddison, "A Comparison of Levels of GDP Per Capita in Developed and Developing Countries, 1700–1980," *Journal of Economic History* (1983), pp. 27–41.

The most comprehensive article on the mainland colonies is Marc Egnal, "The Economic Development of the Thirteen Continental Colonies, 1720 to 1775," *William and Mary Quarterly* (1975), pp. 191–222; a rebuttal of his thesis is John R. Hanson, "The Economic Development of the Thirteen Colonies, 1720 to 1775: A Critique," *ibid.* (1980), pp. 165–72. For New England in the seventeenth century, see Terry Anderson and Robert Paul Thomas, "White Population, Labor Force, and Extensive Growth of the New England Economy in the Seventeenth Century," *Journal of Economic History* (1973), pp. 634–61; Terry Anderson, "Economic Growth in Colonial New England: 'Statistical Renaissance,' " *ibid.* (1979), pp. 243–57; Anderson, *The Economic Growth of Seventeenth-Century New England: A Measurement of Regional Income* (New York: Arno Press, 1975); and Bruce Daniels, "Economic Development in Colonial and Revolutionary Connecticut: An Overview," *William and Mary Quarterly* (1980), pp. 427–50. An important article on the middle colonies is Duane Ball and Gary Walton, "Agricultural Productivity Change in Eighteenth-Century Pennsylvania," *Journal of Economic History* (1976), pp. 102–17.

Three excellent papers on the tobacco region were given at a conference at the Hagley Library in Greenville, Delaware, in 1977. They were later published in Glenn Porter and William Mulligan, eds., *Economic Change in the Chesapeake Colonies*, Working Papers from the Regional Economic History Research Center, vol. 1, no. 3 (Greenville, Del., 1978): Russell Menard, "Secular Trends in the Chesapeake Tobacco Industry," pp. 1–34; P.M.G. Harris, "Integrating Interpretations of Local and Regionwide Change in the Study of Economic Development and Demographic Growth in the Colonial Chesapeake, 1630–1775," pp. 35–71; and Lois Green Carr and Lorena S. Walsh, "Changing Life Styles in Colonial St. Mary's County," pp. 73–118. Additional data are presented in Walsh, "Urban Amenities and Rural Sufficiency: Living Standards and Consumer Behavior in the Colonial Chesapeake, 1643–1777," *Journal of Economic History* (1983), pp. 109–17. Allan Kulikoff stresses economic growth in the third quarter of the eighteenth century in "The Economic Growth of the Eighteenth-Century Chesapeake Colonies," *Journal of Economic History* (1979), pp. 275–88; see also Kulikoff, *Tobacco and Slaves: The Development of Southern Cultures in the Chesapeake, 1680–1800* (Chapel Hill: University of North Carolina Press, 1986).

The sources of productivity growth in the trade sector are identified in James Shepherd and Gary Walton, *Shipping, Maritime Trade, and the Economic Development of Colonial North America* (Cambridge: Cambridge University Press, 1972), and Paul Paskoff does the same for the manufacturing sector in "Labor Productivity and Managerial Efficiency against a Static Technology: The Pennsylvania Iron Industry, 1750–1800," *Journal of Economic History* (1980), pp. 129–35. A thorough discussion of the literature on per capita growth rates is found in chapter 7 of Alice Hanson Jones's *Wealth of a Nation To Be*, cited in the first paragraph of this essay.

An overview of growth and welfare and an extensive bibliography on related topics are in John McCusker and Russell Menard, *The Economy of British America, 1607–1789* (Chapel Hill: University of North Carolina Press, 1985).

NOTE ON PRICE AND INCOME ESTIMATES

T H E conversion of sterling prices into current U.S. dollars is based on data series in Alice Hanson Jones, *American Colonial Wealth* 3 vols., 2d ed. (New York: Arno Press, 1978), table 3.5, 3:1719, which carries the exchange ratio up to 1975. By that date, £1 British sterling was valued at $45.19. I have adjusted that figure upward for subsequent changes in the consumer price index. My rough conversion rate is $90 to £1 sterling in 1985 dollars. Such numbers are imprecise but do serve as useful guidelines for relating monetary values in the colonial era to prices and incomes in modern times.

The same degree of tentativeness applies to estimates of incomes and living standards in the colonial period. The estimates of mean incomes in this book are based on the application of a 3.5 to 1 capital-to-output ratio. The capital figures are the wealth data from the research of Alice Hanson Jones. For a discussion of why she selected the ratio of 3.5 to 1 as the appropriate one for colonial America, see appendix A in her *Wealth of a Nation to Be* (New York: Columbia University Press, 1980).

All estimates of median incomes, which represent more typical incomes and living standards for an entire population, are my own. Today, in the late twentieth century, U.S. median income and wealth figures are around 80 percent of the mean, and I have allowed that general standard to guide me in producing estimates for the earlier era. The mean per capita figure for the whole free population was approximately £12 ($1,080); therefore I have assumed a median income of roughly £10 ($900).

Estimating the incomes of slaves required even more imagination. I began with an analysis of diet. Several sources suggest that the cost of providing an adequate diet, including at least one-half pound of meat per week, ranged from £3 to £4 ($270–$360) per annum.

Food normally accounted for about 50 percent of the cost of maintaining a slave. They also received additional income in kind from the receipt of coarse clothing, a housing allotment, occasional medical services, and other incidentals. Most slaves also had sufficient free time to chop wood for cooking and heating. (In his study of lower-class workers in Philadelphia, Billy Smith discovered that urban families typically spent 10 percent of income on wood energy.) I finally settled on a figure of £7 ($630), and I assumed no significant differences between mean and median incomes for slaves.

For indentured servants, I simply picked a figure between the numbers for the slave and free populations; in this case I settled on £9 ($810). Families who purchased indenture contracts invariably had incomes above the median and thus were in a position to care adequately for bonded workers. Servants usually consumed more meat than slaves, and male servants expected generous allocations of alcoholic beverages. Finally, servants ended their service with freedom dues in hand. In Pennsylvania in the mid-eighteenth century, prices for servant contracts were about one-fifth the cost of buying a slave; part of that difference was accounted for by the length of service but much of the differential was a reflection of higher maintenance costs for servants. My guess is that, all things considered, servants probably had incomes only slightly below the median for the free population.

In estimating the incomes of slaveholders, I assumed first that slaves and free workers produced on average about the same amount of output. For the south as a whole that figure was around £10.5 per capita. Second I assumed that the rate of profit on slaveownership was somewhere in the range of 8 to 15 percent, depending on region and dates of ownership. By acquiring five slaves, a planter could expect to realize a per capita income for his family on the order of around £15 ($1,350). Owners with approximately 100 slaves probably realized incomes about equal to the median figure for white Americans in 1985, or $11,700 per capita.

SUBJECT INDEX